Keep Fighting

THE Fighting

BILLY

BREMNER STORY

Keep Fighting

THE Fighting

BILLY
BREMNER
STORY

PAUL HARRISON

BLACK & WHITE PUBLISHING

First published 2010
by Black & White Publishing Ltd
29 Ocean Drive, Edinburgh EH6 6JL

1 3 5 7 9 10 8 6 4 2   10 11 12 13

ISBN: 978 1 84502 324 9

Typeset by Iolaire Typesetting, Newtonmore
Printed and bound by MPG Books Ltd, Bodmin

CONTENTS

ACKNOWLEDGEMENTS

This book could not have been completed without one outstanding individual, namely William John Bremner. Footballer, family man and a decent all-round human being. Billy was a true gentleman off the pitch and a colossus and leader of men upon it. His every football performance was filled with passion and a genuine desire to succeed, not only for himself, but for his club, his country and more importantly for the tens of thousands of fans who would spend their hard-earned money to marvel at his consistent top-quality performances. To thousands of football supporters around the world Billy Bremner was (and remains) a hero, a legend and a god. Anyone arriving at Elland Road football stadium, home of Leeds United AFC, is greeted by the brilliantly captured clenched fist (Keep Fighting) life-size statue of Leeds' favourite son. His name and image are synonymous with the West Yorkshire side's football successes of decades past. Elsewhere around Elland Road one can find a commemorative plaque bearing his name, Billy's Bar and an abundance of Billy Bremner memorabilia on sale in the Leeds United club shop, bearing testament to the influence and adulation he is still awarded by the Leeds faithful.

Such memories are not solely confined to the postcode LS11; in the district of Raploch in his home city of Stirling there exists a further commemorative plate and the annual Billy Bremner Regeneration Trophy, a youth football competition that was first introduced in 2006 to commemorate Billy Bremner. It would have given him some satisfaction to note that the 2007 winners of the trophy were Raploch-based Castleview.

This book was originally penned in 1998 but never made the bookshelves at that time. Now, over a decade later, it is with the utmost pride that I am able to put into print the results of dozens of those interviews I held with Billy since I first met him back in 1968 and the thoughts, recollections and anecdotes of many of the real football superstars of the Billy Bremner era, but more of that later.

This work could not have been achieved without the help of an entire Premier League size-squad of support. I would like to thank each of the following for their contributions, thoughts, opinions and assistance in the completion of this work and in particular: Mandy, Mark Daniel and Paula Jayne Harrison. Sincere appreciation must go to: Bingo, Angel and George, Mason and Blossom, Will Scott, the late Don Revie OBE, Mrs Isabel McDonald, Howard Wilkinson, Sir Alex Ferguson, Pele, the late John Charles CBE, the late Bertie Mee OBE, the late Brian Clough OBE, the late Albert Johanneson, Eddie Gray, Peter Lorimer, Paul Reaney, Norman Hunter, Franz Beckenbauer, Billy McNeill MBE, Bobby Lennox MBE, the late Jimmy Johnstone, the late Willie Henderson, the late Bob Stokoe, John Greig MBE, Jimmy Hill OBE, the late Don Weston, the late Ian Hutchinson, Dave Mackay, the late Alan Ball MBE, the late Keith Newton, the late Derek Dougan, Craig Brown CBE, Tommy Gemmell, the late Bobby Murdoch, David Hay, Gordon McQueen, Jimmy Armfield CBE, Trevor Francis, Jim Smith, Graham Carr, the late Joe Baker, Barry Fry, Dave Bassett, Howard Kendall, Michel Platini, Joe Royle, Sammy McIlroy, Gordon Strachan OBE, Colin Todd, Graham Taylor OBE, Graham Kelly, George Burley, Glenn Aitken, Dickie Guy and Raymond Blaylock. Many thanks also go to the Football Associations of England and Scotland and in particular to Catherine Smith of the latter, Donald Morton of the *Stirling Observer* and staff of the British newspaper library (ex-Colindale). Finally, my eternal thanks go to the thousands of supporters of Leeds United who have shared terrace and seat space alongside me at countless stadiums across the United Kingdom and Europe. I hope each and every one of you enjoy this treasure trove of football nostalgia as a fitting tribute to, and courtesy of, the late great Billy Bremner.

Paul Harrison

Now little Billy Bremner is the Captain of the crew,
For the sake of Leeds United he would break himself in two.
His hair is red and fuzzy
And his body black and blue
As Leeds go Marching On.

———————————

His eyes they shone like diamonds
Lived a man, who played for Leeds,
Billy Bremner was his name,
The best wing half you've ever seen.
We all live in a white Scratching Shed
A white Scratching Shed.

———————————

There's a red-headed tiger known as Billy,
And he goes like a human dynamo.

———————————

One Billy Bremner
There's only one Billy Bremner.

———————————

THE BALLAD OF BILLY BREMNER

There's a tale I'm goin' to tell you
All about a brave young man
Who was born and bred in Scotland,
That's where history began.

He once cheered the Glasgow Celtic
Just the soon as he could talk;
And he'd kick a paper football
Just the soon as he could walk.

And his name is Billy Bremner
We will never forget his deeds;
He was made to play for Scotland,
Now he captains United of Leeds.

So he came to Leeds United,
And they made Don Revie the boss;
All the Elland Road fans were excited
And wor gain was Celtic's loss.

Many giants have tried to slay him
When he fights for every ball;
But he knows the famous saying
When they're big the harder they fall.

And his name is Billy Bremner
We will never forget his deeds,
He was made to play for Scotland,
Now he captains United of Leeds.

When they talk of Matthews and Pele
Of Lawton and Finney and James,
Like a whisky in your belly
He will glow amongst those names.

He will lead our lads to glory,
He will lead our lads to fame;
When they sing United's story
You will always hear the name.

And his name is Billy Bremner
We will never forget his deeds,
He was made to play for Scotland,
Now he captains United of Leeds.

And his name is Billy Bremner
We will never forget his deeds,
He was made to play for Scotland,
Now he captains United of Leeds.

Dedicated to the football fans of Scotland,
Leeds United, Hull City and Doncaster Rovers

PREFACE

(BY THE LATE JOHN CHARLES)

When Paul Harrison approached me to write a few words about my old friend, the late Billy Bremner, I didn't hesitate to say yes and agree. Both Billy and Paul had one thing in common, a genuine passion for Leeds United, and it is a real privilege for me to be able to add my own thoughts.

If there is one person who truly sums up all that Leeds United stands for, then that person has to be Billy Bremner. Throughout the years I knew him, Billy remained extremely passionate about three things in his life: his wonderful family, Leeds United, and his beloved Scotland. I've never known a more committed and driven person, in everything he did Billy gave his everything. Never more so than when he pulled on the legendary all-white shirt and playing kit of Leeds, or blue and white of Scotland.

As a footballer, he was tough and resilient, never failing to give anything but 100 percent he would run through brick walls for the sake of Leeds United and Scotland. Loyal and genuine, he was admired as both a man and as a sportsman. Very few people in life deserve to be called a legend, Billy Bremner is the exception to the rule. To this very day, the mere mention of his name commands immediate respect.

Billy may be gone, but he will never be forgotten, and this book is a fine tribute to him, immortalising his spirit and fine character as only a true fan and supporter could.

John Charles
Summer 2003

xv

INTRODUCTION

Billy Bremner was someone I hugely admired and one of my first childhood heroes. Along with Batman, he provided me with a huge amount of positive childhood memories and happiness. Unlike the caped crusader, Billy was tangible. Week in, week out, he thrilled football audiences with his passion and desire to win. He was the perfect role model for a young aspiring footballer – strong, resilient and determined, he could score goals too. In fact, on a football pitch it seemed to me that he could achieve anything.

I wasn't alone in my adulation; he was revered by all football supporters and, even if they weren't Leeds fans, privately Billy Bremner was the player they would all have loved to have had in their team. Even the late Brian Clough found it in himself to tell me in a private interview:

'Billy Bremner was the greatest ever footballer and man to play for Leeds United. When he spoke everyone listened, including me, and it takes someone very special to get me to shut up and listen. Billy Bremner had that quality. I didn't always agree with his aggressive playing style but he was the most influential footballer of his era and the mainstay of the Leeds side through-out two decades.'

The football fraternity in general has been more than keen to provide glowing testimonials to a very special person and to one of the most gifted footballers of his generation; a player who many still refer to as the 'wee man'. The impact he had on people was immense and some of those interviewed for this book openly wept whilst discussing their own personal memories of him as a footballer and man. Billy Bremner was not simply a footballer or a football manager, he was a genuine human being, a devoutly loyal husband, father and a man who cared for and put his family first and foremost. He was a friend to many and a figurehead to entire communities in what was essentially viewed as a working-class game. We shall never truly know how many youngsters and adults Billy Bremner inspired but the great respect in which he is still held is rarely so consistently sustained in the memory of football fans. Billy is a qualified member of a most elite football body, 'the greatest ever', an accolade afforded to less than a dozen British football icons since the game first began.

Despite the popular image of him being a 'hard' and 'angry' footballer, emotions that are possibly better described as passionate, Billy was in fact a thoughtful schemer, with a tactical awareness that instilled fear into the most disciplined of opposition. Chris Balderstone, the ex-Huddersfield Town and Carlisle United player (and professional cricketer) described Billy as:

'the most difficult player to mark in football. You couldn't stick with him throughout an entire game, he was like "Will o the Wisp", one minute he would be right in front of you shouting for the ball, the next he was gone, ghosting past players and running into gaps that he had created. He had incredible stamina and vision, an awareness of what was happening on the pitch around him. The complete package really.'

Whether it was for Leeds United, Hull City, Doncaster Rovers and not forgetting his beloved Scotland, Billy was fiercely competitive. He wanted to win, to succeed. It is no coincidence that the title of his 1969 autobiography is *You Get Nowt for Being Second*.

Off the field he continued to display his leadership qualities. Management and motivational skills are not something that you simply buy off the shelf, read about in a book or are trained in. It takes a variety of skills and experiences to be able to consistently lead and inspire, not the least of which is respect. No one could ever suggest that Billy didn't command respect. He naturally motivated everyone through his enthusiasm be it team mates in training, the women who washed the playing kit or the staff of the Elland Road café where playing staff congregated before and after training sessions. He knew full well that a kind and supportive word here and there made a difference, and one of the things he truly enjoyed was making people happy.

Of course he was no angel on the pitch. He could and did mix it with the best of them, yet to a man, each and every player I have spoken with who played against him in a competitive game or during a training session reiterated the same thing – that he generally gave as good as he got. If someone kicked him during a game, rarely would you see him rolling about on the floor feigning injury. He would simply make a mental note of who it was and would get up and play on, all the while biding his time and awaiting the opportune moment to return the kick. And he would often retaliate twice as hard so that the offending party would think twice about doing it again! Reasoned justice, one could say.

There can be no doubting the fact that he was very often targeted by opposition managers, players, fans and even match officials before a ball was kicked. With his fiery red hair, vocal opinions and exuberant character, he had the ability to wind up opponents in pre-match warm-ups, as he confidently strutted around the pitch displaying his 'Keep Fighting' attitude; motivating colleagues with the odd snippet of personal detail about opposition players. He was a warrior going into battle and few teams could boast such players in their ranks. Without doing anything untoward or wrong, Billy Bremner could intimidate any opposition in their own stadium.

Managers and experienced players would openly say in pre-match talks that they were going out onto the pitch with the intention of stopping Bremner from playing his natural game. If successful, and his threat was eliminated, the chances were that this would temporarily stall the finely tuned cogs of the Leeds United football machine and prevent it from operating efficiently. Not that Leeds was a one-man team, but the Billy

Bremner influence was so great that his mere presence on the pitch would often raise the standard of his colleagues' game.

The late Don Revie once told me that Billy Bremner's presence in the dressing room and on the pitch would produce a charged atmosphere throughout the Leeds team (never mind their opponents), making them an even tougher, motivated and focused proposition to encounter:

'Billy liked to generate passion in his team mates; he could lift their spirits or dampen them with a solitary glance. If we didn't play well then some of them would be more concerned as to how he would react afterwards in the dressing room than they were of me as manager. In the build-up to every game he was driven and focused, inspirational. He knew the strengths and weakness of other teams and the individual players; his own game would revolve around exploiting those weaknesses. He was a visionary and I never managed a footballer or a man like him. An exceptional person.'

Once on the field, it was time for battle. Afterwards, irrespective of what had occurred previously or during the ninety minutes, Billy would very often be the first to greet and shake hands with his adversaries. The infamous encounters with Dave Mackay at White Hart Lane, in August 1966, and with Liverpool's Kevin Keegan at Wembley in August 1974, are now part of football folklore. Yet neither incident created serious disharmony between any of those involved. The Wembley incident with Keegan was part of an ongoing spat that had been present from kick-off, and whilst many supporters of Leeds and Liverpool believe it to have been a nonsensical refereeing decision, it wasn't quite as innocent as it appeared. Keegan had given out, and taken, a few whacks (often retaliatory) throughout the game. He had earlier tangled with and felt the full force of Johnny Giles' wrath as the two clashed, resulting in Giles lashing out at the striker whose response was to react as though he had been struck at close quarters by a charging hippopotamus. This reaction certainly riled some of the Leeds players, whilst their Liverpool counterparts pleaded complete innocence.

Later in the game, Keegan attempted to outmuscle Bremner on the edge of the Leeds penalty area and once again he came out second best – not only losing the ball but taking a retaliatory smack to his upper body, Bremner's response to the attempt to force him off the ball. He took his frustration out on the Leeds captain and puffing his chest out like a turkey cock he elected to confront him. Both men exchanged expletives in a face-to-face encounter. Then, without warning and in full glare of the match officials, Keegan threw a right-fisted punch that landed on the left side of Bremner's face. For a split second time stood still and Wembley stadium fell silent, only to erupt moments later as a scuffle between the two players ensued. Leeds players Norman Hunter, Gordon McQueen and David Harvey moved swiftly to break up the spat and hold back both men. The rest, as they say, is history. Match referee Bob Matthewson intervened, calmly pulled both players to one side and gave them a stern dressing down before sending the pair of them off. It was Keegan's second sending off in four days.

In emotionally petulant displays both players pulled off their club shirts and threw them to the ground in blatant disgust, before walking disconsolately from the pitch. From Bremner's point of view the shirt removal was symbolic – he had let down his manager and the club. He was genuinely ashamed of the incident, the shirt removal was one of respect that he wasn't fit to wear it after his actions.

'I don't have any regrets in football. I loved every moment of my career though perhaps I could have done things a little differently. The sending off at Wembley is not something I am proud of. There had been a lot of name calling and comments made in the tunnel before we walked onto the pitch. We were reminded of comments our new manager [Brian Clough] had previously made about us and certain Liverpool players were also going on about Don Revie abandoning us. It was nothing unusual, just the general winding up of the other team. I made a couple of comments about them being nothing special now they were losing Bill Shankly and it seemed to set the tone for the rest of the game. There was a few late tackles and fouls going on that the referee missed, and I think we all sensed and reacted to the intense atmosphere of the occasion.

'Kevin [Keegan] was a good player and we always seemed to have a tussle during a game, it was nothing unusual. I was genuinely shocked when he reacted the way he did and tried to put me on the floor. I could tell by his eyes that he had lost it; I tried to calm him down. I actually apologised to him on the pitch, for what it was worth I could have been proposing to him. He wasn't about to listen to someone he had tried to flatten. Bob Matthewson the referee didn't really have an option, we both had to walk. I tried to call Kevin back to apologise but he was already gone. I felt really bad for the Leeds fans, I had let them all down.

'The manager wasn't too happy with me either, he told me I deserved to be sent off and refused to listen to me; he said that we had no reason to cheat our way through games and we could win them fair and square without resorting to other tactics. He used the phrase "cheat" and I didn't like that at all and told him so. I apologised to him later but I don't think he really forgave or forgot it. I made a point of looking out Kevin and apologising to him afterwards. It was made all the more difficult for me by the fact that we lost the game [on penalties] to our old rivals as well. I really wanted us to take revenge for the 1965 FA Cup final defeat they inflicted on us.'

Keegan was clearly unhappy and frustrated about the treatment he received and even threatened to quit football altogether.

At the subsequent Football Association disciplinary committee hearing, both players were punished for the Wembley outrage and both received hefty eleven-game suspensions and £500 fines. Shocked by the severity of the punishment, Bremner, in a most characteristic emotional outburst, swore at the members of the adjudicating panel that included the chairman of Nottingham Forest, Harold Alcock. Bremner recalled:

'It was a ridiculous punishment, we had publicly apologised to supporters and to the Football Association, what else could we do? There was a feeling that some of the discipline committee had personal agendas and by punishing the league champions [Leeds United] in such a drastic manner, it gave the clubs they were involved with an advantage. These types of committee hearings are necessary but back then they tended not to be objective but extremely subjective in their decision making. They were archaic and institutionalised with an "Old Boys Club" mentality. Any player or manager going before a discipline panel was fighting a losing battle. I told them I thought they were a bunch of wankers and the judgment was shit. The look on their faces was one of horror, like they had never had anyone swear at them before.'

As for the incident with Dave Mackay, it was nothing more than over-enthusiasm; both players were winners and battlers, both were influential and inspirational and as usual in midfield emotions were running high. It says a great deal for both men that later they played down the incident as a brief flirtation with confrontation borne out of a desire to win. Much to the chagrin of the media, who thrive on such on-the-field rivalry and attempt to regurgitate it at every opportunity, both maintained a friendship long after the event. Both were patriotic Scots with much more in common than most footballers and there was mutual respect.

Bremner, when pressed to talk about it, said:

'Naturally I was shocked, Dave was angry, very angry, but he was an honest player. I had been a bit of a pain in the arse to him during the game, just winding him up a bit. A bit of chit chat and the odd knock and push is all part of the game. I knocked an injury he had on his leg. I had no idea he was going to react like he did and I got one hell of a fright when he grabbed me.

'To be fair I knew I was in the wrong and that it would not be right for me to inflame the situation, and in all likelihood get us both into trouble, so I held my hands up and said sorry to him. It worked and he let me go. He had quite a temper on him and, rightly so that day, as I had been giving him a lot of stick. Dave Mackay is someone I highly respect; he looks hard, he is hard, but underneath all of that he is a really nice guy – apparently.'

Mackay's version is not too dissimilar:

'In general Billy was a good honest professional. He could be a real wind-up though and I had just about taken enough of him that day. He says it was an accident, but he went to hurt me on an injured leg. It was a stupid thing to do and I wanted to let him know that he can't do that to me. Looking back on it now it was just one of those things. Too much has been made of it since and if that photograph [see picture section, page 1] didn't exist then it would have probably gone away without any fuss or further mention.'

The 'win at all costs' image of Billy Bremner has reached almost mythical proportions in some parts of the media and in the terrace legend, as has the 'dirty Leeds' tag. There can be no denying that Bremner and his Leeds colleagues liked to win. A collective and competitive mindset to achieve first place permeated throughout the football club. To be second best or to suffer defeat in any form was unacceptable.

The 'dirty Leeds' tag could never be associated with such exquisite and skilful footballers like Eddie Gray or South African, Albert Johanneson. In fact no Leeds players of the era could ever be described as a 'clogger'. All possessed great levels of skill and one need only review some of the games of the era to see how they destroyed teams with their pure footballing ability.

As team captain, Bremner was the focal point of the side; football supporters often quite incorrectly regarded him as tough, reckless and unsympathetic, a destroyer. Nothing could be farther from the truth.

In what may have been his last ever interview, shortly before his sad death in 1995, Albert Johanneson described to me Bremner's influence on him as a person:

'Even when staring directly into the face of adversity I can rely on Billy Bremner to put matters into perspective. I may not always like what he says but he never hides his feelings, he has always been straight with me. He helped me overcome many of the battles facing what was a rare commodity in the 1960s, a black footballer. In many games the players we faced would call me offensive names and some even asked me to clean and polish their boots. It hurts me to think that they did not see me as an equal; after all we were all footballers. Billy would always come to my defence and tell me I was better than such people and to ignore all the comments. He would tell me that the best way to hurt them was with my skill and pace and goals. Many times I cried and it was Billy Bremner who would lift my spirits, even after we finished with the game; I sometimes feel ashamed that I am not as strong a person as him. He is a fine man and he has helped and supported me through some difficult times in my life.'

Kind words indeed. I can only hope that this work appropriately conveys the love of football, life and sincerity Billy Bremner possessed. His passion in particular for Leeds United and later Doncaster Rovers is unquestionable. This book is a unique tribute to the greatest ever footballer to don the club shirt of Leeds United, Hull City, Doncaster Rovers and, arguably Scotland. His passing in 1997 was not only a huge loss to his family and friends but to the world of football too. Long may the legend of William John Bremner live on.

1

IN THE BEGINNING, THERE WAS . . . BILLY BREMNER

On Saturday, 16 March 1968, as a mere eight-year-old, I realised my first life ambition. On that particular day Leeds United were playing a game in the old First Division at Newcastle United and I attended my first Division One football match. Arriving at Newcastle station with my uncle, we made the walk through some narrow and hilly cobblestone streets on a grey drizzly day. The route to St James' Park felt claustrophobic and intimidating, raising my anxiety and trepidation at seeing two of football's biggest clubs. After what seemed dozens of miles, we eventually emerged into open space and I caught my first glimpse of St James' Park, home of Newcastle United AFC. It looked spectacular and resplendent and just a little run down, altogether bigger and somehow more complete than the only other football ground I had visited, Brunton Park, Carlisle.

The first thing to grab my attention were the giant floodlight pylons that stood aloft at the corners of the ground – the lighting frame on each pylon giving the appearance that they were looking down on the stadium below, literally standing guard. Elsewhere there was a garish-looking black and white grandstand that ran the entire length of one side of the ground. As we neared the stadium, the sight of seemingly never-ending rows of steps that led up to the roofless Gallowgate End sent the butterflies in my stomach into lunar orbit. I had seen dozens of pictures of St James' Park in magazines and books, yet none could deliver the thrill of seeing it in real life. I was hooked, and in my nervous excitement, began to shake. Walking into the main car park, I suddenly became aware that we were not alone. Hundreds of other people, mainly Newcastle supporters, were milling around and waiting for something. Quite what, I had no idea.

By now all I wanted to do was get inside and to see the ground, the luscious green pitch and to savour the smell of the freshly mown grass and the build-up to the match itself. I wanted to see my idol, Billy Bremner, and his fellow Leeds United team mates in real life.

Suddenly, a man shouted, 'Here they come', sparking a flurry of activity in the car park. A less than state-of-the-art, sandy-coloured charabanc pulled into the car park and stopped close to the concrete steps leading into the rear of the main stand. There was a mad dash as everyone ran towards the bus. I had no idea what was happening but ran alongside my uncle, as fast as my skinny little legs would carry me. We stopped by the front of the bus where he turned to me and said in an excited tone, 'It's Leeds United, they're here, it's the Leeds players.' Being small, I was able to work my way through the crowd and pushed through to the front to stand as close to the bus door as possible.

Moments later, the door jerked open and they emerged, one by one, the management and playing staff of Leeds United Football Club: a stern-looking Don Revie, a grinning Paul Reaney, a thoughtful Paul Madeley, a laughing Mick Jones, a serious Mike O'Grady, a smiling Johnny Giles, a curious Terry Cooper, a loud Jack Charlton (how tall he looked, a giant of a man), and a friendly Jimmy Greenhoff. It was thrilling, I stood motionless and speechless, my eyes like saucers as others clamoured for, and got, the autographs they so desperately wanted. Gary Sprake, one of my great heroes from the Leeds team, climbed down from the bus. Seizing my chance, I plucked up the courage to speak and offered him my programme, politely asking him to sign it. The Welsh keeper wasn't interested, he sneered down at me (I will never forget the look) before pushing me to one side adding 'Get out of my way,' as he did so. Sprake rudely pushed through the crowd and made his way towards the main stand. He was obviously not in a great mood that day and I was absolutely mortified and close to tears. For a brief time, Gary Sprake had been someone I admired. Not any more.

I did manage to get my own back on him some years later when I was in a Leeds restaurant with a couple of fellow Leeds supporters. One of them recognised him and asked for his auto-graph. Begrudgingly, he obliged before turning to me, 'I expect you want one as well?' My reply was brief and concise, it was meant to be dismissive: 'No thanks, not for me.' He was clearly unhappy with that response and moved away without reply.

Back at St James' Park, Terry Cooper had witnessed the downright arrogance of his colleague, took my programme from me and signed it, giving me a knowing wink as he handed it back. Don Revie was there and he gladly signed it, as did Jack Charlton. Then it happened – suddenly I was face to face with Billy Bremner. By now, I was shaking uncontrollably. There before me was the greatest footballer ever. Worse still, I was suddenly competing with dozens of adults who had arrived and wanted his autograph. I lunged forward, was able to get his attention and handed him my programme. He took, it, smiled graciously and asked me, 'What is your name, son?' He was speaking to me; Billy Bremner was actually speaking to me. My throat went dry as my vocal chords seized, I tried to speak my name, but all that came out was a frog like croaking noise. I blurted out 'Paul, sir,' at which he laughed and said, 'Pleased to meet you, Paul,' signed my programme and handed it back to me.

I couldn't contain myself and without any thought made the most inane comment imaginable: 'Billy, I have posters of you on my bedroom wall.' I don't know why, but the comment seemed to take him by surprise, and he talked (whilst signing dozens of other autographs) to me for what seemed an eternity. I explained that it was the first time I had seen Leeds United in real life, and that my uncle had brought me. He asked me to point out my uncle and I then heard Billy say to him, 'Follow me over here.' We pushed our way through the throng and made our way towards the stadium. Climbing the steps, Billy turned round to my uncle and told him that he would be back in a moment then disappeared inside the stand. My uncle was grinning from ear to ear. 'I can't believe you,' he kept repeating. Moments later Billy reappeared, clutching several programmes that had been signed by both Leeds and Newcastle players. 'Here you are son, come back after the game and tell me what you thought.' I agreed that I would do just that and he returned to the inner confines of the stadium.

We moved off and entered the ground taking our place in a paddock-style terraced area that sat below the main stand; we were close to where it met with the Gallowgate End. To be honest I can remember little of the game, it was over in a flash. The final score was 1-1 and the records show Norman Hunter had scored for Leeds before a crowd of 49,190, of which proudly, I was one. As we exited the ground my uncle told me that we had to be quick in order to catch the train home. My mind wasn't fixed on any train or going home – my thoughts were on Billy Bremner. Wouldn't Billy be waiting for us? My tiny world collapsed as it dawned on me that we weren't going to meet the Leeds captain again, at least not that day.

Whether it was through feelings of guilt or a simple desire to make me happy, unbeknown to me, my uncle and my mother carefully crafted and posted a letter to Billy Bremner at Leeds United, apologising for our failure to meet with him after the game at Newcastle. Within a week, a reply was received. I was then told of the communications. I can't remember the precise wording of the response, but it was signed by Billy Bremner and it was on Leeds United headed notepaper. Essentially, it said that they were to let him know when I was next coming to Leeds and to Elland Road to watch a game. My mum, proud as punch at getting such a response, refused to allow me to take it to school to show it off to my mates, instead she took it to her work and let everyone see it. Parental logic!

The belief a child places in a hero should never be under-estimated; many children select fictional superheroes, or film or popstars as their role model. I was truly fortunate. For me, my hero was the best of them all, he was the ultimate role model.

My next encounter with the superstar was on 4 May 1968, before a 2-1 defeat at Elland Road, by Liverpool. Somehow we (I was escorted by my mother) had arranged to meet Billy prior to the match, in the main reception of the ground. I expected others to be there doing the same thing but I was wrong. Billy came out smiling and greeted us, and without waiting a moment, whisked me off on a whirlwind tour of the stadium, leaving my mother sat in reception. It was surreal, I met player after player before finally being paraded before team manager Don Revie, nervously answering his questions.

Let me tell you, no matter what anyone may say about him, Don Revie had an immense presence. It was like meeting God himself. He held out his hand to shake mine, he was courteous and polite yet clearly much focused on the game. He told me how he loved Leeds United and in turn, he expected his players to be as passionate about the club, as much as each of its supporters. I explained to him how one day I wanted to play for his team. Smiling he said he would look forward to signing me on. I was thrilled, it was a truly unforgettable experience and, sublimely, all the time Billy Bremner was there with me, guiding and supporting me through my obviously excited yet nervous state.

The one thing I learned from the Elland Road experience was that Billy Bremner always made time for the important things in his career and life. The supporters of Leeds United meant everything to him, and he was tireless in going out of his way to achieve success for those same people. There are few who are naturally blessed with an aura that causes those around them to feel in awe, yet at the same time can make people relaxed, comfortable and very much their equals. Billy was one such individual. Throughout the entire time I knew him, he never changed his manner or attitude, maintaining the same respect for others, whether he was with the Queen of England, with a football supporter in a pub or to fellow locals in the tap room of the Woodman at Halton. He had the uncanny knack of making others feel important and crucial to the team's success.

Over the years that followed I kept in touch with Billy, meeting up with him on countless occasions and always talking football and his love of Leeds United. Throughout this time he remained honourable, honest and open, taking time to talk to and often meet with his critics head on. Rarely did he walk away from any encounter, both on and off the field, without a smile and a shake of the hand. A genuine person indeed.

2

THE EARLY DAYS

William John Bremner was born in Stirling, Scotland on Wednesday, 9 December 1942 and raised in the district of Raploch. Raploch's history dates back to the 1100s and is on the site of the Battle of Stirling Bridge. According to Bremner himself:

'Raploch was a tough part of Stirling. Raploch was a hard place, not criminally, but one of those places that as a child you had to learn the rule of street law very quickly. Nothing came easy and you had to stand your ground and never show any weakness, even if you were scared to death. Once you had established your level on the streets you became part of the pecking order, a league table of respect really.

'I had my fair share of scrapes and incidents with some of the bigger lads who would try it on to see if they could bully you. Whatever the size of bully who fancied a go at me, I always gave as good as I got and defended the honour of my family and friends above everything else. After a time no one picked on me any more and I knew then that I had established my place amongst the kids of Raploch.

'The nice thing about Raploch was, that despite its local tags of "Little Chicago" or "Raptap", it was in fact a loyal community. If a family was struggling with anything, without any prompting whatsoever, other Raploch families would automatically help them out. I learned a few harsh lessons on the streets of Raploch and Stirling but the one thing that remained with me was that no one was better than anyone else, we were all equals. To me that's a fundamental lesson of life, we are all people, human beings, we come into this world with nothing and we sure as hell leave it with

7

nothing, so we should enjoy and make the most of it while we are here. I wouldn't want to have been raised anywhere else. Raploch was my home and will always remain very special to me.'

Billy's parents both hailed from a working-class background. John William (more commonly known as 'Pop') worked as a storeman at a Ministry of Defence establishment in Stirling, while his mum, Bridget (Bess), was an excellent mother and wife and managed all things relating to their home.

From a football perspective the young Billy Bremner (nick-named Brock) was quite an adept player, appearing for his school football team, St Mary's Primary under-11s at the age of just nine. The school wasn't far from his Weir Street home, literally round the corner.

Weir Street still exists but the semi-detached council home that Billy shared with his mum and dad no longer stands, demolished as part of the recent Raploch regeneration programme. This is not the first time Raploch has endured major regeneration. During the 1920s and 1930s the council commenced slum clear-ance and built council houses to replace the older slums at Raploch. It was in one of these modern replacements that Billy lived. Today a modern urban-style property stands on the site of number 35a Weir Street which was once Billy's home.

As a schoolboy footballer Billy Bremner shone like a lighthouse beacon amongst his contemporaries. He was so skilled and determined that by the time he was thirteen (and attending St Modan's Secondary School) he was playing in an adult league for the Gowan Hill under-21 team. He had shown sheer persistence by turning up to watch the team train in all weathers and helping collect and recover footballs that had gone astray. He would pester the club coach George McDonald, constantly telling him that he was better than some of the other players he had in his team. Giving in to the claims of the young red-haired boy and to one of the Gowan Hill players, Alex Smith, McDonald eventually relented and allowed him to train with the team. He was so impressed that he was at once signed up as a player and given a regular place in the first eleven.

Isobel McDonald, his cousin and best friend, told me a story that sums up the ingenuity and commitment of a young Bremner, determined not to let anyone down:

'Brock was going to be late for the Gowan Hill team training session one evening. He didn't like to be late for anything; he saw it as letting people down and he hated doing that. When he arrived he was on a bicycle. Now the strange thing was that Brock never owned a bicycle. So that he wouldn't be late he had taken the bike from a neighbour's garden without permission. In his own mind he had borrowed it and he was always going to give it back. When he finally got home and he had the bike with him he received a royal telling off from Pop and Bess, and from the neighbour as well. The biggest punishment to him was that he was grounded for a week for taking someone else's property without first asking. He never did it again and although everyone knew that it was not a disingenuous act, he felt very guilty about the whole thing for months after.'

Another tale recounted by Isobel involved Billy's liking for certain sweets:

'He was dreadful for eating sweets as a young man – he had a real liking for Mars bars and Rhubarb Rock. One of his neighbours, Mr Wheater, used to make toffee apples to sell in the street and when they were cooked he would place them out on his kitchen window to cool down. The smell of those toffee apples was wonderful even though the window where they sat was two storeys up. Billy and I would wait until we saw him put them out on the window sill to cool then quickly climb up a drainpipe and help ourselves. To this day he never knew it was us that did it.'

During those formative football years the diminutive Bremner was forced to work harder, committing himself to the tackle with greater strength and displaying greater courage and determination on the football field than many other players. He had decided that his size was not something that was going to hold him back:

'I loved playing football as a youngster and I hated defeat. I was not going to allow myself to be classed as too small or too slight. I wanted to be noticed for my skill and ability so I worked harder than most to improve my game. Football was becoming my life. Pop knew the game better than most people in Raploch and Stirling and played a great role in my physical development and improving my ball control and skills. He would say that I was never happier than when I had a football at my feet and I agree with him on that point.'

The quality of his performances caused many of the best local coaches and football scouts to keep an eye on his progress. A number of appearance for Scotland schoolboys followed, four international games in his final year at St Modan's School, including a Wembley appearance against England schoolboys:

'It was a marvellous thrill to represent my country at such a young age, something I will never forget. I am a devout Scotsman and the thrill of representing my country filled my heart each time I pulled on the national team jersey thereafter. It still gives me a real lift when I think back to each of my international appearances. At schoolboy level you don't really know how to savour the moment or enjoy the occasion, you have a lot of fun and you are playing football in different places, different countries, and not many things can beat that when you are young.

'Yet underpinning that side of it is a more serious tone, you are after all representing your country and any Scot worth their salt would never give less than 100 per cent for their country. It's an honour and a privilege to represent your country or your respective club side and footballers across all divisions and leagues should always remember that fact. Anyone who gives less than 100 per cent in each game is deceiving not only themselves but the supporters too.'

Such a prodigious talent was clearly destined for a career in professional football and, to all who knew Billy, it seemed a natural progression. His tiger-like aggression and ball distribution as a youngster were described by one local commentator as 'well in advance of his years. Young Bremner plays with maturity and looks to have the effectiveness of an experienced professional. If he can overcome his physical slightness, then he may well forge a good career for himself in the game.'

Club scouts were constantly on the lookout for fresh emerging talent and the bigger clubs had excellent communication networks across the British Isles that alerted them to up-and-coming young talent. Together with his pal Tommy Henderson, Bremner was invited for a fortnight of trials with Arsenal and Chelsea, two giants of the English club game. Chelsea had in fact been the English league champions just three years earlier. Managed by the ex-England international Ted Drake, the club must have seemed an attractive proposition to both young men. Both clubs made tentative offers in the hope that they would eventually join them but, astutely, neither Bremner nor Henderson would commit themselves until given time to discuss the long-distance move:

'We took part in a couple of trial matches and training session during a two-week, all expenses paid, stay down in London. Everything about the place was very different from Scotland. I didn't like it, nor did I feel comfortable about how we were treated. There were a lot of other players on trial, mostly from England, and they seemed to get a lot more attention and stuck together. They were clearly more settled than we were as two Scottish lads. It was such along way from Raploch and Scotland.

'You get a feel for a place and London didn't do it for me at all. When I had been to Wembley and seen small pockets of it, it looked a bleak and unhappy place and from experience I knew that it was filled with very rude and ignorant people. I think Tommy would have fancied it though.

'The other thing that I didn't like was that both clubs made comments about me being of small stature and perhaps therefore not able to compete with bigger, better built players! I thought to myself, "How rude, bugger this, who do you think you are questioning my ability like that?"

'Pop always said to me that good things come in small packages! That apparently isn't the case in London, size matters there! I was determined from that point on to work hard and to prove that size doesn't matter when you can play football. My big fear in signing for a London club was not making the grade;

11

a wrong choice could ruin my entire career. I didn't trust the London thing at all, it wasn't right.'

On returning to Scotland there came the news that there had been interest shown by the Glasgow giants, Rangers and Celtic. The Rangers scout had made little more than a tentative inquiry and never returned once he realised that Bremner was a Catholic. Not that such matters bothered the Bremner family. Celtic followed up their enquiry with an invite for both Henderson and Bremner to attend a training session at Parkhead the following Tuesday. Being a Celtic fan, Billy, by his own admission, desperately wanted the Bhoys to come through with a firm offer:

'We still had Arsenal and Chelsea showing interest but Celtic would be the one I would have chosen and preferred. The thought of playing for them really excited me. I didn't dislike Rangers mind, I would often go and watch them at Ibrox, but the whole Celtic thing was really appealing. It was an unbelievably incredible time for both Tommy and me. I couldn't take in what was happening and genuinely had to keep pinching myself to make sure it wasn't a dream. I once said to someone that it was like a giant wave that just seemed to carry us on to new heights every day; it was like reading an adventure story, but it involved me.'

Further offers arrived, this time including Leeds United. A Leeds director, Harry Vennels, and team manager Bill Lambton arrived in Scotland and were keen to secure the signatures of both Bremner and Henderson. Lambton had previously seen both representing Scotland in a schoolboy international at Wembley and had been greatly impressed by Bremner's tenacious attitude and ball control. Leeds weren't about to stand on ceremony, and just days before the Celtic training sessions, they invited the two boys down to Elland Road to see for themselves what the club was like. At this point in time, Leeds United was hardly a prominent force in English football. Bremner admitted that he had never even heard of Leeds United:

'I thought to myself, "Who the hell are this lot, Leeds United, which league do they play in?" I wasn't being critical or cynical but outside the first division and with living in Scotland, I hadn't really any idea about many, if any, of the lower level football teams, other than the grand-sounding Exeter City! Pop was keen for me to go to England as he thought it was a better standard of game down there, especially in the top two leagues. Whatever Pop said was always right and I knew he had my best interests at heart. The Leeds people were persistent; they told us they were family focused and looked after all their young players and their families. They were looking to the future. I liked what I was hearing and my family agreed that I should go and see the club and the place for myself.'

At Elland Road, Leeds Chairman Harry Reynolds took a personal interest in both players and guided them through his own personal ambition for the club, making no elaborate claims or promises but assuring the boys that Leeds was an ambitious club with some great young talent. Bremner recalled this encounter:

'He seemed a down-to-earth and a likeable, open character. I don't really know what it was about Leeds United which impressed me so much, but at the time I felt it was the right decision to join them. They had quite a few youngsters with them, and these lads were honest, like my pals up in Scotland. I liked that.

'It certainly wasn't a case of first impressions that attracted me. The Elland Road stadium was hardly a patch on its present almost regal state and, to be honest, it was depressing and reminded me of the banks of a coal quarry. When I signed I really found it difficult to settle in the city. The people were great, friendly and welcoming, and the club and the officials were good to both Tommy and me, but it wasn't Scotland, it wasn't Stirling. Everything I knew and missed was back in Stirling, my family, my pals and the fun times. Now I had to prove myself to be a man and to make a new life for myself in Yorkshire. I knew it wasn't going to be easy, but never did I envisage how home sick I would become.

'Poor Tommy couldn't handle it at all, and he decided that he had to go home. Cyril Williamson, the Leeds general manager, held a lot of meetings with us and gave us a weekly pep talk. I didn't want to let anyone down, not Leeds, not my family and

13

definitely not myself. As if that wasn't sufficient pressure, I knew that just about all of Raploch was behind me, willing me to succeed, so for them I decided to stick it out. Tommy got fed up with it and went home. I felt so sad for him, yet I still believe he didn't give it anywhere near enough time. I was more determined and something inside told me that it was right for me to stick it out at Leeds, at least for a wee bit longer.

'My gut instinct was to prove right and it wasn't too long before I was told that I was being given a run-out in the reserves at Deepdale, Preston. It was a midweek game. I felt fantastic and on a real high. If only Tommy had waited he would have been lining up alongside me. For the first time in my football career I felt that I had actually achieved something for myself.

'Even though it was only the reserves, I fully intended to treat it as importantly as any game in which I had ever played. I thought I did alright; I kept it simple, and always made the easy pass. Because I was generally smaller than many of the players on the pitch that day, I was quickly on the receiving end of a few rough and unfair tackles. At first I looked for the sympathy of the referee, but found my protestations to him ignored. So I thought to myself, "Right Bill, it's sink or swim time, you have to keep fighting." Pretty soon I was holding my own and then started to impose myself on the game. It wasn't pretty or beautiful, but it worked for me that day. When we came off at the end, the staff were really pleased with me and told me I was the best player on the pitch. I felt great, but my legs ached and were covered in cuts and bruises as a result of the rough treatment dished out by the Preston boys.'

Billy continued to work hard at his game. However, with the undoubted quality of the Leeds first team, he remained very much a reserve-team player. Manager Bill Lambton, who had been handed the post in December 1958, resigned just three months later. By May 1959, rumours were rife that Lambton was to be replaced by Headington United manager Arthur Turner. For whatever reason the move didn't happen and Jack Taylor, then manager of Queen's Park Rangers, joined Leeds as manager instead.

The managerial merry-go-round was giving cause for concern to those within the club, including Billy:

'It was a bad time for everyone at Leeds; players were unsettled and team tactics were all over the place. I was really fed up. It was great playing regularly for the reserves but after a while I wanted more, I wanted a place in the first team and that didn't look very likely. I would have accepted a move back home to Scotland; I was becoming more and more restless at the lack of opportunities and felt I was never going to get the chance.

'With Bill Lambton gone, I wondered whether I would slip completely out of the first-team picture. I would often talk over my worries with my cousin Issy and my mate Alex Smith. They were excellent pals, and told me to keep at it, to stay focused and to take the opportunity when it came along. They would remind me how grim life in Raploch could be, and how I was gifted and had a chance to make something of myself.'

Billy had little need for concern, as it wasn't too long before the new manager called him into his office for a quiet chat:

'I had a couple of conversations with Jack Taylor. He had showed some interest in keeping me on the fringes of the first team, but he didn't feel I was yet capable of holding down a regular first-team position. So I told him that I felt I should have broken into the first team by now, I was consistently performing well for the reserves, yet for whatever reason it hadn't happened for me – I was being overlooked. I told him I was thinking about getting myself a move back to Scotland. I was surprised to hear him say that he knew every club in Scotland and many in England would want me. He listened to me and understood my frustration. His parting advice was that it would be in my best interests not to seek a move away from Leeds but to stick it out, as bigger things awaited me while he was manager. I wasn't at all sure what he meant, but he was a Yorkshire man and seemed genuine enough. He was experienced in the game and had a great playing record behind him at Wolverhampton Wanderers and Norwich, so I decided to wait a wee while before formally asking for a transfer.'

3

MARCHING ON TOGETHER

The moment Bremner had waited so patiently for arrived on Saturday, 23 January 1960. Winger Chris Crowe was forced to drop out of the first team through injury and Billy Bremner was added to the first team to play Chelsea at Stamford Bridge:

'I thought, "Christ what a coincidence, making my debut against a club that had shown a bit of interest in signing me before Leeds had come in." It was also a club who said I was too small to make it in the professional game in England. A comment I was not to forget.'

Jack Taylor selected his first eleven: Wood, Ashall, Hair, Cush, Charlton, Gibson, Bremner, Revie, McCole, Peyton and Meek. It was the vastly experienced centre forward Don Revie who roomed with the young Bremner the night prior to the game and whose advice and guidance were to be so influential on him:

'Don the player was professional and sincere; he was grateful for possessing football ability and did his utmost to make sure he was fit and ready for every game. He insisted on getting an early night, and told me that a good night's sleep before a game was extremely important if you were to perform to the best of your ability. I had a lot of respect for what he had achieved as a player so listened to him and acted on a lot of what he said. We did have an early night but it didn't matter as I didn't sleep a wink. I was so excited and couldn't wait for the game and to get out onto the pitch.'

In the Leeds dressing room, as he pulled on the number seven shirt, both Wilbur Cush and Revie advised the youngster to play it easy and to stick to the easy option, two-touch football:

'Don Revie was with me all the way, he told me how Stamford Bridge had a shit hole of a pitch when it was wet or evenly mildly damp. Wilbur said that the Chelsea fans were an unsporting, noisy and abusive lot and I was told to ignore anything they yelled at me or the team. Neither were wrong, Chelsea, not just the pitch, was a shit hole, and over the years I was to find that with the slightest rainfall, puddles would build up on that surface, causing the pitch to cut up until eventually it resembled a ploughed field more suitable for keeping pigs than for football, an environment that would be like home to their fans!'

Prior to kick-off, heavy rain fell, and the Stamford Bridge pitch began cutting up during the pre-match warm-up; huge divots of turf were present across all areas of the pitch. The more experienced Leeds players knew how physically exhausting ninety minutes on that surface could be. Neat passing football was totally out of the question, hard work and determination were needed if any kind of result was to be ground out. The rain continued to fall throughout the game and it was surprising that an attendance as high as 18,963 turned out in atrociously wet conditions.

Some of the Chelsea staff and players mocked the diminutive ginger-haired Leeds winger making his debut, crudely referring to him as the 'ginger-haired dwarf-kid'. It was to be a game that Billy would never forget:

'It's difficult to know what to think when you make your first-team debut; the pitch was dreadful. I thought other teams would be as professional as we were, but instead I found that Chelsea would stoop to any level to intimidate and bully. It riled me and ensured that I was all the more determined to get one over on them.

'All I wanted at the start was to get my first touch of the ball out of the way. Fortunately this happened fairly quickly and when I laid a pass on to Don Revie I immediately settled down into my game. Wilbur Cush constantly reminded me to ignore abusive and foul comments made by the Chelsea players and their crowd. He reminded me that the abuse should be taken as a

17

back-handed compliment, as it meant they saw me as a threat and that I was playing well. By the end of the game I was being nasty to the Chelsea players who had been having a go at me and they didn't like it one bit!'

With Revie and Cush playing alongside him, Bremner displayed composure and finesse with his possession and passing. The two experienced professionals literally nursed him through the game, ensuring that simple passing options were always available. In fact he almost snatched a goal. When a misplaced Chelsea clearance fell to him he at once turned this into a Leeds attack, pushing forward at the Chelsea defence, before shooting at goal. The press reported of his performance: 'The lightweight boy came through well; he used the ball speedily, generally accurately and always intelligently.'

It may not have been the most spectacular of debuts, but Billy Bremner had not looked out of place. He had achieved what he wanted, to get one over on Chelsea. Leeds had been too good for the west London outfit, and had comfortably won the game by three goals to one. Afterwards, he was to recall:

'It was excellent, everybody congratulated me on having a good solid game. I had been rattled by the abuse, but first and foremost stayed focused on my game. It was nice to walk off that pitch a winner and letting the Chelsea losers know the utter contempt I had for them.'

The following week Billy made his Elland Road league debut, at home to West Bromwich Albion, and again he was wearing the number seven shirt. The thrill of a winning start to his first-team career disappeared before 23,729 despairing Leeds supporters, as the home side capitulated against an unusually rampant Albion, who ran out winners by four goals to one.

'Oh Jesus,' Bremner recalled, 'it wasn't a game I can recall with any fondness. That day, if I am to be honest, West Brom ran us ragged, and the Leeds crowd really got on our backs, which made us all a bit nervous. I couldn't assert myself on the game and struggled to get into any rhythm. The Albion boys were fighting for every ball. I wasn't ready for it and it was a relief when the final whistle sounded, to get off the pitch, albeit to a chorus of booing and angry swearing of discontented Leeds supporters. In the dressing room afterwards there was absolute silence. We were shit; we played like shit and felt like shit. It was horrible and I vowed that never again would I want to endure such bad emotions and an awful dressing-room atmosphere.'

With Chris Crowe again fit, Bremner found himself dropped from the first eleven for the following two league games:

'When I was dropped I asked the manager and players if I was being blamed for the result against West Bromwich. He told me I wasn't to blame, and that I had to realise that a player of Chris Crowe's quality couldn't justifiably be left out of the first team. I was disheartened. I knew inside that I was being made the scapegoat for the defeat. I also knew that I hadn't made enough of an impact to prove myself a capable alternative. I knew that I was a better player than Chris Crowe but opted to keep my own counsel on that belief and to keep fighting to win back a place in the first team.'

Within the space of a few weeks, Chris Crowe was sold to Blackburn Rovers for a fee of £25,000. The club accepted the bid as they knew that in Bremner they had an all-round better player. Finally, the youngster from Stirling had secured a regular first-team place, making a total of eleven league appearances during the remainder of that season and scoring two goals. His euphoria at breaking into the first eleven was dampened by the club's relegation from the First Division:

'It was an awful feeling. Being relegated is the worst feeling in the world. The mood throughout the club was miserable and I have to confess that I still missed Scotland and was looking at sounding out a move to Stirling Albion. My mate Alex Smith put me straight on that one and told me not to be so bloody stupid and to give Leeds a chance. Everyone seemed to be saying the same thing to me – give Leeds a chance.

'Jack Taylor must have realised how I was feeling, not that it was any kind of secret, because he went out of his way to make me feel comfortable about everything at the club and assured me that I had a bright future in the first team at Leeds. Going into the summer I felt fairly confident about how my career was mapping out. I believed Jack Taylor was going to be instrumental in that career. I was very wrong.'

Despite Taylor's apparent warmth towards him, Bremner made just two league appearances in the first thirteen fixtures of the 1960-61 season:

'I had taken a knock or two in training and needed some treatment – nothing too serious, but enough for Jack Taylor to drop me from his plans. I was really pissed off about it but continued to train hard. I often stayed behind after sessions to try to build up my fitness and body strength. Still Jack Taylor ignored me.

'It got to the stage where I had to take the bull by the horns and confront the manager. In straightforward language I asked him why I wasn't playing in the first team. It was my first glimpse of a manager under duress. I was expecting a blazing row but, instead, he told me I had been dropped because it was character building, adding that I would be back in the first team for the next game and it was up to me to prove that this was where I should be every game.'

It goes without saying that he did impress as it marked the start of an ever-present run of thirty-two consecutive first-team outings.

'Despite everything else, I still missed the comfort Raploch offered; I went home as often as I could to see my family and mates. On one trip back I went out for a night to the Plaza in Stirling. Issy, Alex and a couple of other mates were there too. I saw this lovely looking girl and asked Issy if she knew who she was. Issy told me that she was known as Vicky Dick, and that she had won a John Player Beauty Competition. I wasn't surprised, as she was a real stunning-looking girl and still is. I was reluctant to approach her so I did the cowardly thing and asked Issy to ask her to go out with me.'

Isabel takes up the story: 'Billy asked me to ask her to go out with him and I told him not to be daft and to ask her himself. A short time later I went to the toilet to get myself ready to go home and Vicky came in. I spoke to her and she asked me if I knew anything about the young lad with reddish-coloured hair from Raploch who had asked her out. She said he had given her some story about playing for Leeds United and owning his own car. She didn't believe him as no one from Raploch owned a car – if they needed one they just stole one. I put her straight and told her that he did own a car and he did play for Leeds United. It didn't impress her at all. Eventually she relented to his advances and they became a couple, and a really nice couple too. After a short romance they married in November 1961. Both of them were nineteen years old when they wed. Alex Smith was Brock's best man on the day. I couldn't make the wedding ceremony as I had joined the forces and wasn't allowed leave to attend. I was really upset at missing it.'

On the football side of matters, it was all change at Leeds once more, as manager Jack Taylor resigned on 13 March 1961. Just four days later he was replaced in the manager's office by a new personality.

4

ARISE SIR DON!

The new manager of Leeds United was soon revealed as Bremner's team mate, and room mate, Don Revie. It was a move which was to prove more than influential to the football career of Billy Bremner:

'I couldn't believe it when Jack left and Don got the job. There were a lot of rumours about the new manager of course, but no one really expected Don to be given the job like that. He had a great relationship with the directors and staff, so maybe that is what swung it for him in the end; whatever, it came as a bit of a surprise. I wasn't sure how he would treat me or the rest of the boys. He had been good to me as a player but now things were going to be different, he was the boss.'

Don Revie recalled his first managerial talk with Bremner:

'He was an impudent little sod at times and I thought he may give me a bit of trouble. Keeping all his enthusiasm in check was a full-time job. I talked to all the players and they were right behind me as manager. I told Billy that I wanted us back in the First Division and that his role in that was pivotal to the team's success. He told me he wanted to be part of that success but he still missed Scotland. I told him that he should focus on himself and Leeds United and put Scotland behind him for now. He said he would, but I didn't really believe him He was so patriotic and devoutly loyal to his family and friends up there. I was fortunate to have him at Leeds and didn't want to lose him. I realised at that early stage that it was going to be a real battle keeping him at the club.'

Bremner recalls Revie's first managerial talk with the players who were previously team mates and pals:

'It was a bit strange, none of us knew how he would be. He had our respect as a player and a colleague but now he was the manager things had to be different. He called all the players together for a meeting, and informed us how he wanted to make us formidable opponents. That got a bit of a cheer. At some point he told us that we could no longer call him "The Don" (which was our nickname for him), or any other personal title or pseudonym. Someone piped up and asked whether we could call him Mr Revie. He didn't like the term "Mr Revie" – he thought it still had an air of informality about it! Finally he said, "I want you all to call me Boss." He seemed embarrassed to be making the request, but as a group of players, a family almost, we were all okay with it. So Don Revie was no more, he was now the boss!'

The following season, 1961-62, saw Billy Bremner notch his highest-ever goal tally for a complete season, twelve in all competitions. His consistent and battling performances in the Leeds attack hadn't gone unnoticed, his quick feet and vision had attracted many admirers. Hibernian manager, Walter McMurray Galbraith, had heard the rumour that the player was unsettled in England, and was yearning for a return to Scotland. Hibernian, who were regarded as a very good side, made a cheeky bid of £25,000 for the player.

'I was actually quite keen on the move north of the Border, the boss knew I wanted to go home and a move to Hibs seemed a good move to me. I was going in the right direction. The boss told me that Hibernian had formally submitted a bid for me – he looked devastated when he told me. I honestly believed that my days at Elland Road were numbered. The next day the boss had me in his office. He clearly wasn't happy one little bit about the move and told me that he wanted me to stay at Leeds. He looked at me straight in the eye and told me that I had "what it takes to make it to the top." There was something about the way he said it that made me realise he believed what he was saying. For someone like Don Revie to say something like that to me was a real compliment. He stood looking at me, almost pleading with me to stay. For a few seconds I wavered a little and had misgivings about wanting to leave but, for me, I was still a slip of a lad, Scotland was my home and I believed that home was where I would be happiest. With a heavy heart I had to tell him that I was interested in the move to Hibernian. He looked a broken man.'

Revie later recalled: 'It was a dreadful situation, here we had a player who had the makings of being a top-class footballer and he didn't really know how highly his colleagues across the game regarded him. As well as that, just about every manager of the teams we played would comment on how good a player he was, and subtly ask whether he was available on transfer. I always gave a resounding "No" to that question and would have to tell them to bugger off.

'Unfortunately, the board of directors were keen to accept the bid, it was a good fee, and the money would help the club. I was dead set against it; it filled my thoughts every day. I wanted the directors to realise how much I wanted him to stay with us, how important he was to my team-building plans. Hibernian gave a deadline for the response and the directors said they would wait for my decision before responding. I waited until the last possible moment then told them to take not a penny less than £30,000. It was a gamble, but my sources in Scotland told me that they were stretching their finances to their very limits at £25,000, so an extra £5,000 would hopefully be a bridge too far and end their interest.'

The manager was right, the transfer faltered and never progressed, the £30,000 fee terrified Hibernian and they eventually withdrew the original offer of £25,000. It was not the news Bremner had wanted to hear:

'The boss called me in the next morning and he seemed a lot happier. He wasn't looking at me when he said it, but he told me that Hibernian wouldn't meet the club's asking price for me so, until that happened, I would remain a Leeds player. I was absolutely fuming and disappointed that the move was off.

'As I stood there I wanted to tell him to shove Leeds United up his arse; my emotions were about to explode when he looked up

24

and told me to sit down. Eye contact at last. This, I thought, would be my opportunity to let him see my dissatisfaction. Instead, I began to listen to what he was saying. First, he told me that he felt it was in my best interests to see the job through at Leeds, and that he wanted success and would not settle for anything less from any of his players. I had heard that story before from different Leeds managers. This time, I have to say, I believed it. He casually added that he wanted to build the team around me, a team capable of winning and challenging for the Football League Championship and European honours. At that moment I realised that I was going to stay and help him achieve success, and would give everything to attain it myself, even though I still I yearned for Scotland!'

So began the manager-player relationship that was built on respect and was to last for a lifetime. It has been well recorded that Don Revie was so keen to keep Bremner within the ranks of his Leeds team that he drove to Stirling and personally spoke with the player's wife, Vicky. Explaining his long-term plans for the club and for her husband Billy Bremner. Whatever was said between the two appears to have worked as Billy Bremner, the footballer and person, settled into his Yorkshire surroundings and began to enjoy his new life.

The 1961-62 season was one of struggle, and much later, in 1973, it became the subject of much controversy. Then Bury manager, Bob Stokoe, made public allegations that Don Revie had tried to bribe him, with £500 for his team to 'go easy', before a league game on Good Friday 1962. Stokoe claimed to be incensed by Revie's cheating, and so began his professional and personal hatred for the Leeds boss that was to last his lifetime. Stokoe was to cash in on the story when he later sold his version of events to the *Daily Mirror*.

Bremner was quick to defend his manager:

'I know the history of the whole Bob Stokoe thing. I never quite got on with him as a person or a manager, and he was a bit eccentric and very much a loose cannon. That's why he never managed at the very highest level. I crossed paths with him

25

many times and on each occasion he would hurl abuse towards me, calling me Don Revie's favourite son and a mini-cheat.

'It got so bad that eventually I had to confront him at a Football League event somewhere in Park Lane, London. I was sat in the reception of the hotel talking to a couple of reporters from a football magazine. Up comes Stokoe, mad as a hatter and says to the reporters, "You want to believe nothing this cheat tells you." Then he struts off. That was it for me. I jumped up and followed him into the gents toilets and asked him what his problem was. He turned on me again, this time his face was all gnarled up in anger, spittle flying from his mouth. He looked at me and said, "You are nothing but a little shit, Bremner, Revie's ponce, doing his dirty work. Now get out of my sight before I f—— drop you." I laughed at his comments and replied by telling him to f—— off to see his mate Brian Clough, who curiously enough he had also accused of being a cheat. Stokoe was really angry now and I was waiting for him to thump me. Instead, the dirty bastard spat at me but thankfully he missed. I didn't. I wasn't privy to what happened between him and the boss, the boss rarely talked about Bob Stokoe, but when he did it was clear he believed him to be irrational, out of his depth and out of control. Someone else said he was an attention seeker, an underachiever as a player and destined to a life in the lower levels of the football league. I never told the boss about what had happened between me and Stokoe – he would have had a fit at me for reacting to his inane ramblings.'

The following 1962-63 season saw a marked improvement on the previous season's endeavours. A Second Division final placing of fifth was to provide the platform for greater things. For Bremner it was another season of solid performances topped with ten league goals: 'The boss had us working as a unit, instilling self-belief in everything we did. He wanted us to be a big family, with complete trust in our fellows and team mates. Honesty and openness in debates and discussions were introduced to team talks and post-match inquests. To lighten up some of the meetings we would introduce card games and other light-hearted family games and entertainment. It was all good fun and the lads would look forward to the team meetings.'

The 1963-64 campaign was indeed a glorious one as Leeds romped to the Second Division championship, losing just three of their forty-two league games. Elland Road became a fortress as not a single league defeat was suffered at home. For Bremner it was a consistent season; he appeared in all forty-two league fixtures and four cup games.

'It was a great season, one of the finest,' he recalled. 'The boss drafted a lot of youngsters into the team and we gelled and never really looked back. We knew we had to work for each other, not only as a team, but as a club. Everyone was committed to the cause and we got to know each other's game. At times it seemed almost telepathic. There was a real understanding between us as a group; more than anything I think it was the belief that the boss was behind us with everything we did and tried.

'As for my role in that group, it just happened, I felt comfortable in midfield, with players like Jack Charlton, Norman Hunter and Johnny Giles playing alongside me, and with the presence of Bobby Collins, I couldn't really go wrong. To say that I was an influence on that side is unfair on the rest of the lads. I was still learning my trade, we were as one, and the entire team influenced and looked after each other. I think Bobby Collins was the main inspiration of that side, he was a competitor and didn't know when to stop. What many players would view as a lost cause, he would chase, hassle and harass, intimidating the opposition into virtual submission. The younger ones in that side learned a lot from Bobby, I know I did. We all seemed to realise that we were part of something very special at Leeds.

'I've always had fond memories of the 1963-64 season not only because of what we were achieving as a group at Leeds, but because I finally found my favourite position at wing-half or half-back or, in the modern game, midfield.

'It was also special because I got my first of what was to be four

27

Scotland under-23 call-ups for a game against the "auld enemy", England, at St James' Park, Newcastle. It was a cold February night and it wasn't the most atmospheric of evenings, though more than a few Scots had made the journey over the border to cheer us on. We had a united belief within the Scotland team that we had the individuals who, if they could get it together on the night, could beat England. We went close to doing just that, and had it not been for the killer instinct of Everton and England centre forward Fred Pickering, we would have got at least a draw. Pickering was hard as nails, and was a real handful that night; he got himself a hat-trick. I had a good crack with him before, during and after the game. He could take a bit of stick, and he could give it too. He stood on my foot for a few moments when we were waiting for a corner to drop into the penalty area. So I pinched his arm really hard. I'll never forget it; he yelped like a dog and soon got off my foot, holding his arm like he had been wounded by a gunshot. The referee had seen the lot and was laughing at the pair of us.

'Afterwards in the dressing room we couldn't believe we had lost 3-2 and vowed our revenge the next time we faced them. My other appearances for the Scotland under-23 team came against England (again) at Pittodrie, Aberdeen. In the England team were my Leeds pals Norman Hunter and Paul Reaney. I was working my butt off trying to keep Alan Ball in check, he was a livewire and I thought it funny that people often compared our game and style. For heaven's sake, he was English and couldn't possibly have the heart of a Scot. He was a good little player though and a right handful whenever I faced him. He had sprinting pace as a youngster and managed to turn me a couple of times, but kept away from me after I told him in no uncertain terms that he would end up in 'row Z' of the stands if he tried it again. The daft thing was, as soon as I said it, I heard a voice I instantly recognised, threatening to put me up there alongside him, if I tried it. When I looked round it was only Norman Hunter!

'To be fair, the game was a bit of a non-event and we drew 0-0.

I played and scored against Wales when we won 3-0. That match was played at Kilmarnock. It felt good scoring a goal for Scotland and although it was at under-23 level, it still meant a hell of a lot to me. I played in the game against France which we again won, this time 2-0. I don't think that's a bad under-23 international record; played four, won two, drawn one, lost one, scored one.'

5

MOVING ON UP

If the 1963-64 season was classed as a good one, then the 1964-65 one could only be described as unbelievable. The media, as is now generally the case, believed that the newcomers to football's top league would simply aspire to nothing more than stability. It was predicted that Leeds would find the pace and quality of the First Division vastly different from that of the Second Division and would struggle. Yet Revie and his players felt differently. Bremner recalls:

'There was self-belief running throughout the team. We all knew that it wouldn't be an easy season, but we actually believed in each other, and that made a difference.

'One enigma was South African winger, Albert Johanneson. Albert had joined the club in 1961; in training the things he could do with a football amazed us. Ball juggling, flicks and tricks, he could control a football like no other person I had seen. He had the potential to become one of the game's greatest players of the era. We called him the Black Flash because he was so quick, and he weighed in with goals too. The problem was he had very little self-confidence. No matter what we told him, as soon as an opposition player or the fans got onto him, he began to doubt his ability and would hide in games where we needed him. We all had belief in him, none more so than the boss. Saying that, we had players of real quality who couldn't get a regular first-team place, we had strength in depth and the best supporters in the land to back us.'

The season began with a 2-1 win over Aston Villa at Villa Park; this was followed by a midweek Elland Road clash against reigning league champions, Liverpool, as Bremner explained:

'I don't believe we openly classed the Liverpool game as any different from any other league clash, although it's always nice to beat the reigning champions. The supporters were relishing the chance to see us match them. Privately, I think the boss and the rest of us saw it as a benchmark of how we would cope with life in the first division. It was a great game to play in, a real battle from start to finish, and something else to win 4-2. We left the field that night absolutely drained but emotionally high. The belief and confidence we gained from that one result set us up for the rest of the season.'

An eighteen-match unbeaten run between late November and mid-April proved Leeds' resilience to cope with top-flight football. Two defeats in April, at home to Manchester United (0-1), and away at Sheffield Wednesday (0-3), coincided with the two league games Bremner missed that season.

'Oh, I don't think you can relate my absence to those two defeats. Manchester United was a strong side, always capable of beating anyone on their own turf. As for Wednesday, it was just one of those games, they unsettled us, and Hillsborough is a tough place to go when you are Leeds – Yorkshire rivalry and all that. Those two results effectively killed off our championship aspirations.'

Despite the undoubted quality of the football they consistently delivered, the media, fuelled by information contained within *FA News*, condemned the club for their 'dirty' style of play. The *FA News* had published a league table of clubs with the worst disciplinary record for the previous 1963-64 season, Leeds were top. The club ignored it and declined to comment on the abuse directed at them from certain quarters of the press and also from their opponents, many of whom would refer to them during games, particularly the Southern-based sides, as 'dirty northern bastards' or 'cheating Yorkshire thugs'.

Bremner in particular found himself identified as an instigator of the so-called 'dirty Leeds' style:

'I remember being asked by one journalist why I was such a dirty player and why I seemed to encourage my colleagues to kick lumps out of the opposition. It came as something of a surprise to be confronted by such inane and insulting questioning. I was really offended by the accusation thrown at me and it hurt. Without thinking, I asked him why he was such a shit writer and why he wasn't writing for one of the top national newspapers. He went bright red and didn't answer, he couldn't. I followed this up by advising him that it was because he lacked any professionalism and that as long as he had a hole in his arse he would never make a good football correspondent. For good measure I told him that he was a complete and utter wanker and not to be bother me again. He was obviously very upset by my comments as he abruptly turned on his heels and walked away.

'I wasn't always a dirty player, sure I was tough and I always wanted to win, and yes, I admit it, I was enthusiastic, perhaps a little too over-enthusiastic on occasions, but I firmly believe that every footballer should give his all for his club. He gets to wear the club shirt on a match day because he has earned the right through individual qualities. That reporter was intimating that I possessed little in the way of talent and had got to where I was through fouling, cheating and kicking. To my knowledge, I never saw him again.

'Don't get me wrong, I have nothing against football journalists or writers, many of them are extremely good at what they do, but there are limits as to how far anyone should pre-judge any individual, especially when the majority have never played professional football.

'I remember Chelsea players (again) trying to have a go at us during a game at Elland Road. Each time we went into a tackle they would hit the ground as though they had been struck by a scythe; they were shouting out "cheats" and "dirty northern bastards" so the referee could hear. It was ridiculous. Eventually I had a word with the referee and explained that Chelsea were play acting. He told me that from where he stood, I needed to calm my players down, as they were being overtly clumsy in the challenge. What a prat – "overtly clumsy" – what kind of stupid talk is that! Why did he not come out and say – "I think you are dirty northern bastards too"? I told the boss at half time and he went to speak with him

32

about some of his decisions. A minute later the boss reappeared shaking his head from side to side. He looked at me and said, "Bill, we're playing against twelve men today, the ref has to be a Chelsea fan. He can see no wrong in anything they do and he says we are abusing and intimidating them."

'That was it. In my short time in the game so many incidents were Chelsea related. I knew that Chelsea and I were never going to get along. As we came out for the second half one of the linesmen said to me, "Don't worry Billy, we've spotted the play acting and are onto it." So tell me, in these instances who actually were the cheats, Leeds, Chelsea or the match official? It still pains me that the "dirty Leeds" tag stuck with us long after we had all finished playing, and still continues.'

As the 1964-65 season progressed it was evident that the race for the Football League Championship was going to be between Leeds and Manchester United. Leeds had beaten the Red Devils in a replayed FA Cup semi-final so had one eye on the club's first ever FA Cup final appearance at Wembley stadium. Incredibly, the final game of the league season had seen Leeds needing to win to win the league. It wasn't to be, as a ten-man Birmingham City side, with nothing to lose or play for other than pride, were 3-0 up after 51 minutes of the game. The title dream was dwindling away, but not the Leeds spirit. In an incredible fight-back, goals from Johnny Giles, Paul Reaney and Jack Charlton earned a 3-3 draw and a solitary point, insufficient to secure the championship. Leeds had to be satisfied with the runners-up spot:

'The game against Birmingham City wasn't the reason why we weren't league champions that year. We couldn't afford to lose two of our last five games and then expect to win the league, especially as one of those defeats was against our closest rival, Manchester United. Yes it was disappointing, yet when I look back and think of what we had achieved in a relatively short space of time, it was quite incredible. We were seen as serious contenders and despite what our critics and the cynics said, we played some really good football and won games because we outplayed our opponents in every position.'

The FA Cup provided a real opportunity for the team to collect some silverware. First Southport, then Everton (after a replay), followed by Shrewsbury Town and Crystal Palace were suitably dispatched, before Manchester United, proclaimed by the media to be the mightiest team in the land, were slain in the semi-final:

'I loved playing in the FA Cup, it was never easy going to smaller clubs and those nasty little grounds where it was impossible for us play our usual football. We were building a decent reputation for ourselves as a team and club, and some lower league teams saw us as a team they couldn't compete with football wise. Instead, they would resort to trying to kick lumps out of us. It was hilarious to see supreme footballers, like Albert Johanneson, skipping past players trying to kick him into the stands, dancing past and round them like he was Rudolph Nureyev. Albert had all the football skill in the world and the dirtiest of players couldn't get anywhere near him when he was on his game.

'Then there was Terry Cooper. The sight of him with his head down and in full flow, sprinting up the wing with the ball at his feet, he would leave everyone in his wake. I swear, sometimes Terry didn't know where he was going to end up when he set off on those mazy runs. Invariably he got a cross into the penalty area where we had forwards who could stick away half a chance. It was exceptional and, when I look back, so many teams simply couldn't compete with what we had in our armoury.'

The Manchester United FA Cup semi-final was no classic. Indeed, it took a replay to decide the issue. Both games were littered with niggling little incidents which detracted from what many had hoped would be an epic encounter. The first game was played at Hillsborough before 65,000 spectators. One reporter recorded that during the game there had been '32 fouls, 2 bookings, 7 prolonged injuries and no goals'.

The match referee, Mr R. H. Windle, suffered heavy criticism in the pages of the national press. His all-too-lenient approach to both sets of players was deemed to have encouraged the ill-tempered attitude displayed by both sides. At one point a group of seven players, four from Manchester and three from Leeds, squared up to each other and included in that mob was, of course, Billy Bremner:

'I was being kicked all over the place by Paddy Crerand and little Nobby Stiles. My legs, my arse and even my back was covered in cuts and bruises. I took what I could until it was time to put a stop to it. It was a bit of a tame challenge that caused me to have a go in return, Paddy had been winding me up all game, kicking at my calfs and grabbing my shirt, holding tight onto me so I couldn't move, adding "f—— off Bremner" when he released the hold.

'I decided to have a dig back at him, it was a simple elbow to his ribs, not hard but just a reminder that he shouldn't mess with me. Then it all kicked off, name calling, slapping, shirt pulling, but there was not one punch thrown, we had far too much respect for each other to punch. Everything else was okay, but no punching.'

Despite the continual skirmishes all over the pitch and the media damnation of the referee, surprise surprise, the Football Association stood by the match official and announced that he would officiate the replay at Nottingham Forest four days later.

The replay was by far and away the better of the two games; from the first whistle both sides attacked and defended in equal proportion; more importantly, both played some neat passing football. The two teams were deadlocked and it was going to take something very special to win the tie.

There was a number of fine individual performances, none more so than that from the most outstanding player on the field that night, Billy Bremner. He covered every blade of grass and totally controlled the midfield area of the pitch and beyond. From defence to attack, Bremner was involved with everything for Leeds. The *Yorkshire Post* reporter, Eric Stranger, said of his performance; 'Bremner had one of his most outstanding games.'

It was somewhat fitting that with just two minutes of the game remaining the familiar form of Billy Bremner latched onto a forty-yard free-kick that had been lofted deep into the Manchester penalty area by Johnny Giles. The irrepressible midfield dynamo launched himself toward the ball, twisting and stretching every muscle and sinew in his neck and upper body, in a desperate attempt to make contact. He succeeded, the ball bulleted off his head and into the roof of the net, giving Leeds the lead, and ultimately a place in the 1965 FA Cup final.

'At first I thought Johnny had taken it too quickly and overhit it. I remember reacting first and seeing the Manchester United defenders stood still. I was thinking, f—— me, I'm in mid-air leaping like a salmon, and that f—— ball is going to sail right past me and out of play. As it dropped I realised I could get my head to it and said to myself – go on Bill, head the f—— thing into the net, you can reach it, you can do it. The ball seemed to drop down in its trajectory, beside, yet behind my head. I twisted myself backwards and sideways in mid-air, and managed to divert it into the Manchester United goal! To this very day I still don't know how I got to that ball, yet as soon as I did, I knew it was going in. Johnny always said he had dropped it right on my head. That's not true. He hit it in my general direction. Before I landed on the ground I could hear the Leeds fans let out a huge roar, what a noise. I think it was Tony Dunne who was closest to me, and I heard him shout, "You lucky Yorkshire bastards, Bremner, you little shit." Boy did I feel good. As I got to my feet I reminded him that luck never came into it, the best team wins. The Manchester United fans were screaming all kinds of abuse and throwing coins at us. I didn't care, it was the greatest moment of my Leeds career up to that point.'

Sadly, the game was marred seconds after the Bremner goal, when a Manchester United fan ran onto the pitch and knocked out referee Mr Windle with a clean punch to his head. Despite the despicable behaviour of the Manchester Red Army, behaviour that was to get much worse as the decade progressed, the night belonged to Billy Bremner and his Leeds United colleagues:

'What happened to the referee was all wrong; the man could have been seriously hurt. That aside it was a great moment for us all, to get to a Wembley Cup final, a first for Leeds. In the dressing room after the game, I was trying to have a relaxing smoke and a bit of time to reflect but it was pandemonium. Everyone was hugging each other and in the end I realised that I wasn't going to be able to enjoy a fag and it was a complete waste of time trying to grab five minutes for myself.

'I had done Wembley before in a schoolboy international back in April 1958 when we beat the England boys on their own soil, but I knew it wasn't going to be remotely comparable to appearing in an FA Cup final.'

The Wembley final against Liverpool was played on a filthy, wet afternoon on 1 May 1965. The pitch, green and lush at the beginning of the encounter, resembled a mud bath at the end of ninety minutes, as the teams fought out a 0-0 draw in normal time, thus ensuring that extra time was necessary in an FA Cup final for the first time since 1947.

'It had been a long old season for us all and I was bloody knackered at the end of the ninety minutes. The Wembley pitch saps your energy and strength. It's the Cumberland turf, it was like a sponge, and it's great in the dry, but like a quagmire when it gets damp or wet. I thought we had matched Liverpool in every area in the first ninety minutes, and in the back of my mind I wanted us to hold out for a draw and a replay at Maine Road the following week. That would give us all time to rest and do battle again.

'I could see other players were shattered, and poor Albert Johanneson was a bag of nerves with some of the Liverpool crowd shouting racist comments at him. That unnerved him, but so did the fact that he was the first black footballer to appear in a Wembley FA Cup final. Someone, a reporter, had reminded him of the fact in the tunnel area before the game. As he walked into the dressing room I could see something was bothering him. He looked like he had the weight of the world on his shoulders. So I asked him what was wrong. "Sir, they say I am special and the eyes of the world will be on me today, as a black footballer in an FA Cup final." Most people would see that as an honour and challenge to be the best on the day. Not Albert, he shit himself and when some of the crowd made Zulu noises each time he got the ball that finished him. It wasn't only Albert who was struggling. As a team we had ran out of steam at the final hurdle. Just when it appeared that we could hang on for a draw, it happened, they scored.'

That initial blow came after ninety-three minutes when Roger Hunt dived in to head the Merseysiders into a 1-0 lead. The goal looked as though it had settled the tie. Both teams were clearly weary through their exertions, yet despite suffering from exhaustion and cramp, continued to strategically outmanoeuvre each other. Leeds, with nothing to lose, pushed forward at every opportunity, only to be snuffed out by the strong Liverpool rearguard. On 101 minutes, a dishevelled-looking Billy Bremner, soaked to the skin, and with one sock rolled down to his ankle, giving him the appearance of a lost waif as opposed to a professional footballer, put a temporary halt to Liverpool's somewhat presumptive celebrations. His sweetly struck shot from the edge of the penalty area flew high into the Liverpool net, past the clawing and clutching fingers of the despairing goalkeeper Tommy Lawrence. Bremner threw his arms out high and wide and began his celebratory sprint. Jack Charlton meanwhile leapt high into the air, punching his right arm towards the heavens. Wembley stadium erupted into a sea of white, gold and blue:

'I have scored a few goals in my time, but the two goals in the FA Cup that season are the most memorable. The diving header against Manchester United gave me a great feeling of relief and achievement. The goal in the final against Liverpool was without doubt the one which gave me the greatest amount of satisfaction. When they first took the lead in extra time, I think we all knew that it was going to be hard for us to get back into the game. I looked round at our players and could see in their faces that they were physically drained. I ran round to each of them and reminded them that Liverpool looked knackered too; I kept telling them that I was going to give it one final push and to get behind me in doing that.

'Many were too tired to speak, others gave an understanding wink. When I equalised I thought my goal would generate that lift, that additional rush of adrenalin you sometimes need to keep going. When the ball came out to me, I looked up, I was a good distance away from the goal and reminded myself of something John Charles had once told me: "Power and accuracy lad, that can beat any goalkeeper from any distance, if you can see the features on the goalkeepers face, then you are close enough to shoot and score." I really smacked that ball and I felt all my energy going through my leg and into the shot. It was a great feeling – watching it sail by Tommy Lawrence and into the back of the net. There was a split second of silence, probably through disbelief more than anything else, before my goal celebrations began, it was a wonderful moment. It felt like we had won the damn Cup, not just equalised.'

The revival lasted just ten minutes. An unmarked Ian St John headed the Merseysiders back into the lead to virtually kill off the Leeds challenge. The FA Cup was on its way to the Anfield trophy cabinet for the first time in the club's history. As the final whistle blew, many of the Leeds team collapsed to their knees, mentally and physically shattered by the afternoon's exertions.

It was a defeat which Bremner was never to forget:

'When I left the Wembley pitch that afternoon, I was really pissed off. The boss came up to me and gave me a reassuring hug, he thanked each and every one of us for our efforts. It is a dreadful feeling losing at Wembley, an emotional void that I would often recall, in order that I would give my everything, just to prevent it happening again. At the time I could not really understand why the boss had said "Thank you" to us at such a moment. He later explained that he felt that we had given our everything and could give him no more, and no man could ask for anything more.

'At the post-match banquet, which was more like a funeral, the boss explained that the game and the result was gone, part of history, and we had to put it behind us, learn from the experience, and not to repeat the same mistakes that cost us both the game and the Cup. He also reminded us that very few people ever remember the losing Wembley finalists. How right he was.'

6

SCOTLAND THE BRAVE

The week following the FA Cup final defeat, Saturday, 8 May 1965, the rollercoaster ride that was Billy Bremner's football career reached a new summit, when he was called up for his first full Scotland international cap, by the then Scotland manager Ian McColl. It was an international challenge match against Spain at Hampden Park, in Glasgow:

'What an honour, and it was like I was coming home and making my Scotland full international debut at Hampden Park. I was so excited when Ian McColl gave me the call to tell me I had been selected. What you must remember is that playing for Scotland back then really meant something special. The team was full of world-class players who could cut it at any club in the world. From goalkeeper through to substitutes, we were a match for anyone on our day. For me, it was the ultimate accolade, I cried with joy and pride. Me, Billy Bremner from Raploch, representing my country at football, fantastic. It was a good way for me to end the football season. I was roomed with wee Willie Henderson, what a footballer and man he was, so much skill, and quicker and stronger than a steam train, too.

'Willie was a really nice guy who everyone liked. He was a master piss taker too; nobody was safe from his practical jokes or impressions. It was lovely having such a great guy alongside me. The team that day is one which will stick in my mind for eternity: Bill Brown, Alex Hamilton, Eddie McCreadie, Billy Bremner, Billy McNeill (captain), John Greig, Willie Henderson, Bobby Collins, Denis Law, Alan Gilzean, John Hughes. What a great line-up that was. We had an abundance of football talent and most of us were good pals as well.

'Even though the game ended 0-0, it is a memorable game in the history of Scottish football, if not world football, sadly not for any football reason but through its classic comedy value. Up front, Denis Law had been putting himself about a bit, typically challenging for every ball and generally hassling the Spain defence. One of the Spanish defenders thought that Denis had gone into a challenge too hard, so he punched him in the head. The referee saw everything and ran up to the Spaniard and sent him off. On receiving his marching orders, the Spanish player flung himself to the ground and lay there feigning injury. The referee didn't know what to do next, so allowed the Spanish physio to come onto the pitch to give him treatment. For a few minutes it was bedlam, Spanish players were arguing with the referee and a linesman, neither of whom could understand a word of what was being said to them.

'All the time this was going on, the Spanish player who had lumped Denis Law was receiving treatment for an injury that didn't exist! Eventually, everyone calmed down and the game restarted, and both teams still had eleven players on the pitch. The referee either forgot or ignored the fact that he had sent a Spanish player off, and he remained on the pitch for the rest of the game. What a palaver to be involved in on your full inter-national debut. It did give me an insight into the mentality of European footballers and what some of them were capable of. We were all able to have a good laugh about it afterwards. What else could we do?

'As for the referee, well, despite his major cock-up, nothing truly happened to him. I should say that in my opinion, and in the majority of instances, the standard of refereeing didn't really improve throughout my career.

'I loved playing for and representing Scotland, it was totally different from club football; players who were your enemies in the football league were able to put that animosity behind them, and become their true selves, genuine Scotsmen. Throughout my international soccer career, I played alongside and against the world's greatest footballers and met some really high-powered dignitaries.

'I remember the game against Spain for another reason. I was standing near to Willie Henderson as we were introduced to some royal official with an unpronounceable name from Spain. Willie had secretly imbibed a drop of alcohol before the game, not a lot, just enough to take away the nerves. Anyway, there we were standing almost to attention when the dignitary comes along and shakes our hand. He said something to me, I didn't know what it was, so to save embarrassment, I smiled and nodded. As he reached forward to take Willie Henderson's hand, I heard the noise that makes everyone giggle, an emission of wind from the backside, it came from behind us. It was Willie! Embarrassed, he immediately said, "Ooh shit, sorry." The official smiled and swiftly moved on.

'Great times, you couldn't do that now with all the cameras on you. There was another time when Willie kept getting one of our player's name wrong. Throughout training he would be calling him Bob, eventually the player came to him and said, "Will you stop calling me Bob, my name isn't Bob." Quick as flash, Willie, said, "Oh, okay sorry pal." Thereafter he called him "Touchy sod". That was Willie through and through.

'Jimmy Johnstone was another who liked a dram or two. What a player he was, I don't know another player who could drink as much then go out and play a full game on a belly full of ale. Jimmy is such a lovely guy, and back then, drinking and smoking wasn't the sin it has been made out to be now. Most players enjoyed a fag and a pint, in moderation of course. It's natural when old pals get together to represent their country that there is going to be a bit of daftness at times. I remember Jimmy getting so drunk once, that he took a rowing boat and went out to sea. He was pissed. The tide carried the boat out away from the coastline, Jimmy was drifting away. There was a lot of panicking, and the coastguard was called out to rescue him. It was all good humoured, although a bit dangerous too; the press got hold of it and tried to malign us all. The end result was Jimmy playing the game of his life for Scotland and it was even nicer that it was England we beat, 2-0. I remember Jimmy running up to the press pack as each goal went in, and giving them the salute they deserved. Agitators the lot of them.

'I don't think it's worth disguising the fact that Jimmy and I had a bit of a reputation for a enjoying a drink or two, and a game of cards after. It was good for bonding. Yes, there were a few scrapes and incidents we got ourselves involved in that, looking back, maybe weren't the wisest moves we ever made. Like the night in Oslo in 1974, we were well and truly enjoying ourselves and thought it would be good to give some of the locals a rendition of "Flower of Scotland". We were staying in student accommodation, there was none of those swanky hotels for us Scots on our travels; as long as we had a bed, a bar and each other, then we were content. As it was, the bar stayed open for us and we crooned them Norwegians with some wonderful Scottish songs. Unbeknown to us, they hated it and complained. One chap seemed keen on trying to fight with us but we weren't having any of that. So I reminded him how my team, Leeds United, had beaten local side Lynn Oslo 16-0 a few years earlier. Not the wisest thing to do; the management were called, and we were given a stiff telling-off and warning. We were both full of apologies, of course. And went out of our way to appease the locals and show ourselves to be great ambassadors. A few of them even spoke up for us. That was nice. I remember telling Jimmy that we should maybe keep off the juice in future get-togethers. He laughed and said, "Nice sentiment Bill, you've been down in England for too long, pal."

'Well, a year later, the game was up. I had pissed off a lot of Scottish Football Association officials with my outspoken and honest ways, and some of the extra-curricular drinking and celebrations I had with my colleagues. I was told by a few folk, players and managers that there was a groundswell of these people who wanted me out of the Scottish international equation, they saw me as a loose cannon.

'The incident in Copenhagen gave them all the ammunition they desired. I went out with Arthur Graham, Pat McCluskey, Willie Young and Joe Harper. We had a disagreement with a member of staff in the hotel, and a drink got spilled – thrown – whatever, she ended up getting wet. We celebrated and had fun in the bars and clubs we visited. It was all innocent fun, so we thought anyway. But the cops were called and, as usual, the matter was blown out of all proportion.

'There was also a bit of a bedroom trashing to a Scottish Football Association official's room (Jock McDonald), nothing damaging, just the odd bit of blanket throwing on the floor, and it was said by him that someone crapped on his bed. He got anxious and upset by our behaviour and I told him what a boring fart he was and to loosen up a bit. He told me he would make sure I never played for Scotland again.

'Next thing, I am on the floor – he had smacked me one! We each got five-year Scotland international bans, mainly courtesy of McDonald's report; though our behaviour did warrant some punishment, it was way over the top. The worst thing was I heard that a couple of the players were told privately not to appeal, as their punishment would be reviewed and lifted. Not so mine, and whilst I formally and publicly apologised for my behaviour, McDonald was so influential that he was not about to allow my punishment to be rescinded. It was a sad end to my Scotland career, and I felt as though I had let so many people down, not least my family.

'There were many great players and characters around that time. Jim Baxter for instance – what an arrogant man he was on the football field, and off it too. He had a very definite way about him, Jim. Confident, and focused all the time, especially on himself. You were never sure whether he was being funny, as in funny peculiar, or whether he was pulling your leg. He always said it as it was. He once told Alf Ramsey, the England manager, that he (Ramsey) didn't have any personality, and that he found him really boring as a person. Jim meant it, and Ramsey knew it. Next thing I hear is that Ramsey rang Jim up and said that he was worried by what Jim said, and asked him what he meant by boring. Jim had told him straight: "You put people to sleep when you talk." To which Ramsey had said, "Oh" and replaced the telephone receiver. Jim loved playing for Scotland and would have gladly given all he had for a Scotland win. It was like that for all of us back then, though I'm not so certain in today's game we see the same level of commitment.'

As someone who has witnessed for himself how proud and committed Billy Bremner was to the Scottish cause, it is perhaps worth noting how things have changed, not for the better, in the international game since the days when Bremner, Henderson, Johnstone, and cohorts were thrilling crowds with their skills and football prowess. In today's international game, players retire for a variety of less than orthodox reasons; because they are displeased by tactics, or at being substituted, or because they don't like another player in the squad. Some even come out of international retirement when a new coach is appointed. This isn't something unique to Scotland. In England, Wales and Ireland too, the commitment and pride at being selected to represent your nation seem to have been ignored, as players often churlishly put their own needs before that of the nation they are called to represent. I can tell you now, Billy Bremner and the majority of players of his era would have freely given up their time and walked hundreds of miles to represent their countries at not only football, but anything. The thought of voluntary premature retirement from international duty would be quite unthinkable to the likes of Billy Bremner, as would not giving 100 per cent commitment and effort when wearing the country's colours in a game. Quite what he would have made of some of the Home Countries international performances during the most recent 2010 World Cup qualifying and competition is open to debate but it's doubtful that he would have been accepting of any of the players' attitudes or performances. There was a lack of passion to their game.

Certainly in the Scotland team Billy captained, each and every player would be focused and would deliver their all throughout the entire game. Representing their country, Scotland, was important to them, their families, their people. There would be no shirkers of responsibility, no excuses, just honest and tireless effort and at the end, great pride that they had given their all.

With incredible foresight and vision, Bremner once told me of his take on the future of the Scottish game in general.

'I blame the Scottish Football Association of the 1970s for not having the foresight to develop young football talent at junior school level. The Scottish clubs themselves have to take a look at themselves; far too many home-grown young Scottish footballers were allowed to join English clubs from school. Outside Celtic and Rangers, and occasionally Aberdeen or Hibernian, no club was seriously investing in, or encouraging youth into the game. It has to change, otherwise Scottish international football will stagnate and it will take decades to catch up on other countries' emerging youth policies.

'Willie Ormond was another great character as the Scotland manager. Willie was a Hibs (Hibernian FC) man, he had represented Scotland and appeared in the 1954 World Cup finals, so he knew his football. As a manager he was tough, or tried to be. To be honest, we gave him a bit of a run around, albeit we were respectful and generally did as was asked of us. We were once staying in a hotel in the middle of nowhere, good for focused training, Willie would say. We were told to get an early night, and to be up for an early start the following morning, a run and some light ball work before breakfast. Will escorted us to our rooms and bid us a goodnight. It took about half an hour before the tapping at the bedroom doors began – a few players fancied a late night tot to help us sleep. So together, we sneaked back downstairs and into the bar, ordered our rounds and quietly sat down in the corner to drink them. I took a drink out of my pint to find it was shandy and gradually everyone realised that we had been served with pints of shandy, and not what we ordered. One player thought he was drinking rum and blackcurrant, it was in fact just blackcurrant!

'We complained to the barman and he said he would fetch the

manager. A few seconds later, out comes Willie Ormond, wearing a broad grin on his face. He looked at us all and said, "I knew I couldn't trust you buggers. Now off to bed with you all. I'm staying up all night, guarding this bar." As far as we know he did too, least ways he looked rough the next morning. Willie wasn't a fool, nor was he a stooge for the bureaucratic ways of the Scottish Football Association. He began to speak out against their ways, and, for his rewards, he too was effectively shown the door, being allowed to leave to manage Heart of Midlothian.

'I played under a few authoritarian managers for Scotland and Tommy Docherty wasn't a man to cross. He had a real temper on him, added to which, he knew how it was, he knew the tricks and fun players got up to when away on international duty and you couldn't pull the wool over his eyes one little bit. I got to know Tommy over the years. He is an amazing after-dinner speaker, players of all ages and eras just love listening to him. It's such a pity that a great Scot such as him should have had a club career at Chelsea and Manchester United.

'Of course, the man I would really liked to have played under was Jock Stein. He had a short stint in 1965-66, but by the time he was permanently appointed in 1978, my international career was over. Unfortunately, I missed him at Leeds too. I was gone by the time he made his brief visit to the club.

'Another would have been Alex Ferguson. That man is a wonderful role model for future potential managers to study and emulate. Alex is a devout and thoroughbred Scotsman, the greatest manager in the modern-day game without any shadow of a doubt.

'Scotland is my homeland, no one will ever insult or discredit it in front of me; if they do, and few have tried, then they will learn from me what makes Scotland so superior to all other nations. Our passion, loyalty and bravery are a good place to start!'

It's sad that modern-day football fans will never see or realise the absolute passion and commitment players of the Billy Bremner era had, when representing both club and country. It wasn't about money, ego or self-publicity and marketing, it was about a love for the game and loyalty to the club and country they represented. There was no badge-kissing heroics before the fans, or feigned affection; this was an era when men played football with honesty and integrity. It was rough and you had to be tough, it was all about winners and losers, and for a select few, collecting trophies. Players were both approachable and accessible, and in general, enjoyed mixing with supporters and making them happy. Today, the marketing people in football tell us that the game is more fluent, action packed and entertaining than it has ever been. Anyone who watched football through 1960-1970 era will know different. It was the golden era of the game and it's no coincidence that so many recognised all-time football greats come from that era. For Scotland and Leeds United, Billy Bremner stood out among his peers, and continues to do so to this day. Class is permanent.

7

WE LOVE YOU
LEEDS – LEEDS – LEEDS

Don Revie held a great belief in his team and not least in Billy Bremner, who he saw as the lynchpin around which he could build his side. However, other managers could spot a 'wee gem' as well, and Revie was not alone in his respect for the player. With Leeds still aspiring to succeed, and with no silverware to boast, other top First Division sides began to express an interest in signing the Leeds star. Everton came in with an offer of £25,000. Once again the Leeds board spoke to their manager and intimated that they were interested in reaching an agreement with Everton. According to writer Eric Thornton, 'Revie was incensed by such business and in no uncertain terms told the board: "If you go through with this transfer of Bremner, I'm through too. I shall be out of this club."' In consequence of this show of support from manager to player, the board brought transfer negotiations to an immediate halt.

In the late 1970s Revie recalled the incident:

'At the time I thought the board of the football club was acting improperly. They seemed hell bent on cashing in on playing assets; they wanted the silverware and the trappings of success that went with winning trophies, yet hard cash seemed to be a bigger attraction to them. As a manager you tend to forget that the football club side of things is run as a business. I was upset by them – first we had Hibernian, then Everton sounding out moves for some of my best players, and instead of turning them down, the board implied that they were open to, and would assess, individual offers. It sent the wrong message out to our competitors and my players. I wanted stability throughout the team, players who knew they were wanted and were treated with respect and loyalty. I wanted them to feel part of one big family. Transfer speculation does nothing but cause unrest and disharmony within a football club so I told the directors that if any player was sold to a rival club without my blessing then they would need to find another manager. Of course, they were shocked by my outburst, but I meant it, and if they had sold Billy Bremner, then I would not have hesitated in resigning. The chairman wasn't slow in changing his mind and in telling me that niether Billy Bremner, nor any other Leeds player, would be sold in the immediate future. Thankfully that was the end of the matter.'

The 1965-66 season was not as dramatic as the previous one, which had ended in failure at Wembley. Leeds were gradually forging a good reputation for themselves and being accepted as a force and championship contender within the First Division. Despite this they still had many critics, each of whom tended to concentrate solely upon their tactics rather than football performance. The Liverpool manager, Bill Shankly, once described their style as being similar to that of a 'rugby team, more akin to Hull Kingston Rovers than a football team'. Whether this outburst was borne out of the fact that Leeds had just inflicted a 1-0 defeat over his side in front of Liverpool's own fans at Anfield, on the day after Boxing Day, is open to debate. Nevertheless, such comments offended many of the Leeds team, and if anything were to make them a more committed unit.

Highlights in the league included the 6-1 defeat of newly promoted Northampton Town, and a 5-0 demolition of West Ham United, with Bremner scoring in both games:

'Northampton Town were a bit of an unknown quantity to the First Division. They had made a meteoric rise from the Fourth Division to the First in consecutive seasons. Although we really thrashed them, they had some decent players in their team but on the day they couldn't compete with us over ninety minutes. We exploited their full backs and defensive weakness time and again.

50

I think I am right in saying that Northampton were relegated after just one season and dropped straight back through the leagues and back into the Fourth Division as quickly as they rose from it.'

Perhaps the best league result of that season was the 3-0 victory over Arsenal at Highbury, a game that took place before just 4,554 spectators. The game had been rearranged and was played on the evening of Thursday, 5 May 1966. On that same evening, Liverpool were facing Borussia Dortmund in the final of the European Cup Winners Cup and that game was being shown live on national television. This, combined with Arsenal's dismal form, resulted in Highbury's lowest First Division crowd since the First World War. Goals from Jim Storrie (two) and Jimmy Greenhoff secured the victory. Arsenal manager Billy Wright was humble in defeat, and later told reporters:

'It was a bad result for us, Leeds were beatable today but we failed to capitalise on their frailties. They are a rugged outfit, not very pretty to watch, but they have an extremely strong midfield. Billy Bremner strikes me as the kind of player who will forge a good career for himself, I wish we had half a dozen of his sort playing for us.' Good fortune appears to have deserted the Arsenal manager who was removed from his position the following summer, after Arsenal finished a lowly fourteenth in the league, their lowest position since 1930.

There was a lot of comment about Bremner by this time:

'By now, many people were making comparisons with my style of play and that of other more experienced players. Other than those who counted, such as my dad or the boss, I never really listened to anyone else about my play. I realised through bitter experience that some journalists and outsiders tended to be deliberately cynical and more critical about individual performances. If Pop and the boss thought I was playing alright, then that was good enough for me. I always gave my best and if you do that in all you do, then no one has any right to criticise.'

As previous season runners-up in the First Division championship, the team had qualified for European football. The challenge of pitting their skills against some of the best football opposition in the world beckoned Bremner and his colleagues. The first round of the Inter Cities Fairs Cup competition saw Leeds paired with Italian side Torino, who visited Elland Road in the first phase of the two-legged tie. It was a far from easy draw but Leeds pulled off a 2-1 victory courtesy of goals from Bremner and Alan Peacock.

The second leg, in Turin, however, was an entirely different proposition:

'We knew that Torino would come at us as soon as the whistle blew. We had more than a few ball winners in our side, certainly enough to unsettle them, and perhaps give us the chance to hit them on the break.'

In the fiftieth minute of that game, United skipper Bobby Collins was clattered to the ground in a vicious tackle by Torino full back Poletti. As a result Collins suffered a broken thigh. With substitutions not yet introduced into European football, Leeds were forced to play out the remaining forty minutes with just ten men. Hang on they did, right through to the final whistle, to win the tie 2-1 on aggregate.

Don Revie believed that the performance of the team in Turin was as good as his side had ever produced. Bremner was less than complimentary in his assessment of Torino:

'They were the dirtiest set of players I had ever come up against, kicking, punching, pinching and spitting at us. They were a bunch of spoilers and the foul on Bobby (Collins) was sickening. I swear you could hear the bone break. To lose a player of his influence was a real blow, but we did our bit and resolutely fought on.'

The second round provided opposition in the form of SC Locomotiv Leipzig. United repeated the first-round formula, taking a 2-1 lead to East Germany, and once again Bremner netted in the Elland Road triumph. A dour 0-0 draw in East Germany ensured further progression in the competition.

Spanish club side Valencia were next on the European agenda:

'I don't think any of the team could really believe that we were successfully marching through Europe. There was a different atmosphere about the European games and even when we played in Leeds it felt like we were in some far-off cosmopolitan district of Europe. The night we played Valencia there was a peculiar, almost hostile atmosphere around the stadium. Some of their players ignored us when we met them during the pre-match build-up. It was not unlike two boxers winding each other up before a fight. I cannot stand rudeness in any form; there is no excuse in the world for ignoring someone who acknowledges you. A few of our players made comments about it and I told them to ignore the foreign bastards.'

Little could anyone have realised how such a glamorous-looking European tie would be recounted for everything but football memories. Valencia knew all about how to win European encounters, having won the Fairs Cup in 1962 and 1963, and had only been narrowly beaten by Real Zaragoza in the 1964 final. An injury to centre forward Alan Peacock in a league game at Sunderland had left Leeds with few options up front. Revie toyed with the idea of moving Bremner forward, but didn't want to upset the equilibrium of the team too much. Instead he opted to play an inexperienced youngster, Rod Belfitt, as centre forward. Valencia were clearly aware that Leeds could rough it up with the best of them, and so applied their tactics accordingly. One commentator stated: 'Valencia's tactics smacked more of the bullring than the football field. They were the roughest continental side I have ever seen.'

An eleventh-minute Valencia goal silenced Elland Road early on, giving the visitors a 1-0 lead which was consistently defended; at times all eleven Valencia players were committed to protecting the lead from the edge of their own penalty area. The Spanish giants undoubtedly used every trick in the book to suffocate the Leeds threat, with blatant strong-arm tactics, and they brought down a Leeds player with every tackle. It was a nasty and hostile atmosphere both on and off the pitch. Supporters yelled at referee Leo Horn to bring the Spanish side to rights for their continued fouling. The match official ignored all shouts from the crowd and from the players and, ultimately, his refusal to act fairly caused the game to degenerate, as scenes of violence were witnessed all over the Elland Road stadium, not least amongst the players on the pitch. Leeds continued to push forward but couldn't break open the heavily manned Valencia rear guard. Trailing 1-0 at half time they left the pitch looking disconsolate and clearly wound up.

In the second half there was some reward for their efforts, when a Bremner cross was met by Peter Lorimer, who gleefully fired home the Leeds equaliser. It was game on and it was Leeds who were clearly in the ascendancy. As the match moved into its final quarter, Leeds continued to attack. During one such raid, Jack Charlton was clearly punched and kicked by a Valencia defender. Charlton recalls the incident:

'What had been a sizzling atmosphere became downright white hot, as we threw everything into an assault which, we hoped, would bring us a winner. Fifteen minutes to go, and I raced upfield to add my weight to one of our attacks. As I challenged an opponent in the Valencia penalty area, I was kicked. This angered me, of course – but before I knew where I was I found myself having to take much more when one of my opponents slung a punch which would have done credit to Cassius Clay. Right there and then, my anger boiled over. I chased the culprit around that penalty area and I was intent upon only one thing – getting my own back. I had completely lost control of myself after these diabolical fouls upon me, and neither the Spaniards nor the restraining hands of my team mates could prevent my pursuit for vengeance. Then I saw police appear on the field, they were there to stop this game of football from degenerating into a running battle.'

Finally, on police advice, referee Leo Horn walked from the pitch with both of his linesmen and he signalled to club officials of both sides to get their players off, too.

Charlton continues: 'I was still breathing fire when I reached the dressing room – then I got the word that I need not go back. For a moment I thought the referee had called off the match . . .

then it sank home that it was only Jackie Charlton's presence which was not required any longer. For eleven minutes the teams remained off the field, to allow tempers on both sides to cool down. By that time, I was beginning to feel sorry for myself, and not a little ashamed of the way I had lost my temper.'

Bremner recollected:

'It was an awful night; some Valencia players were more keen on kicking us rather than the ball. It was complete mayhem; no one seemed to know what to do. Jack was very angry, the worst I have seen him, but he was right to be so. I was trying to tell everyone involved to calm down but I don't think the Spaniards could really understand an angry Scotsman.

'The referee had lost control; the police were pulling players apart and pleading for common sense to prevail. When we were ready to return, we got the word that Big Jack could stay where he was – he'd been sent off, and so had a Valencia man. We all assumed it was the number five, who had started the trouble which had angered Big Jack. But when we got back out onto the pitch, there, large as life, was their number five! The man who the referee had sent off was the left back; I don't think it was a coincidence that the same left back had been given a real roasting all game by Jim Storrie, who skinned him time and again. Valencia risked very little by losing the left back. Whichever way it was, this case of mistaken identity was worked to their advantage.'

Seven minutes from time Valencia inside forward Sanchez-Lage felled Storrie and was promptly dismissed and the game, if that is what it can be termed, ended 1-1. The situation deteriorated further when referee Leo Horn inflamed proceedings by claiming to reporters of several daily newspapers around the world, that Leeds players were on a £1,500 bonus to win:

'Money was the cause of the trouble; you could see it in the nervousness and the excitement of the players. There was something in the air . . . something unpleasant . . . there was too much at stake. It was unbelievable. I was reminded of South American cup finals I have taken, where players were on a bonus of 3,000 dollars. It was the same then. Since European football began we have seen this sort of thing spreading. These games have become too important for the players.

'When Leeds lost a goal this nervousness spread among them. Valencia had nine men in front of their goal. They too were gripped by this terrible feeling. I understand professional players, but they have changed. Money has made them too eager. After sixteen years of international refereeing I believe money causes all the trouble . . . all the nervousness and desperate play. It is no use clubs expecting referees to impose discipline. The referee is there to control a match. Players must be taught to control themselves.

'I have always regarded Charlton as a fine man. He was the cleanest player on the field, until he lost all control. I saw a Spanish defender kick him, and if Charlton had given a reprisal kick, I could have understood it and let it pass, because it happens so often. As captain of Leeds, and an international, he should have been the first player to exercise complete self-control.'

Don Revie later refuted the allegations of the match official:

'It's untrue. My players were on no special bonus. Mr Horn is guessing, or has been misinformed. I resent these allegations, but I am saying no more now. It's time for the whole thing to simmer down. The referee was a complete fool and an attention seeker. He had no control of the game at Elland Road. It was funny, mind you, seeing Big Jack chasing that Spaniard around the pitch. If he had got hold of him, I dread to think what he would have done to him, all hell would have broken loose.'

The referee, just as he had during the game, failed to take responsibility for his part in the débâcle. It was not his place to question or discuss players' financial incentives; he continued to apportion blame for the violence, anywhere and everywhere, but not on his own performance. He did not escape criticism for the integral role he played in the affair. Not only was he replaced for the second leg of the tie in Spain, he was also told that any ambition he held to officiate at the forthcoming World Cup finals had completely evaporated.

Some of the comments made by Horn display him in a poor light but the official was well known for his behaviour and verbal outbursts, as recorded in his 1963 autobiography. He continually demanded from FIFA that referees should be provided with five-star hotel accommodation. On another occasion, he took a corner kick himself, as the player concerned was dithering. What he says about Leeds doesn't even compare with how he described Chilean football supporters. 'Nice friendly, even pious people until they enter the stadium, then they turn into devils.' It seems that Horn believed himself to be greater than the teams and fans in any game he officiated. Hardly a man whose opinion could be considered well balanced, one would think.

The second leg was a much less volatile affair with a Mike O'Grady goal sufficient to give Leeds a 1-0 victory in Spain and a mouth-watering quarter-final tie with Ujpesti Dozsa. A lively attacking performance against the Hungarians saw Leeds run out 4-1 winners at Elland Road, and once again Bremner added his name to the score sheet. The result was followed by a 1-1 draw in Hungary. A 5-2 aggregate victory saw Leeds through to play Real Zaragoza.

Bremner was loving the European excursion:

'It was amazing stuff; after the battle of Elland Road against Valencia, Ujpesti were a much more controlled and skilful side. We wanted to take a lead with us into the second leg in Hungary, so pressured them the entire game, the crowd really got behind us and we looked like scoring every time we went forward. It finished 4-1 to us and again I got myself a goal.

'I thought we delivered a much more disciplined performance in the second leg in Hungary. I was impressed by Ujpesti; they looked a really good football side and had we not been on top of our game they would have punished us. Thankfully we held them to a draw and went through to our first European semi-final against Real Zaragoza.'

The semi-final was not to be a straightforward affair. The first leg in Spain ended in defeat. Bremner was cruelly adjudged to have handled the ball in the penalty area, giving the Spaniards a penalty which was duly converted:

'It was an absolute bloody joke that penalty, I never used my hand to intentionally stop it or control it, if someone strikes a ball at you there is little you can do to stop it hitting you, sometimes your reflexes cause involuntary actions. It was never a penalty. The referee got it wrong and I told him so; I told him he couldn't manage a game of tiddlywinks. I don't suppose he knew what that was! Ultimately, he bowed to player and crowd pressure in my opinion.'

The second leg at Elland Road resulted in a 2-1 Leeds victory, meaning the semi-final had finished all level at 2-2 on aggregate. A play-off game was necessary. Jack Charlton, who had been handed temporary captaincy following the injury to Bobby Collins, won the toss to give Leeds home advantage in the third and final game. From a Leeds perspective the game was very much a non-event. Zaragoza scored three times in quick succession, all inside the first thirteen minutes, to kill the game dead. As a spectacle the game was over but the fans did at least having something to cheer when a late consolation goal from Jack Charlton added a little respectability to the scoreline:

'It was a depressing result, we quite simply did not get out of the starting blocks until half time by which time it was too late. We were taught a bitter lesson that game by a team with immense quality and focus. Thankfully we were willing scholars and profited from all of the experiences we encountered.'

8

'LEADING LEEDS UNITED
WAS MY DESTINY'

The European tie against Torino was to have a great impact upon the playing career of Billy Bremner, far greater than he could ever have anticipated. He recalled a meeting with manager Don Revie shortly after the tie:

'The boss asked me to give him half an hour for a chat and a catch-up meeting. He was worried about how the loss of Bobby's influence on the pitch had affected the rest of the lads. Big Jack had done a good job in covering the role, yet by his own admission, he had lost it completely against Valencia. It was obvious that Bobby was going to be out for a long time and that the boss wasn't comfortable with Big Jack as acting captain. I told him not to worry about it – as a set of players we would keep fighting and do our bit to make sure we pushed on. He said to me, "Bill, I like that attitude, keep fighting. How do you feel about taking over the captaincy?" It came as a bit of a surprise as I hadn't considered the situation. He told me that he thought I was the natural leader of the team and that I would make a great team captain. I told him that I would not do it if Jack (Charlton) was going to be upset by the decision. I had a lot of respect for the big man, we had an excellent understanding on and off the field and there was no way I would deliberately hurt or offend him. The fact that he was about four foot taller than me hadn't escaped my attention either!

'Looking back, I can see that the boss was using his own management tactics to instil a more positive side to my game. I had, at times, an excitable temperament on the pitch, some people called it a short fuse. One reporter said I was a keg of gunpowder waiting to explode, but that was far from true in my opinion. If anything, I was too honest. If I saw someone commit a foul against a fellow Leeds player and the referee missed it, then I would have a word with the player, but sometimes, very often really, the other player disagreed with my opinion which would end up with me getting into trouble. As team captain I had to lead by example so if I was sent off or was too hot-headed then this would affect the team. I had to take responsibility and show self-control.

'From the day I took on the captain's role I felt that I matured as a person, it was a great honour. Looking back upon it now, it was my destiny to lead Leeds United; I feel I was born to be part of what I consider the greatest club in the world. How fortunate was I to hail from a great nation, too. I accepted the role and told the boss that I would maintain the high standards expected of an individual, given such an honour. I thought to myself, "Now I've got the captain's role I am not relinquishing it to anyone else." I was rightly very proud – what an honour to captain Leeds United. It wasn't long after that I had the "Keep Fighting" number plate hanging above my dressing-room peg. I wanted it to be a constant reminder to the rest of the lads that no matter what we are faced with in life we will keep fighting until we can fight no more, and even then, defeat wasn't an acceptable option for us as individuals, as a team, or for Leeds United.'

The following season was in many ways less eventful. In the League Cup, West Ham United inflicted a 7-0 thrashing at Upton Park, and a few days later in a league game, Leeds went down 5-0 to Liverpool at Anfield. The FA Cup offered some solace, as the team battled through to the semi-final stages. Chelsea were the opponents in a game that took place at Villa Park. Trailing 1-0 to a Tony Hateley goal, Leeds mounted serious pressure on the Chelsea goal, yet, as was so often the case, they were denied by some poor refereeing decisions, one of which, to this very day, defies all logic and evidence of common sense. Leeds had reason to feel aggrieved when a Terry Cooper strike was disallowed for a player being offside, yet worse was to come. Later, in more dramatic circumstances, a Peter Lorimer 'special', with just two minutes of normal time remaining, was cruelly ruled out. No one, not even the Chelsea players, knew why the goal had been dismissed by referee Ken Burns. The Leeds players remonstrated with the match official, but he would have none of it. He later said that he 'wasn't ready for the free kick to be taken'. This despite the fact that Chelsea were lined up in a defensive wall, whilst others took up positions marking the Leeds attackers in the penalty area. Clearly, the goal was a good one, yet incredibly, Leeds were punished for what should have been a free kick to their advantage. Billy recalled the game and the poor refereeing decision, with some harshness:

'F—— Chelsea again, fair play to them, they did get at us in their usual dirty way. Name calling, over the top tackles and elbows in your ribs were very much part of their tactics. We just couldn't find a way through them. The free kick that Peter [Lorimer] fired home was as sweet as you will see anywhere, nothing wrong with it. Chelsea thought it was a good goal, so did everyone else, even the television commentator. The one bastard that mattered though, the referee, well he had other ideas. He was a bit of a larger than life character was Ken Burns, but I always thought he cheated us that day. I never forgave him for that and would never miss an opportunity to ask him if he had his spectacles with him whenever he refereed us after that. He would say, "We all make mistakes, young Bremner." If that doesn't tell you something about what he realised, then nothing will.'

In Europe, it was once again the Inter Cities Fairs Cup competition. Aggregate victory over DWS Amsterdam (8-2) brought another tie against Valencia. All supporters of Leeds had been concerned about the return of Valencia to Elland Road, and the potential clashes that may occur on the pitch. I always recall my uncle telling me how the local police were apparently preparing for a situation not dissimilar to a war. They typically over-dramatised the whole situation, something that still often occurs to this day, but now affects kick-off times and dates. Thankfully back then policing was usually a bit more sensible and individual officers took responsibility, part of which was ensuring that the crowd enjoyed the game. A strong police contingent was present and as a result, nothing untoward took place among the spectators. On the pitch, both managers were said to have warned individual players about the manner in which the game was to be played. Whatever was said, it influenced both teams, and when compared to their previous encounters, there were no incidents of any real note. Both sets of players had sensibly put their history behind them.

After beating Valencia (3-1), victories over Bologna (toss of a coin) and Kilmarnock (4-2) put United into the final against Dinamo Zagreb. There the success ended, as Zagreb ran out 2-0 aggregate winners:

'We were disappointed when we lost the Zagreb first leg; it was the first time we had conceded two goals on foreign soil. It just didn't happen for us – we seemed to have a lot of the possession but didn't forge any chances. After the game we talked about where we had gone wrong, but to be honest apart from scoring there was nothing more we could have done. Both Zagreb goals were well executed and not down to any individual errors. In the second leg at Elland Road we were virtually camped in their half for the entire game, but they again shut up shop and defended too deep for us to exploit them. It was disappointing to lose the final but we had to recognise that we were beaten by a more clinical team.'

If the 1966-67 season was one of disappointment, the 1967-68 season was one of great celebration as two major trophies were brought back to Elland Road. In the league it was a lack of consistency that proved to be United's downfall, although a final league position of fourth was still attained. Some good league results were achieved, especially the 7-0 against Chelsea, in which Bremner's performance was described as 'simply outstanding'. January saw back-to-back 5-0 victories over Fulham at Craven Cottage, and Southampton at Elland Road, but it was the Chelsea result that Bremner recalled most vividly:

'Oh that Chelsea result was simply fantastic, we completely outplayed them and I was teasing and hounding their midfield. We seemed to move to a new level in the 1967-68 season and we were maturing as a group, and as individuals and players. Some claimed we were too mature for our age, as we all enjoyed a game of bingo after training or when we were on our travels, and then there was carpet bowls! I'm not kidding you, we genuinely did play those games, and it was great for relaxing and taking your mind off everything. I still hated losing though.'

Once again it was in the cup competitions where United showed their resilience and determination to succeed. The FA Cup semi-final was again reached, after victories over Derby County, Nottingham Forest, Bristol City and Sheffield United. The semi-final paired them with Everton at Old Trafford, the end of the trail as far as United were concerned. The Goodison Park outfit clinched the tie 1-0, by virtue of what was fast becoming a typical Gary Sprake error. Clearing the ball whilst under no serious pressure he kicked straight to the feet of Everton's Jimmy Husband, who lobbed the ball back towards Sprake's goal. The retreating Jack Charlton did a better impression of being a goalkeeper than Sprake. The big centre-half was forced to handle the ball to prevent it going directly into the net. The referee instantly blew his whistle and pointed to the Leeds penalty spot. John Morrisey lined the spot-kick up, casually winking at a nervous looking Sprake as he drove the ball into the Leeds net. And with that woeful error went United's dreams of an appearance in another FA Cup final:

'Big Jack wasn't the only one fuming with the blithering idiot. Gary was prone to making basic errors and not for the first time Jack and I tore into him in the dressing room afterwards. Typical of Gary, he refused to accept any responsibility whatsoever, and in his usual arrogant manner, threw insults back at Jack and anyone else who got involved. Gary believed that Jimmy

Husband should have been more closely marked, and if he had been then he wouldn't have scored. There's his stupid f—— logic for you!'

In some of the interviews we did, Billy would occasionally reflect on his colleagues, and clearly Gary Sprake was not one his favoured team mates:

'To me, Gary Sprake was so bloody infuriating, he could pull off some fantastic saves and just occasionally, he was as reliable as any keeper in the land. Yet on other days he wasn't with it at all, his attention was all over the place, and his catching, kicking and communication were non-existent. As a set of players out on the pitch we could sense his poor attitude and it did make us very nervous as to how he would cope throughout the game. I had plenty of bust-ups with him over the years and I don't think I was alone either. He had a "couldn't give a damn" attitude that tended to wind a few of us up. In his world there was just one player of any note and importance at Leeds United and he would think of no one else but Gary Sprake. It was a great shame really, a waste of goalkeeping talent. Quite a few of the team felt that he was massively over-rated by the boss; he got too comfortable in his position and cost us some very big games, and the trophies that went with them. The thing is, if you are a centre forward and you miss a golden chance, you get other opportunities to put it right during a game. As a goalkeeper one mistake can prove vital, and sadly, that's what Gary Sprake will be remembered for. I'm not saying he was universally crap, he did pull off saves that kept us in matches, and in some games I saw the world-class goalkeeper that he could be. Yet overall, he was an absolute liability to the team and the club, he was our Achilles heel, our weakness that other teams and supporters exploited.

'I say supporters, because amongst them, outside of Wales, he was regarded as something of a joke. In one game at Liverpool he threw the ball into his own net and, at once, and in unison, the Kop and thirty thousand other people in the ground began to sing the Des O'Connor hit, "Careless Hands" to him. At Chelsea and Leicester they would scream whenever he went near the ball, trying to make him nervous and put him off his game. He did react a couple of times, turning on the crowd to show his displeasure. We all told him to ignore everything but the game being played out in front of him. Sometimes he saw the funny side of how the fans related to him and he got a rapport going with them, other times he just didn't seem to concentrate.

'It might well be that this made him even more prone to making mistakes. I don't know, he was so arrogant and full of himself, I couldn't be doing with it half of the time. Saying that, I wouldn't want to be a goalkeeper at any price.'

I had witnessed Sprake's arrogance as a supporter and, as sad as it was, he didn't always endear himself to the Leeds fans, despite many remaining loyal to him because he represented Leeds United. It was only after he left and sold his version of events to a national newspaper that we saw him in a different light. I lost most of my respect for him when I was a child meeting him at Newcastle, but I did occasionally feel sorry for him when he dropped one of his clangers. Billy Bremner had very definite views on this:

'The boss had this thing that he had plucked him from obscurity as a teenager and nurtured him, and Gary would play on that, abusing the boss's loyalty to his own advantage. He reckoned he had film-star looks and at times was more concerned about his appearance than saving bloody shots. He was always chewing gum, too, and that would irritate me, trying to talk to him and his bloody jaw jerking from side to side.

'To be honest, I always felt much safer with David Harvey in goal; David was a sensible and level-headed lad who quietly went about his goalkeeping without any fuss. In games, he did the simple things and made the most difficult saves look very easy. David was reliable and instilled confidence in the defence, whereas Sprake was so wrapped up in himself that he would miss important moves.'

Oddly enough, during that previous season Sprake had been replaced in the Leeds goal by David Harvey for a Football League Cup tie at West Ham. Leeds had lost the game 7-0:

'In no way was David Harvey responsible for the way we were comprehensively beaten by West Ham. We defended like amateurs in that game and West Ham played us off the park. As infuriating as it was, they well and truly stuffed us.'

In the League Cup competition of 1967-68 there was far greater success as Leeds marched on to Wembley, overcoming the challenge of Luton Town, Bury, Sunderland, Stoke City and Brian Clough's Derby County before a final encounter against Arsenal:

'By the time the season was over we were well and truly shattered; I think the successes of the cup competitions arrested our league progress. Not that we failed at all, but we all felt we could have achieved more. It's fair to say that the majority of us believed that we could have won just about every competition we went for. It may sound arrogant or big-headed, but not many teams will ever come as close as we did to achieving a clean sweep of domestic trophies and a European success into the bargain.

'The semi-final against Derby County wasn't the tough challenge we expected. I never liked playing at Derby County, it was one of those intimidating little grounds, where the stands feel like they are going to fall on top of you on the pitch. That was my first brush with Brian Clough. He stood by the side of the pitch calling me a Scottish ginger-nut, telling his players to kick the cheating Scottish ginger-nut and finish his game. I thought that's rich coming from someone whose playing career was ended through injury. As I ran past him I told him what an arsehole I thought he was and he yelled back at me, "Who are you talking to, little man? If it's me, then you call me sir, you understand." I called him an English prick and got on with my game.

'Afterwards, the boss told him in no uncertain terms that he ought to concentrate on his own team and players, and not those at Leeds. He (the boss) gave him a friendly pat on the shoulder as he did so and winked. Clough was visibly angered by this. As we walked out of the ground the boss advised me that it was a lesson learned – some people are able to manage themselves, others aren't. Brian Clough, at that time, fitted into the latter category but, to be honest, it mattered little to me at that time. I just wanted to get home to my family.

'The second leg at Leeds wasn't easy for me. It was obvious that Brian Clough had targeted me and some of his players were throwing themselves like cruise missiles into tackles where I was involved. The comments coming from some of them were as foul as I had encountered, so I thought to myself, "Bill, you either go down without a fight, or you give back as good you get." I chose the latter and "inadvertently" clattered into a couple of their players. They soon backed down and our football won the day. Brian Clough was incensed and vocally abusive. I gave him a friendly nod and a wink as we triumphantly walked off. "I won't forget this Bremner, you little shit" he said to me. So I asked him who he was and if he was talking to me? And if he was, he was then to call me "the winning captain". He quickly disappeared into the dressing room, muttering all kinds of things as he did so.'

The final was a close-fought affair. Revie and his players were almost desperate to collect their first silverware, but in Arsenal they knew they faced formidable and tough opponents. The pre-match team talk consisted of the manager telling his side, amongst other things, to match Arsenal for effort and in the physical challenges and encounters. The uninspiring final was settled by a hotly disputed Terry Cooper goal, a sweet strike from the edge of the Arsenal penalty area which flew past the Gunners keeper Jim Furnell. The goal was immediately contested by the Arsenal players who hounded and surrounded match referee Mr Hamer, bitterly complaining that Furnell had been impeded and fouled by Jack Charlton.

The match official stood firm in Leeds favour and the goal stood:

'It was ridiculous the way the Arsenal players reacted. Big Jack never deliberately went into any challenge intent on fouling an opponent – he always went for the ball and nine times out of ten he won it. He never fouled Jim Furnell that day. Likewise, I can't remember too many occasions when Terry [Cooper] struck a shot so well. He could be devastatingly accurate in training, yet in matches he never got much opportunity to shoot so, as you can imagine, we were all really happy that he chose that game to have a go. Bobby Charlton would have been proud of that shot and goal, it was a real screamer.'

Arsenal never gave up fighting but Leeds were their match and deserved their first Wembley victory, and the club's first major domestic honour:

'It was fantastic getting hold of our very first major trophy. I remember looking around the ground from the podium where I collected the trophy and Wembley was a sea of white, blue and gold. It was a joy to celebrate our success with the supporters.

'When we returned to Leeds, thousands of people were out to welcome us. I was so proud and as I looked round the rest of the team I could see how much it meant. The boss didn't stop smiling for a couple of days. That was unusual because it took something very special to get him to smile in the first place.'

The victory assured qualification into European competition again. In the Inter Cities Fairs Cup, Spora Luxembourg were beaten 16-0 on aggregate and, once again, Billy Bremner was among the goals at Elland Road in a 9-0 first leg demolition. Partizan Belgrade were beaten 3-2 on aggregate, followed by Hibernian, who went out 2-1 over two legs: 'I was keen to play well against Hibernian. After all, they didn't think I was worth £30,000. It was a tough two games we had against them and I thought we were lucky to come through.'

Unlike now, clubs like Hibernian, Kilmarnock and Dundee were frequently participating in European competition. They were challengers too – Celtic and Rangers didn't have it all their own way in Scotland. Hibernian's team was filled with well-known stars of the Scottish game, legends like Pat Stanton, Colin Stein, Peter Cormack and Pat Quinn. Hibernian in particular could boast European victories over great clubs like Real Madrid and Barcelona to name a couple. Perhaps the most incredible victory the Hibees achieved came in the round prior to meeting Leeds, against legendary Italian goalkeeper Dino Zoff's Napoli. After a disastrous 4-1 first leg defeat in Italy, they produced one of the most scintillating European performances of all time, thrashing Napoli 5-0 at Easter Road and winning the tie 6-4 on aggregate.

These weren't games that Leeds saw as easy and they were as tough, if not tougher, than any overseas opposition. In the first leg, Leeds took an early lead through Eddie Gray, yet it was Hibernian who looked the more confident side, forcing Leeds back at every opportunity. They were worthy opponents and caused mayhem in the Leeds defence. Colin Stein had a goal disallowed, before leaving injured, while Peter Cormack played what many believed was his best ever game. Despite everything, Leeds were resilient and won the first leg 1-0.

A few weeks later, 40,000 partisan Hibernian fans filled Easter Road, creating an intimidating atmosphere for Bremner and his colleagues:

'It was as tough a game as I can recall in Europe. Edinburgh was filled with green and white and we were given a raucous welcome when we arrived at the ground. Nothing sinister, just lots of anti-English chanting. I couldn't help but laugh with the fans screaming "Scotland, Scotland" – that's my boys I thought, passionate and devout, good on you.

'The game was frantic to say the least. It was wave after wave of Hibs attacking, we couldn't get near them and I feared that we were going to be overrun. I think it was Colin Stein who scored to level the game. We were hanging on. I can honestly say that I realised that not all referees are poor. Clive Thomas was the man in the middle for this game and he had been tough on both teams, telling players that he wouldn't stand for any nonsense. I thought we were going to extra time and I remember the ball being with their goalkeeper, Willie Wilson. Clive Thomas suddenly blew for an infringement. Back then the four-step rule had been introduced for goalkeepers. Apparently Willie took five and we won a free kick. The result was Big Jack equalised and we went through 2-1 on aggregate. Poor Clive Thomas took the brunt of the fans' angst, the Easter Road stands were vibrating to a chorus of booing. I didn't take much satisfaction in seeing a Scottish club being knocked out. Though my football love belonged to Leeds, my football heart belonged to Scotland.'

Next came a tie against Glasgow Rangers:

'I was thrilled to be playing against Rangers. We held out for a 0-0 draw in front of 80,000 raucous spectators at Ibrox Stadium in Glasgow. As a Scotsman, and with my background, to play Rangers at Ibrox was the stuff dreams were made of. Apart from the emotion I felt as a Scotsman, it was a marvellous occasion to savour. As we made our way to the ground in the bus, supporters lined most of the streets surrounding the stadium. Many had come all the way from Leeds and were yelling and waving to us. The Rangers fans, normally regarded as partisan and hugely biased, applauded our team, and from what I saw, made our supporters very welcome in Glasgow – at least that was before the game.

'Once we got inside it was clear Ibrox was buzzing. Many of the Rangers boys, some of whom I would class as good friends, were trying to play down the game, in an attempt to disguise the pre-match nerves we all suffer before such an important encounter. A few of us knew the Rangers players and had a laugh with them; it was all part of the psychological build-up to the game itself. As we took to the pitch, the Ibrox roar filled our ears. It was as intimidating a ground as I have played on. I remember the smell of fag smoke, Oxo and cigars. I was mighty glad to hang on for a 0-0 draw, privately, and I knew that at Leeds it would be a different game altogether.'

The second leg saw Leeds progress, with a competent 2-0 victory, goals coming from Johnny Giles and Peter Lorimer. With two Scottish club sides dispatched, a third awaited in the semi-final. Dundee proved themselves to be much more difficult football opponents. A Paul Madeley goal was enough to earn a draw in Scotland, and an Eddie Gray strike in the second leg put Leeds through to the final for the second year in succession:

'It was nice to beat Hibernian, Rangers and Dundee; there were those who said that we had managed to get to the final by avoiding foreign opposition. What a load of rubbish that was, the sides we met were more of a match for us than any overseas club and there was British pride at stake which made the games all the more difficult.'

The final of the competition saw United face Ferencvaros, a Mick Jones goal was enough to give United a 1-0 advantage to take to Hungary. A sterling defensive performance saw off the Hungarian challenge as United tasted European success, and brought home to Elland Road the Inter Cities Fairs Cup, making them the first British club side to do so.

Bremner recalled:

'I often look back on that season as one of the best. We were accused of being the bridesmaids and falling at the last hurdle. Sometimes we did stutter, but people forget what an achievement it was to get there in the first place. Two Inter Cities Fairs Cup finals on the trot, and two FA Cup semi-finals in succession is not a bad achievement by anyone's standards. Yet we were condemned by the media for not winning everything. In hindsight, I can now see how highly regarded we were. If the press believed we were capable of winning everything then we can't have been a bad side, but try getting one of them to admit that and you have no chance. Instead they will remind modern Leeds fans of our "too physical attitude", but mark my words, we were a damn good football team, the best. Leeds United could, and did, compete with the best that European football had to offer – how many clubs can say that?'

Incredibly after the European success of the 1967-68 season, United were forced to begin their defence of the crown just one week after winning it. The first round of the 1968-69 Fairs Cup campaign was a particularly sticky and uncomfortable one. After a 0-0 draw against Standard Liege in Belgium, many thought the Elland Road second leg would be a formality. They were wrong. Liege took a 2-0 lead at Leeds, however, and showed their true

European pedigree before Bremner and company rallied and came back to win the game 3-2. It was Bremner who scored the winner. If that wasn't enough to cause concern, then a trip to Napoli in the next round did. The first leg had been settled by two Jack Charlton goals, but in Naples, United crumbled losing by the same deficit, meaning a toss of a coin to decide who went through. Bremner called it right and Leeds progressed.

There was no such tension in the following round, as Hanover '96 were thrashed 7-2 on aggregate. The fourth round threw up an interesting challenge against Ujpesti Dozsa, a side that Leeds had beaten previously. There was to be no repeat as, on this occasion, the Fairs Cup holders crashed out of the competition, 3-0 on aggregate, putting in two lacklustre performances: 'It was disappointing to lose to Ujpesti Dozsa but it allowed us to concentrate on the domestic front. We had been crowned as Inter Cities Fairs Cup Champions, now we wanted to go one stage further, Football League Champions, and later, European Cup Winners.'

In the league it was jackpot time, as Leeds reached even higher levels and new heights:

'There was feeling throughout the team that we could go all the way in the 1968-69 season. I remember a pre-season friendly, played at Hampden Park against Celtic. There were 75,000 inside the ground creating a terrific atmosphere. The boss didn't want to lose and fielded more or less the full first team, and we won the game 2-1. It was as good an all-round performance as we had given and it instilled an incredible amount of self-belief into our challenge.'

The season started with a winning run of league results, before being brought to a temporary halt at Nottingham Forest when the game was abandoned at half time:

'Christ, the game at Nottingham Forest will always stick with me because it was one of those strange incidents which just seems so surreal and thoroughly unbelievable when you look back at it. It all seemed fairly trivial at the time, but later, the seriousness of it all struck home.

'It all happened in slow motion really, wisps of smoke, the smell of wood burning and the sensible approach of the supporters. The main stand, beneath which stood dressing rooms, was on fire. The referee went into a panic, we all did, our belongings and clothing was all in there. It was something you didn't expect to happen, another chapter in my wonderful football career. It was obvious that complete evacuation was necessary, so we all, as players, made our way into the main car park. These were the days before Health and Safety became important, wooden benches in wooden constructed stands were the usual seating arrangements for main stands up and down the country. I remember seeing a little boy and his dad looking bewildered, and a little frightened, outside the ground. I wandered over to check they were okay. Quick as a flash, the dad asked for an autograph, I obliged and was soon swamped by supporters asking for my signature. Pretty soon the fire brigade were arriving in numbers and it was obvious that the stand was going to burn down, with much of our property still in there. It did, and miraculously, without one casualty. Albeit, Forest's historical records, all irreplaceable, along with various trophies, were destroyed in the blaze. It was a sad and terrifying moment for us all. They said the fire had started in the dressing room area, probably by a discarded cigarette. A further warning as to the perils of smoking.'

An undefeated run of nine league games came to a halt at Maine Road as Manchester City ran out 3-1 winners. Leeds couldn't get into their game as City pummelled them from the outset. A worse league defeat was to follow, when Burnley trounced them 5-1 at Turf Moor. The media began to foretell of cracks.

'F—— hell, yes it was a shock and not so much a bad performance by us but a fluke by Burnley. It was another of those games where the other team got everything right and there is nothing you can do. It was hardly the beginning of the end though. I remember being interviewed by a reporter not long after that game, and he was talking like we were looking at relegation and telling me how Burnley had overrun and completely outplayed us. I asked him if he had been at the game, he said he hadn't, but he had been told by a Burnley colleague how shit we were. So I told him how shit I thought he was, and his mate from Burnley. They could give it, but they couldn't take it, some of the reporters back then were a f—— nightmare, a disgrace to the profession.

'I had vowed some time earlier that I was never going to allow the press to tell me how it was. I would always tell them and if they disagreed then fair enough. Football is about opinions and it's only right that all sides of a story should be aired to readers and not simply what is on many occasions, unqualified opinions that are extremely biased in order to sell newspapers.'

The debacle at Burnley was followed by three 0-0 draws. Winning ways were resumed on Saturday, 16 November 1968 when Coventry City fell to a solitary Paul Madeley goal to give United a much needed 1-0 victory. The win ignited Leeds and, as they shifted up a gear, the team went on an undefeated run of twenty-seven league games, including a 6-1 victory over Burnley and a 5-1 win at Stoke, during which Bremner netted a brace:

'It was like someone flicked a switch. The players kicked on after the Burnley defeat – we were hurt by the press comments and wanted to show the football public that we were the best. Players like Eddie Gray and Peter Lorimer were showing some sublime skills, whereas others like Norman Hunter, Johnny Giles, Jack Charlton, Terry Cooper and Paul Reaney were reliable and solid. It was a privilege to play alongside them. I recall one goal in particular that was scored by Eddie Gray – mind blowing. With the ball at his feet, he weaved in and out and round and about six or seven Burnley players all inside the penalty area before smashing the ball home. It is easily the best goal I, and probably thousands of others have seen and it was the best piece of skill I ever witnessed from a Leeds player in all my years. Such sublime skill and victories defy the "dirty Leeds" label the press had attached to us. No matter what anyone may claim, in the majority of positions we were the complete team.'

74

Leeds kicked on and showed why they were the best team in the land, clinching the Football League championship on the night of 28 April 1969, after a 0-0 draw with Liverpool at Anfield. The scenes were memorable to say the least, and will long live in the memory of all those who attended the game. The night when the most famous terrace in football, Liverpool's Spion Kop, saluted the champions from Elland Road. It was the night Billy Bremner and his colleagues fulfilled a united ambition: Leeds United – Champions of the Football League:

'It was a wonderful occasion. People tell me they shed a tear, who didn't? We were worthy champions, even our closest opposition said we were the best and deserved to win the championship.

'When the final whistle blew I was overwhelmed; I think every Leeds supporter in the ground and back home in Leeds or anywhere else, found it hard to believe that we had done it. All I wanted to do was get in among them and shake each and every one of them by the hand to thank them for their incredible and undying support. They really are the best supporters in football. I don't know if there is any other emotion in football that could equal the joy of being champions of the entire Football League – perhaps lifting the World Cup as a winner for Scotland, but that's a different story altogether. I have to say that the Liverpool supporters were immense that evening, cheering and clapping us and singing our names and acclaiming us as champions. It was the perfect surroundings to be crowned as the best team in English football. Bill Shankly was a fine and honourable man, he had champagne delivered into our dressing room and he was first to congratulate us, adding that we were worthy champions. Coming from him, that's what I call a real compliment.

'The boss was all smiles and when he told me to take the players to the Liverpool Kop I shit myself and said to him, "No way, they'll lynch us." He said, "Bill, these are football people, they known and respect good football. Just go over there, stand proud and thank them." As we got closer I was looking at the sea of red and white scarves and faces staring back at us. Then I saw them applauding and congratulating us, shouting out "Well done" and other compliments. It was something else. I was crying, I couldn't believe it and we all thanked them and applauded back. I didn't want to come off the pitch.'

The domestic cup campaigns had ended at an early stage, Sheffield Wednesday putting the team out of the FA Cup at the first hurdle, and Crystal Palace dumping Revie's side out of the League Cup in the fourth round.

9

THINGS CAN ONLY GET BETTER

The following season, the FA Charity Shield was added to the trophy cabinet as the 1969-70 season got underway and FA Cup winners Manchester City were beaten 2-1 at Elland Road:

'It was wonderful times at Leeds United. I remember telling the boss that he would have to speak with the chairman about getting a joiner to build us a bigger trophy cabinet! He wasn't amused and duly told me that true champions are gauged over a continued period of time and not just on the efforts of one season. I didn't need to be told, but he reiterated that we must strive to further achieve rather than rest on our laurels. I know he wanted to see the European Cup in the trophy cabinet and we all believed that we could deliver that for him.'

The league campaign of 1969-70 went as everyone had hoped with just one defeat in the first twenty-five league games. Indeed, just six league fixtures were lost all season. Incredibly, this wasn't sufficient for Leeds to keep hold of the League championship, and they finished runners-up to Everton.

In the FA Cup, after scraping through 2-1 at home to Swansea, victories over Sutton United (0-6), Mansfield Town (2-0), and Swindon Town (0-2) saw the side through to the semi-final stage, where Leeds drew against Manchester United at Hillsborough and Villa Park respectively. The game was finally settled at Burnden Park, Bolton, when a sweet strike from Bremner flew into the Manchester United goal, giving Leeds a 1-0 victory:

'The FA Cup run really took it out of us that season, particularly those games against Manchester United. It was an exhausting and disappointing season, especially as we had done so well on different fronts. The games kept coming, two a week for most of the season.

'As for the FA Cup and the goal that got us to Wembley, it just fell nicely. I had to be quick to get in front of the defender, and I just let fly; the next thing it was in the back of the net and I was being mobbed by white football shirts. I had a real desire to lift the FA Cup trophy at Wembley, and felt that we were ready.'

Before the FA Cup final, the gruelling diary of fixtures continued. First, they faced Celtic in the semi-final of the European Cup, which they had reached by aggregate victories over Lyn Oslo (16-0), Ferencvaros (6-0), and Standard Liege (2-0). The first leg was played at Elland Road, and was settled by a Chalmers goal which gave Celtic a 1-0 lead to take home for the second leg in Scotland. Leeds looked a shadow of themselves, and never truly outwitted their opponents, for whom Jimmy Johnstone was magnificent:

'In Europe you would prefer to play the away leg first, but we didn't get that luck. I was sick as a dog after our performance at home against Celtic. The press called it the "Battle of Britain" and we did everything but score a bloody goal. Celtic had a strategy, stuck to it, and outwitted and outplayed us.

'Jock Stein was a manager to revere, he knew our strengths and weaknesses. Before the game, he actually commented to me that I and some of our players were looking tired. Clever psychological stuff, and it worked. That aside, some of our players had their minds on Wembley, so were focused on not picking up any kind of injury which might rule them out. I felt very bitter that we lost the first leg in the way we did, almost without a fight, but I knew I had to let it go and focus on the next game – the FA Cup final against Chelsea.'

On a rain-sodden Wembley pitch, Leeds twice took the lead but were twice pegged back by a determined and extremely physical Chelsea team. First to score was Jack Charlton, a header that sneaked between two Chelsea defenders on the goal line. This was followed by a 'freak' Chelsea equaliser. A scowling Bremner recalled:

'Oh dear, we had settled into our game and were playing better than Chelsea – everyone was working for each other, covering when needed, and making space for the pass with our typical understanding. Everyone that is, except Gary bloody Sprake. Chelsea had the ball, Peter Houseman, he was well away from goal and none of us saw the attack as a threat. When he hit what can only be described as a "speculative" shot towards our goal I thought to myself, that's as weak as water and is going nowhere.

'Afterwards, he told me that he didn't expect it to come to anything and just hit it towards our goal. As I glanced back following the ball with my eyes, I saw that Sprake looked to have it covered and dived to his left. Everyone in the stadium thought he had comfortably gathered the ball. The next thing I saw was Sprake fumbling and making a real meal out of such a basic save. I remember saying to myself, "Please, not now Gary, not now." In the next second I saw the ball squirming out from beneath him – it was as though it was alive, and it trickled into our net. I remember big Jack saying to me, "What the hell has the f——clown done now?"

'Now I am no goalkeeper, yet even I knew that he had dropped a right clanger. It certainly wasn't his first and it certainly was not to be his last. Boy, of all the places and moments to choose to f—— about and lose your concentration, the clown picks the FA Cup final at Wembley.

'At half time I made a real effort to console him, and told him to focus and to forget the f—— up. Inside I was seething with him for being so incompetent and wanted to hit him. To my surprise he wasn't at all fazed by the incident. All he wanted to do was get on with the game and told us not to mention it. If it had been any other player who had let the team down, they would have been devastated and apologetic. Not him, he was too arrogant to admit his mistake.

'I told the boss I wasn't happy about Gary Sprake and wasn't comfortable with his shit attitude. The boss told me that he would deal with him. I don't think he ever did and that really didn't help us as a unit. By the time he realised what Gary Sprake was, a weakness and an uncommitted part our team, it was too late. A few years later, Sprake, as far as I am concerned, sold his soul to the devil and showed his true self, all for the sake of a few quid, selling poisonous tales to the press about the boss – damning the integrity and reputation of the man who gave him his opportunity in the game, a man who stuck by him when others doubted his ability and had all but lost belief. Gary Sprake gave us very little yet in my opinion took a great deal from Leeds United. He didn't last long at Birmingham after we got rid of him. I'm certain their manager, Freddie Goodwin, must have always regretted signing him for the fee he paid. Birmingham didn't get much value for their money.'

In the second half of the Chelsea game, a Mick Jones goal returned the advantage to Leeds, only for Iain Hutchinson to head home an equaliser for Chelsea. Again some critics have ascribed blame for that goal to Sprake, although poor defensive marking seems a more reasoned and likely cause for allowing the Chelsea striker the time and room to score. With the scores level at full time, extra time was played out. With no further goals, a replay was necessary to find a winner. Another game was just what Leeds did not want, especially as it was a game carrying such importance.

Four days after the Cup final it was back to European Cup action and the second leg against Celtic, at Hampden Park. In the fourteenth minute, Leeds answered their doubters with a stunning Bremner goal which levelled the tie on aggregate.

Gary Sprake went some way to redeeming his dire Wembley performance, and produced a number of top-class saves to deny Celtic a goal. Eventually, with tiredness beginning to takes it toll, the Glasgow side began to dominate. It came as no surprise when a John 'Yogi' Hughes glancing header flew past Sprake into the net. Celtic had regained the advantage. Later, a clash between Hughes and Sprake saw the Leeds player stretchered off and applauded by the crowd for his valiant performance and bravery. His replacement was David Harvey and the youngster barely had a chance to settle when, before he even got a touch, his first and unenviable task was picking the ball out of his net. Bobby Murdoch scored the second Celtic goal of the night, giving the Parkhead side a 3-1 aggregate lead, more than enough to see them through the remainder of the game against an exhausted Leeds United.

Bremner recalled: 'It was a gruelling night at Hampden Park; Celtic were a great team and really exploited our tired state. It was the one game I saw what Gary Sprake could give us as a team. His head was on the game and he knew he needed to make amends for his abject display at Wembley, not only to us but to the supporters. He was really hurt in that collision with "Yogi" Hughes and I felt for him. Afterwards I think we could all see the strain and exhaustion on our faces. It wasn't so much a long season but the amount of big games we had to play in a short space of time. Ridiculous really. Mentally we had to tough it out – if we approached the Chelsea replay in anything but the right frame of mind then we could be punished and lose.'

The Old Trafford replay was no different from Wembley. Leeds had the play and pressed forward from midfield, and in the thirty-fourth minute took the lead through a first-class finish from Mick Jones, after an Allan Clarke pass had split the Chelsea defence. Late in the game came the Chelsea equaliser, a diving header from Osgood, which broke the resilience and will-power of a team running on adrenalin. Again the final went into extra time. Intense Leeds pressure persisted, yet Chelsea stood firm and began to look dangerous. When David Webb 'shouldered' the ball into the net late into extra time, the trophy was heading to Stamford Bridge. Leeds United left the field thoroughly dejected and trophyless:

'I don't think it was so much losing to Chelsea that hurt us, more the way our season ended. We had chased three major trophies – the European Cup, the League, and the FA Cup – and had just failed in all of them. We had too many important games crammed together and despite official appeals we were forced to play them without a reasonable break in between, as dictated by the football authorities. No thought was ever given to the physical strain such a season placed on the team. For the first time in my football career I felt physically and mentally drained and needed a break and a lift.'

The final game of the season closed a decade of first-team football for Billy Bremner. A decade that by his own admission had been a rollercoaster ride, from reserve-team football to lifting the League Championship trophy, the Inter Cities Fairs Cup trophy, the Football League Cup trophy, the FA Charity Shield plus the consolidation of his first-team place in the Scotland international team.

By 1970, the slightly built ginger-haired boy from Raploch had matured into a world-class footballer, and was accepted in football as a true leader of men:

'I don't think I changed as a person during my first decade at Leeds, but I had become more aware of other people's perception of me. At first I found it difficult to understand why the press would wish to undermine the success of a British football club or of individual players but the sad thing is that they did, and to this day they continue to do so. It's a sad indictment of society and the game but success ultimately breeds contempt.

'Leeds were initially despised by some of the press. Condemnation in those printed column inches spread such animosity to football supporters throughout the land that our football was often condemned as cynical, and as an individual I was classed as "dirty". Eventually such tags wear thin and we were forced to maintain an aloof approach with much of the press.

'With that said, you can imagine my surprise and pleasure when I was told that I had been nominated and voted as "Footballer of the Year" by the Football Writers Association. What a fantastic accolade, one which had previously been bestowed to the boss, Don Revie, at the end of the 1954-55 season. By winning this award I had joined some illustrious company, yet not once did I consider myself as good a footballer as some of those previous winners. Billy Bremner, Footballer of the Year – it was unbelievable! Yet it was true, it had really happened, the boy from Raploch had done good.'

10

SIDE BEFORE SELF EVERY TIME

The new decade brought new hope, and with it new promise to Elland Road. An opening-day fixture at Old Trafford against Manchester United provided a distinctly difficult start to proceedings:

'The boss didn't want any hangovers from the way the previous season had ended, but I felt okay. Winning the Footballer of the Year award was an unexpected honour and kept my mind focused on keeping my performances at their very best.

'Old Trafford was always difficult terrain for us at Leeds, the two teams were so closely matched in skill and ability and the supporters had their own enthusiastic agenda on the terraces. Whenever we played Manchester United the noise level seems to lift – it's a game everyone looks forward to, especially the fans of either club.'

The game itself was typically close with Leeds winning 1-0 courtesy of a first-half strike from Mick Jones. The team set off on a run of five straight victories as they stormed to the top of the league before Arsenal snatched a point in a dour nil all draw at Highbury:

'Mick Jones was a great lad to have up front; he put away so many chances, and what an athlete he was. He never stopped running throughout a game, fantastic energy and commitment. Both Mick, and his partner up front Allan Clarke, were a threatening strike force and they took so much pressure off us defensively by holding up the ball and chasing lost causes.

'At the beginning of the 1970 season we were playing some of our best football and everyone looked comfortable on the ball.

Once again there was a general feeling that in most areas (goal-keeper excepted) we were invincible and could go through a whole season without losing. It was never openly discussed amongst the players, but I know that privately, such a belief existed. Whenever I mentioned it to the boss he would say that we had to take one game at a time.'

If the players were feeling unbeatable, then such arrogance was to disappear during one week in September. First they suffered an ignominious defeat in the League Cup competition, losing 1-0 to Sheffield Wednesday. Then, four days later, the unbeaten league start was not so much stopped, but battered from them one afternoon in Stoke. At City's Victoria Ground, the Potters taught Leeds a valuable lesson that football can be a great leveller. Stoke showed concentration, determination and desire for the full ninety minutes, giving Leeds not a moment to dwell on the ball or the opportunity to get into their passing game. Once the home side scored, in a one-sided first half, the result and outcome of the game was never in doubt as Leeds suffered a humbling 3-0 defeat:

'Stoke City were a funny sort of team; on their day they could hammer anyone, they had the players and the determination to cause damage to the most disciplined of sides. I can't say I have many fond memories of playing at Stoke; I never used to like playing against them as they were one of the few teams who seemed to know how to counter our game. Terry Conroy and Mike Pejic in particular were tremendous servants to the club and both were very good footballers. Some people said they were the "Bremner and Giles" of the Stoke team. I don't know about that, but what I do know is they were bloody tough opponents and real characters too. I was always surprised that Stoke did not compete for more trophies, albeit they had this inconsistent side to their game. They would stuff us one week then lose to a team struggling near the bottom of the table. It must have been hugely frustrating for the manager and the fans that that form could not be maintained.'

Gradually, as the season progressed, the odd defensive

weakness or lapse in concentration crept into games and cost the team dearly. In one game at Crystal Palace, and with Leeds leading, Gary Sprake chose to have one of his 'moments'. As the game moved into its final minute Palace defender and captain John Sewell hoofed a clearance up field which went towards the Leeds goal and was never a threat. Cue Gary Sprake. The Welshman moved to catch the ball which sailed through his hands into the net. John Sewell recalled the goal:

'I only scored about nine goals for Palace but that one was a freak. I just kicked the ball up field, there was no thought of shooting or scoring. I was knackered and was relieving the pressure. When it sailed right through the goalkeeper's hands I couldn't believe it. The whole ground was delighted, it was the first time I heard a crowd of 35,000 laughing in unison. After, Sprake wasn't at all remorseful; it was obvious that many of the Leeds players were unhappy with him but he didn't appear to care.'

Unfortunately for Leeds it wasn't to be the only costly error Sprake made that season. Billy recalled the fluke goal at Crystal Palace:

'I would like to say that I couldn't believe what Gary did that day, but that wouldn't be accurate or true. His cock-ups were never far away and were becoming more frequent. Only he can justify why it continually happened, but my belief is that he didn't keep his eye on the ball, and when he had time to think about making a save, he was prone to fluffing it. Anything that required concentration and he was liable to cock it up. No matter how much we tried to lift his concentration levels and spirits, he didn't seem to bother, he just kept doing the same thing over and over again.

'I wasn't alone in feeling unhappy with him but it was the boss who picked the team and not us players, so we didn't really have a lot of say. It was obvious to everyone that Sprake was our Achilles heel.'

Come the end of the season the point dropped at Selhurst Park was to prove crucial.

In January 1971, the team suffered a shock second league defeat, when Tottenham snatched a 2-1 win in front of 43,907 Elland Road fans – a crowd that included an injured Billy Bremner:

'Whenever I was out injured or through the odd suspension, I would watch the games sat in the West Stand with the supporters and cheer the team on alongside them. It was a real surprise to lose at home to Spurs but we never looked in control, or like winning the game, and seemed nervous on the ball. The fans around me were willing me to get back out there as soon as possible. I assured them that it was a one-off result and that the players would be well and truly pissed off in the dressing room. That helped keep things in perspective.'

With Bremner absent through injury, Leeds temporarily stuttered and in early February lost another home game, this time 1-0 to Liverpool. Things were to get much worse before they improved:

'We had got through to the FA Cup fifth round and were drawn away to a Fourth Division side, Colchester United. It wasn't the sort of game that should cause us any problems – we were generally professional enough to treat every opponent the same. The usual preparations were made for the game and the boss pointed out the obvious threat of their forward Ray Crawford, who was well known to most of us from his days and goalscoring exploits at Ipswich and for England. The boss seemed a little out of sorts before the game. I wasn't playing but we had a bloody strong team despite that.'

Revie later recalled the game:

'I've been in some intimidating stadiums in my time but Layer Road at Colchester was claustrophobic as well. There just wasn't any room and the fans were right on top of the players, touching them when they took a throw-in or a corner. It was a Cup upset waiting to happen and I sensed that the minute I walked into the ground.'

Colchester sat seventy-four positions below Leeds in the football league placings and had four players aged thirty-five or

SIDE BEFORE SELF EVERY TIME

older in their team. They had been meticulous in their assessment of the Leeds threat minus Bremner. Manager Dick Graham knew that Leeds like to get the ball wide and to counter this he had chairs and benches placed at a safe distance round the outside of the pitch to make it appear more cramped. In the week leading up to the tie he had his players practising crosses in the realisation that Gary Sprake was the weak link and could prove key to Leeds' undoing.

A partisan crowd of 16,000 crammed into the tiny stadium and there witnessed one of the greatest FA Cup shocks of all time. Leeds weren't able to compete in a first half that saw them fall behind to two Ray Crawford goals. The first was a thumping header and the second a shot that slid past the hesitant Sprake in the Leeds goal. In the second half, David Simmons ran through onto a looping ball and again Sprake hesitated, allowing Simmons to get his head onto it and past the flailing arms of the Leeds keeper to make the score an unbelievable 3-0.

Leeds did pull two goals back in the second half, through Hunter and Giles, but it was too little, too late. 'Grandad's Army' as they were labelled, won the game:

'It was an awful experience. No one knew what to say, we were dreadful and deserved to lose that day. I think the overall performance put things in perspective for us all, there is no getting away from it – we had let everyone down. Even Gary Sprake was disappointed in his game and gave some sort of apology to the boss but that didn't help erase the memory of our nightmare in Essex. There was a belief in the team that if the game had gone on another ten minutes then we would have won. I don't subscribe to that thought. We deserved to lose on the day, and once again Mr Sprake gave us an indecisive performance in goal.'

With the league championship seeming like a two-horse race, between Leeds and Arsenal, and with the season drawing to a close, Leeds sat four points behind the Gunners but with three games in hand. The Gunners still had to come to Elland Road so it was Leeds who were firm favourites to take the league title.

Then it happened, one of those moments that seem to crop up every so often in the Leeds United history of that era. It was Saturday, 17 April 1971, and Leeds faced West Bromwich Albion at Elland Road. On their day, Albion could pose a threat, yet on this day they were not expected to be strong enough to prevent a Leeds victory. With more than a hint of sadness and disappointment in his face, Billy remembered how that day developed:

'It's difficult to put your finger on why some things happen. That game against West Bromwich Albion is a game that everyone associated with Leeds United has indelibly etched into the forefront of their minds. I know I certainly do, and I shall not ever forget or forgive what happened to us.

'For whatever reason, there was an atmosphere inside Elland Road that day, a state of nervousness amongst the crowd that transmitted itself through to us, though it must be said that we didn't have the same confident air about us in the dressing room before the game. The banter and chat was missing. We knew that Albion could be spoilers, they had turned over enough decent teams in their time to be more than competent at stopping the opposition from playing. In the warm-up, Jeff Astle was having a bit of a go at us about the Colchester game and result, saying we were a laughing stock and shit, and he said he would do anything and everything to stop us winning the championship. Jeff was great, a real character, and we had more than our share of spats during our careers but we always laughed about them. He could head a ball with real venom – vicious and stunning power. When the game started, Albion were really coming at us and it was obvious that their manager, Alan Ashman, had told them to push us back. They scored in the first twenty minutes and that really put us on the back foot. Our passing went all over the place and Albion had got us making mistakes.

'The atmosphere grew more and more intense. The referee, Ray Tinkler, wasn't giving us anything, a few heavy challenges on our players had gone unpunished, yet each time we went into a tackle, an Albion player would hit the floor and the referee would stop the game. I tried to speak to him about what was happening but he wouldn't listen and kept repeating the same bloody thing: "Go away – go away Bremner, play on – play on Albion." I began to wonder if he supported West Brom, so biased in their favour were his decisions. Talk about getting me wound up. He certainly did and that was before his blatant and heinous error that still sticks in my throat whenever I talk about it.

'With about twenty minutes to go we were really going for it and pushing forward in search of an equaliser. An attack broke down inside the Albion half when, unusually, Norman Hunter gave the ball away. Tony Brown latched onto the ball and galloped off up field. In front of him, in our half and clearly several yards offside, was Colin Suggett, and not too far away from him was Jeff Astle. It was a clear-cut decision for the referee to make. The linesman immediately flagged for the offside and we all, players from both teams, stopped in anticipation of the referee blowing for the infringement. Tony Brown still had the ball and he too stopped awaiting the referee's whistle for offside. It was like time stood still, the whistle never came, and instead came the inane bleating of the referee – "Play on Albion, play on." Brown couldn't believe it, he was laughing as he raced on towards our goal. Everyone inside the ground knew that Suggett and Astle were offside. I looked towards the linesman who was waving his flag for the infringement, then he suddenly dropped his arm and stopped. My heart was in my mouth, I couldn't believe what was happening before my very eyes. The whole ground went silent as Tony Brown played a forward pass to a clearly offside Astle, who was still ahead of Brown and still offside, and he duly scored their second goal of the game. I don't believe anyone thought the goal would stand, it was such a blatant and obvious offside decision.'

The Elland Road stadium erupted into a frenzy of anger. Many Albion players were laughing at the decision, an act that didn't endear them too kindly to the Leeds support:

'I saw the boss get up from the dugout – he rarely moved during a game so it must have been something exceptional. I ran over and spoke to the linesman, and at first he said he was flagging for offside then he denied it and said it was for an infringement on an Albion player and he put it down and gave advantage. I called him a lying, cheating bastard and he laughed and said, "It's a good goal." I ran up to Ray Tinkler and explained that he had got it wrong, I know it wasn't my place to tell him that, he was supposed to be in charge, but his incompetence in that decision was clear. He told me that he couldn't see anything wrong with the goal, adding: "It wasn't offside at all, it was fair play, a good goal, and it will stand." I was livid, who wouldn't be at such an injustice? I called him a f—— cheat, his response was to sneer back at me and threaten to end my game there and then.

'Around us pandemonium had erupted as some fans got onto the pitch and tried to appeal to Mr Tinkler, telling him he had got it wrong.' My uncle, the same family man I loved who had first introduced me to Leeds United, was one of those so outraged by the decision that he ran onto the pitch and was duly arrested by the police. It wasn't something he was ever proud of, he knew it was wrong, yet his emotions and passion at witnessing such a clear error and the realisation of what it meant to Leeds United and him as a supporter, had caused him to react and try to explain to the referee that he had made an error of judgement. He got nowhere near, and was felled by three burly coppers having hardly set foot on the playing surface. The shame this brought on him remained with him for the rest of his life, and to his last breath, he maintained that Ray Tinkler had got it all wrong. Football is an emotive game, and whilst I cannot condone what my uncle did, I can understand his passion and repulsion at what he saw as a clear football injustice.

'In my opinion, Tinkler had always been regarded as a supercilious prat, full of his own self-importance, and believed himself to be more important than the games he officiated. There was no way he would listen to a fan's opinion, or those of players, or anyone else remotely connected with Leeds United. Jeff Astle sensed the injustice and the potential of supporter rioting as a result of the ridiculous decision. He approached Tinkler and asked him if he was certain that the goal would stand, and if he understood the consequences of the decision. Tinkler was his own man, and like a schoolyard bully he strutted off, ignoring everything being said to him. In his mind he was right and everyone else wrong. The West Bromwich manager was almost wetting himself with laughter, shaking his head at his side's good fortune.'

In a strange twist of fate, Ashman was to tell the author some years later:

'It was a joke of a decision, wasn't it? One of the worst I have ever seen in all my years. Ray Tinkler got it totally wrong, but what made me laugh was the linesman. He held up his flag and was frantically waving it about, then he took it down and changed his mind about the offside. I don't know how or why but it was pure farce. You could never have scripted that, incompetence of the highest degree, incompetence that provided me with some good fortune as a manager under pressure.'

The game ended in a 1-2 defeat, and with it went Leeds' title ambitions. Despite beating champions-elect Arsenal at Elland Road, the title was lost. The realistic truth of the matter was that too many points had been dropped throughout the whole season. In Europe Leeds had again achieved success, winning the Inter Cities Fair Cup by the away goals rule after they and Juventus had fought out draws (2-2 & 1-1) over the two-legged final:

'It was good to win something that season as we had suffered. I was relieved to raise a trophy high into the Elland Road sky. We had been robbed of the league, it didn't help to look back on the Gary Sprake error at Crystal Palace or the misjudgement of Ray Tinkler!'

An inquest into the incidents relating to the West Bromwich Albion game was held by the Football Association and resulted in Elland Road being closed for the first four home league games of the season and a £500 fine. Key to that punishment was the referee's report. Ray Tinkler's report was influential: everything he said was accepted as fact, and as accurate. There was never any suggestion that it could have been his poor judgement and decision-making that had incited the problems. Interestingly, Ray Tinkler later became Chairman of the Lincolnshire Football Association and sat on various Football Association committees. Most recently, in April 2009, he spoke about the decision in a national newspaper and claimed that Brian Clough and Peter Taylor were at Elland Road, they had agreed with his decision and he stood by the fact that he was right to allow play to continue and the goal to stand. That says it all; if such unbiased persons as Brian Clough and Peter Taylor said it was a fair goal, scored within the rules of the game, then it must have been a good decision!

It remains one of the most curious refereeing decisions ever to occur in the English professional game. The fact that Ray Tinkler is in the main remembered for this error of judgement is something he cannot take much pride in. It may well be that Clough and Taylor were at the game and did agree with his decision. As we know, Clough despised that Leeds team and would hardly be likely to help them out.

As a side issue, Jeff Astle later admitted to being a 'mile' offside when he scored and that the goal should never have been allowed. He performed a satirical re-enactment of the incident on the Baddiel and Skinner television show many years later. Ray Tinkler has stood by his judgement from that day. You have to respect him for sticking to his opinions but he must know that he made a mistake.

Unfortunately for Leeds and Billy Bremner, further success was to be blighted by bizarre refereeing behaviour. The punishment handed out by the Football Association for the West Bromwich affair was harsh, but one that the club had to accept.

11

UPS AND DOWNS

The following season, 1971-72, was another rollercoaster ride for Bremner and his colleagues. After an average start to the league season with one win from four games, the team struggled to hit consistent form. Newcastle United were thrashed 5-1 at Elland Road but still the team couldn't get into their usual rhythm. Too many goals were being conceded and injuries to key players such as Eddie Gray and Mick Jones unsettled the side. There was a surprise early exit from European competition when the relative unknown SK Lierse, trailing 2-0 from the first leg, put four past Leeds without reply at Elland Road. Bremner recalled:

'We weren't at our best during the early part of the season. The Lierse game caught the team napping and they [Lierse] were so fired up for it. And perhaps some of our players thought the hard work had been done after we won 2-0 over there in the first leg.

'I can't recall hearing Leeds fan boo the team but they were deservedly booed off that night. I felt sorry for John Shaw, our apprentice goalkeeper, that night. He was a Stirling boy, was thrown in at the deep end and Lierse exposed his vulnerability.

'We did eventually start putting it together that season. I remember us giving Manchester United a bit of a hiding (5-1) at Elland Road, followed by Southampton (7-0) and we beat Nottingham Forest 6-1 as well, so it wasn't all doom and gloom.

'We got caught up in our own success as we were again pushing for the League championship and for the FA Cup, which was to prove our undoing as towards the end of the season important fixtures were coming thick and fast. The powers that be wouldn't budge and allow us to reschedule; they wanted the football calendar completed by a certain date and that was it, we had to comply with that.'

In the final of the FA Cup Leeds met their old foes Arsenal who were not only the previous season's League champions but FA Cup holders too. A team full of 'superstars' is how they were described in an FA Cup tie against Second Division Carlisle United: 'Arsenal can boast players such as Alan Ball, Bob McNab, Charlie George, George Graham, Frank McLintock, everywhere is a household name.' Bremner and Leeds, unlike Carlisle, were acutely aware of the entire Arsenal threat: 'We were pleased to meet Arsenal in the final; after all we had a 100 per cent Wembley Cup final record against them. The game went by so quickly and soon it was just a memory. David Harvey had taken over in goal, and we felt much more secure as a unit. The boss gave his usual team talk asking for commitment and determination and, of course, goals. We knew from experience that Arsenal could mix it so it was never going to be an elegant game as we were really up for the fight that day.

'A fair few tackles were flying in early on and I thought I had better make my presence known and assert myself in an attempt to stop someone from getting injured. The referee didn't like it and he booked me, telling me not to get carried away and to make it good clean final. He booked about four players in the first half to try to get both teams to think twice before jumping in. At half time the boss told us to keep running at them in the second half and not to give them any time or space. We got off to a great start and it wasn't long before Allan Clarke scored with that brilliant diving header to give us the lead. We kept it going and always looked dangerous on the attack. Arsenal did peg us back for a while but the handling of David Harvey was excellent and he played an outstanding game.

'Towards the end of the game, Mick Jones collided with their goalkeeper and fell awkwardly on his shoulder and arm, dislocating the lot. I still cringe whenever I think about how much pain the boy was in. The game was all but over when it happened, and when the final whistle did blow we were all ecstatic but worried about Mick as he was still down receiving treatment by the Arsenal goal. They strapped him up and, in agony, he went up to collect his FA Cup winner's medal. We couldn't celebrate our victory really because we still had one league game to play two days later, at Wolverhampton Wanderers.'

It wasn't just any league game; it was in effect the Football League championship decider with Leeds needing a draw to take the title. Bremner said:

'It was so wrong, we were physically and mentally exhausted and it was always going to be a tall order for us to win a point. Wolves were a physical side, full of cloggers like Danny Hegan. They made us work really hard and exploited our tired legs and minds by running us all over the pitch. Frank Munro and Derek Dougan scored for them and it looked all over for us. I managed to pull a goal back and that gave us our second wind. I went round our players telling them to give it one big push and the boss was shouting to us to attack and force them back. We did everything, threw the kitchen sink at them but Phil Parkes in their goal played a blinder and stopped everything. When the final whistle went it was as though we had lost everything. It was a shattering blow to lose the League championship in such a way but we had the FA Cup and that was important to everyone and to me as I now had winners' medals for each of the three major domestic competitions.'

The Wolves game was later blighted with allegations of bribery and match fixing. In September 1977 a Sunday newspaper recounted and printed the spurious claims of various players of attempted bribery, and there were plenty of people who appeared desperate for any dirt they could dish on Leeds. One Wolves player claimed that Bremner offered him £1000 to give away a penalty, while another said he offered him £5000 – vastly contrasting and contradictory tales that must have humiliated those making them. On 3 February 1982, Bremner won £100,000 libel damages, along with legal costs, after he sued the newspaper for publishing the article. Among those

speaking on behalf of and in support of Bremner were Jack
Charlton, Allan Clarke, Johnny Giles and Wolves centre forward,
Derek Dougan. On the matter, Dougan was to later tell the
author,

'It was absolute nonsense, Billy was a good man, a great
footballer and I trusted him implicitly. I couldn't say the same
about a lot of footballers I knew. The press were hungry for anti-
Leeds, anti-Don Revie stories to undermine their achievements
and efforts. Certain reporters would say anything, pay anything
for a story, no matter how true or untrue it was, just to cause a
sensation. The rumours about Don Revie and bribery had been
about for donkeys' years. Bobby Stokoe started it all off, he hated
Revie and Leeds United. So you can't pay too much attention to
what he claims, why didn't he report it to the authorities when
it happened, not wait a decade later and get payment for his
version of events? I don't know why Frank Munro and Danny
Hegan didn't come clean at the time either, why sell your story to
a newspaper, why say anything at all? It beats me. I saw plenty
of corruption during my time, I spoke out there and then, be it
referees, linesmen, players or managers or club officials, there
was plenty of it going on. It's a disgrace really, Billy Bremner
wasn't corrupt. He cleared his name in court and I helped him
because it was right and proper to do so.'

Others said the claims were nonsense but as Bremner found
out:

'It just wouldn't go away. We had made enemies in certain
quarters of the press, particularly the southern-based reporters.
They despised us, they enjoyed seeing us lose and would rarely
report positively on us. In my opinion, the whole bribery thing
was nothing but smoke and mirrors. There was a groundswell of
reporters who didn't like the boss and he was being looked at as
a prospective England manager. My take is that they were
desperate to destroy his reputation so as to frighten off the
Football Association. As for the Wolves boys making the allegations, well, they were made to look silly when one of their own
team mates, Derek Dougan, spoke out against them and said

their claims were nonsense. For all I know, they were probably looking at some way to top up their pensions but I hold no public malice towards them. And when it comes to Gary Sprake, the f—— clown wonders why the players of our era don't want anything to do with him. He shit on the boss, me and the club. As far as I'm concerned, what will his football career be remembered for? Mistake after mistake after mistake. The sad thing is, it's never his fault, always someone else's.'

The FA Cup was to feature heavily in the Leeds campaign the following season when they again reached the final. This time they faced Second Division Sunderland, who were managed by Bob Stokoe:

'There was that bit of history and bad blood in existence between the boss and Stokoe. I remember there being a few unnecessary comments made by the press, and accredited to Sunderland, in the lead-up to the game, and basically they were questioning our ability to see off opposition in the final stages of competitions. My response is that at least we reached finals regularly. Not every journalist can write for *The Times*, but they would all like to, I would wager. They do their best, but still only get to write about parish fetes in local rags, so what right had they to write about and question our ability?

'It's no wonder we had a mistrust for many reporters. The amount of crap that was written was ridiculous. They seemed to want any scrap of information be it true or not, and they would run with it as if they were trying to undermine what we were achieving – absolute arseholes.

'I think everything about the FA Cup final of that year has already been said. It always f—— well hurts. It would have been great to win it two years in succession but Sunderland had lady luck with them that day and we really didn't do ourselves justice. Afterwards, I went to congratulate some of them on the win and got told to "piss off". They really did enjoy beating us and rubbed it in.

'Jim Montgomery was class that day, both on and off the field. He made that super save from Peter Lorimer and was courteous to us after the game. I did meet up with some of the Sunderland lads a few months later and to be fair they were all okay then. I reckon Stokoe had wound them up so much on the day that they had to be obnoxious.

'My final word is that Sunderland deserved to beat us, we didn't want to lose, we weren't prepared to lose, but we did, and it was no one's fault but our own. I would have ran through brick walls to stop Bob Stokoe from having any success, but that day he outdid us and fair play to him. A few days after the final we took out our angst on Arsenal, who had already finished the season as runners-up, by giving them a 6-1 stuffing at Elland Road. It didn't take away the pain of losing the FA Cup final but it gave us a real lift for the European Cup Winners' Cup final that we were appearing in a week later.'

The route to the European Cup Winners' Cup final had not been an easy one, but Leeds had achieved it and Bremner and Co. now faced AC Milan in Salonika:

'That final was a farce – Leeds really were playing against twelve men. Before the game, John Giles, who wasn't playing, said he had been talking to some of the press who reckoned that the word was, that no matter how well we played, we wouldn't win the game. Corruption was something we had all heard of and suspected, but none of us had so obviously encountered it before a game. With just four minutes of the game gone, the referee, a Greek called Christos Michas, awarded an indirect free kick in Milan's favour. The lads hadn't settled at that time and lined up to defend the kick. The Milan player Luciano Chiarugi ran up and fired a shot directly into our net. No one was alarmed as it was indirect and it was clear that no one else had touched the ball. I couldn't believe it when the referee gave the goal.

'As the game wore on we were denied three definite penalties, I don't mean debatable penalties, but clear-cut and very obvious fouls. It was excruciating knowing that such blatant cheating was occurring in a European final. Every decision went the way of AC Milan and if it wasn't so serious it would have been hilarious. It was more akin to a scene from a "Carry On" movie. Milan were the winners and collected the trophy but couldn't complete the lap of honour because of the abuse they were getting from the Greek crowd, for the obvious cheating and bribery that had gone on. Missiles were thrown at them and they had to leave the field. The Greek referee was also abused and had the Greek equivalent of the word "shame" screamed at him by the crowd; it was obvious to them what had happened. He was subsequently investigated by his own Football Association on suspicion that he had been bribed. He denied the allegations and it was never proved but he received a lifetime ban from UEFA and would never referee another international club game. Bloody referees, you can't live with them, and you sure as hell can't live without them!'

Within a few days of the final and after taking consultation on the matter, Leeds requested a replay from UEFA. The governing body convened to look at the request but it was denied and the result stood.

Most commentators are united in their opinion that the 1973-74 season was Billy Bremner's finest as a footballer. Not only did he feature in all forty-two league games for Leeds, but he also led his team to new football heights in an unbeaten start to the football league season that lasted an incredible twenty-nine games. Bremner was magnificent as his side raced to the League championship with absolute ease:

'What a side that was – we were f—— superb and probably as good and strong as any British team since the Second World War. It was an absolute pleasure and delight to go out and play week in, week out. Of the four league games we lost throughout the season only Burnley really outplayed us. They actually destroyed us 4-1 at Elland Road, which hurt all the more.

'We had a certain swagger about our play and with Gordon McQueen we had found the best and only replacement for Big Jack that existed. Gordon was a superb defender, he marshalled the defence and was strong in the air and on the ground, and it really made a difference having him in there. To be honest, we

99

didn't actually say as much but our concentration was mainly focused on the League championship. Previously we had wanted to win every competition we entered but now we had a more definite focus and if we progressed in other competitions then that would be all well and good.

'At that time there were a lot of rumours circulating about the boss being eyed up by different European clubs. We all knew he had achieved almost everything he had set out to do at Leeds – we were a formidable football team, the best of our era, trophy winners and a team full of internationals, all as a result of the drive and vision of one man, Don Revie. As it was, the rumours were more than mere speculation, and it had become clear to us all for some time that he was going to move on to take over as England team manager at the end of the season. So that Football League championship was for him.'

12

TO ELLAND BACK

'During the summer the boss told each of us that he was leaving the club. I was devastated that it was over. His departure was a blow for everyone, but it was a step up for him and he was the best manager in the game at that time and deserved a crack at the England job. There was a lot of speculation as to who would replace him. John Giles was mentioned, I was mentioned, Big Jack was mentioned, and he had already begun to prove himself as a decent manager at Middlesbrough. Then totally out of the blue we get told that one of our main detractors, Brian Clough, had got the job. Well, I thought it was big joke to be honest. Was this the same Brian Clough who had publicly called us cheats and dirty and had nothing but derogatory things to say about each and every one of us? I believed that the bloody directors of the football club had gone barmy. What an inappropriate and ridiculous choice to replace the boss. I told them precisely what I thought about it, but was told to give him time and a chance.

'It was obvious from the start that the new manager was going to split the successful Don Revie team of the last decade. He brought in new players, such as Duncan McKenzie, John O'Hare and John McGovern, and tried to drop them straight into the first team. I knew them, they were Clough's boys alright; added to that, they weren't good enough for us.

'We struggled as a unit and Clough never seemed to be there when we needed his support. It was a tough time at the football club. We were league champions yet we were in complete disarray both on and off the field. The supporters had been outraged by the appointment of the new manager and quite rightly so, and he regularly suffered verbal abuse from the terraces but he was so arrogant and aloof to it that he seemed to enjoy it and revelled in the attention. We became a distinctly average team overnight and the buzz and dressing-room camaraderie disappeared as the Clough management style was implemented – split and divide.

'I decided that I wasn't about to let some arsehole like Brian Clough ruin the club so many of us loved. People have gone on for years about how player power got him the sack; let me tell you it wasn't player power at all, it was his own egotistical stupidity. The man was completely blinded and guided by his pathological hatred of Leeds United, the Leeds United Don Revie built! I decided one day after training that enough was enough, and asked for a one-to-one meeting with him. He laughed, and said, "You, Bremner, want a meeting with me, your manager, you running away, are you, you after a transfer?" He said he was busy, he had important things to do, like laugh at photographs of Don Revie with the Football League championship trophy, so whatever it was had better be important. I told him it was, and he said to meet him on the training pitches in half an hour.

'I made my way out onto the pitches, and there he was singing to himself; weird thoughts went through my head, it looked to me as though he was cracking up, and for a split second I felt some sympathy for him. Within a moment it had disappeared. "Right Bremner, what is it, what do you want?" he said. I explained that it was my opinion that he was making a complete balls-up of the job at the club, and that he needed to get rid of the monkey that was on his back that was of his own making. I told him he had lost the confidence of the majority of the dressing room and to grow up and to deal with it all sensibly. He erupted like a volcano at such a suggestion. "F—— you, Bremner, f—— Leeds United, f—— all those morons on the terraces who shout abuse at me each and every game. This is my Leeds United, I will f—— destroy it if I want to, it's not like you haven't already." Spittle was flying from his mouth. I took a step back as I thought he was going to have a dig at me. He stood there staring at me,

Lifting the Football League Cup at Wembley in 1968 – the first of many trophies.

Quickly followed by the Inter Cities Fairs Cup – Champions of Europe!

What me? I never did anything! The infamous bust up with Dave Mackay.

Football heaven – League Champions 1969, a fag and Champagne.

Up, up and away – leaping over Liverpool's Tommy Lawrence
in a Division One match at Anfield 1969.

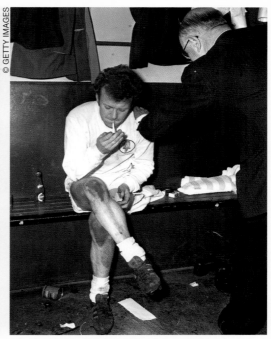

Exhausted – extra time at Wembley in the 1970 FA Cup Final v Chelsea.

After-match wind down and relaxation, Bremner style.

Bedlam – the legendary West Bromwich Albion incident at Elland Road, 17 April 1971, where referee Ray Tinkler awarded a controversial goal.

Being presented with the FA Cup at Wembley in 1972, courtesy of Her Majesty The Queen.

Bremner and the boss – the legendary Don Revie – with the FA Cup at Wembley 1972.

The winning team – Leeds United, FA Cup winners, Wembley 1972.

Room mates – Jack Charlton and Billy Bremner in the hotel
on the morning of the FA Cup Final.

Do I not like that man – 1974 Charity Shield, ignoring Brian Clough at Wembley.

Come on Ref! – being sent off with Kevin Keegan in the 1974 Charity Shield at Wembley.

Exchange of niceties with Franz Beckenbauer - European Cup Final 1975.

Scotland v Brazil – 1974 World Cup Finals and that infamous miss!

Get in! Bremner the manager celebrating another Leeds goal.

Author (centre) with Billy Bremner (right) and Peter Lorimer in 1995.

calling me all kinds of insulting names and generally acting like a right dick-head. I told him he was wrong, Leeds United would always belong to its supporters, and as I was one of those, I wouldn't allow him to drag the club under. He laughed and told me that I was finished, he would see to that. I walked off, reminding him of how big a wanker I thought he was.

'Within an hour, I was sat before Manny Cussins; he told me that Clough had told him that I had said I desperately wanted to leave Leeds with immediate effect. It wasn't true. I told the chairman what had happened, what Clough had said to me. He looked anxious and I think he knew there and then that the directors had made a mess of it in appointing him. "I don't want you to repeat what you have just told me to another soul, Bill, okay. Leave it with me, it'll be sorted very shortly," he said.

'Clough and me never saw eye to eye, I never questioned his ability, but his aggressive attitude and arrogance were fuelled by his hatred of Leeds United. When we heard he had been sacked, well, I for one didn't shed a tear for him. It was like a great weight had been lifted from Elland Road. He had dragged the club and everything it stood for to the depths, a place where none of us wanted to be; we wanted Leeds to be challenging, not the laughing stock he had transformed us into. I hated being at the club during his time in charge, it was like everything we had achieved was being dismantled, freedom of speech was suffocated, and new players had been put into the dressing room to deliberately cause discontent. That was probably the lowest point of my club career. I had never met anyone before who was so manipulative and contriving as Brian Clough. It was obsessive behaviour from him alright, he wanted us all gone, history, players, fans, the lot. He wanted his own version and brand of Leeds United but no man is bigger than the club, as he found out.'

Within days of this incident, Clough was dismissed, but not before agreeing a handsome settlement from the club. He laughed and seemed anything but concerned as he exited Elland Road. Several years later I interviewed him and asked about his thoughts on the Leeds experience. He was unrepentant of his behaviour and actions:

'The board of directors at Leeds United were puppets, controlled by the players. I would have eventually got rid of all of those players at Leeds, they were finished, had their day, time to move on chaps. I wanted to bring real football to the masses of Yorkshire, causing them to leave their terraced homes and get down to Elland Road to enjoy a proper game of football, not the kind of brawlers Don Revie's style had created. They couldn't handle it, they couldn't deal with my honesty, so they forced me out. Best thing that ever happened to me really. Leeds United, who the f—— are they?''

Billy recalls: 'It's funny, but he called after he was sacked, telling me he was now a very rich man, thanks to Leeds United. He said that he wished he had listened to what I had said to him. I thought to myself, "Is this an apology of sorts?" No chance, he followed this up with, "You have the biggest gob at the club, everyone has to listen to your shit when you talk, they have no choice. Our paths will cross again, don't worry Bremner, I won't forget you or your cheating pals."

'The supporters wanted the board of directors and the manager to go and Elland Road crowds dropped to match our performances. There were regular anti-board and manager demonstrations in the club's main car park after games. It was obvious what Clough was doing, creating a "them and us" mentality. I heard deliberately circulated rumours about the various, highly inflated salaries of the new players, which player was signing next and who would be next leaving – it was bollocks. He was a real enigma, a square peg in a round hole, and I did feel sorry for him towards the end of his time at the club. He alienated himself from so many potential allies within the football club, not least the supporters. It was always going to end in tears.'

After just forty-four days in charge, Clough was sacked by the Leeds board and once again press and supporter speculation was rife as to who the next manager would be, Bremner admitted:

'I would have taken the manager's job at that time if I had been asked, and I make no bones about the fact that I wanted it. So did John Giles and I think if they had paired us up as a managerial team we could have worked wonders. Instead the club went for another outsider and Jimmy Armfield was appointed. I was a bit dubious about the change but Jimmy won us all over with his calm manner and knowledge of the game.'

It didn't take the new manager long to start sorting out the dressing room. Players like John O'Hare and John McGovern were moved on as stability returned. League form was patchy but in Europe the team found their best form, beating teams like Anderlecht and Barcelona en route to the 1975 European Cup final where they faced the mighty Bayern Munich in Paris. It was the twentieth anniversary of the European Cup competition and UEFA elected to stage the final in Paris, the scene of Real Madrid's first triumph in 1956, when they defeated Stade de Reims 4-3.

I was fortunate enough to be in Paris with my uncle, a couple of days before the game itself. The build-up was excellent; I remember Leeds fans enjoying the whole atmosphere and being welcomed by the locals in bars around the city. There wasn't a problem until the day of the game. In the afternoon, riot police had been deployed, sweeping bars and ejecting anyone who had any link with Leeds United. Most fans accepted the strong-armed policing tactics and moved on, finding another bar where they could relax and soak in Paris and the thought of a European Cup final.

As kick-off got closer, the police grew antagonistic. Batons were used to clear bars and restaurants, and fans were struck by over-enthusiastic police desperate to avoid trouble, when in fact, it seemed they were creating the problem. I recall seeing Leeds fans laid in gutters and on the streets, bleeding and requiring medical attention, because local authorities deemed the best way to prevent violence was to attack first.

We made our way to the stadium where we were forced by a mounted police branch to congregate into one mass group. No one told us what was happening and Leeds fans were becoming agitated. Eventually we were marched through some gates, into the stadium, no tickets required, no searches, no checks, just get in and stay there until the game's over. The atmosphere was becoming hostile against the authorities; families had been separated during the rounding-up, and now had no way of contacting one another. By the time kick-off arrived, an element of support were looking for a fight. It wasn't a good situation; we were hemmed in like cattle.

The match didn't help proceedings. The final got off to a physical start when a late tackle by Terry Yorath on Andersson ended the game for the Bayern defender. Bayern boss Uli Hoeness later described it as 'the most brutal foul I think I have ever seen.' It served to heat up the already hostile atmosphere, Bayern fans were now throwing missiles at us. Leeds produced some fine football and controlled the game. In an action-packed first half two penalties were denied by referee Michel Kitabdjian: the first when Franz Beckenbauer handled the ball inside the penalty area and the second a much more blatant foul when Allan Clarke was tripped by the Bayern captain when through on goal – a foul that Beckenbauer himself later admitted should have been a penalty. Bremner recalled:

'What the referee was playing at I do not know. It brought back the nightmare memories of games against West Bromwich Albion and AC Milan, when the referees seemed strangely aloof to the reality of what was taking place around them. I clearly saw both incidents that should have been penalties, and so did 48,000 other people. The only one who didn't was the most important one, the referee. I was rattled and extremely pissed off as I could see how it was going to map out.

'In the second half we really attacked Bayern but Sepp Maier was in outstanding form and seemed to get a hand, leg or foot to everything we fired at him. Franz Beckenbauer was a real pain and made no end of tackles or interventions to stop us getting through on goal. On one occasion I hit a shot that I was sure was going in but, amazingly, Maier got a hand to it and parried the ball out through a crowded penalty area. Peter Lorimer was first to react and lashed it back in and at last the ball flew past Maier into the net. I remember hearing our fans going wild and shouting "Goal", then there was an eerie silence. Before we could congratulate Peter on his goal the referee was blowing his whistle and signalling a foul. The linesman had flagged for offside. We were asking who was offside and when I was told that it was me I disagreed. I was certain that I had a Bayern player between me and the goal and another closer to the goal than me. Despite my angry protest to the referee and linesman the goal was disallowed. I couldn't believe it and neither could the majority of our fans.'

As is generally the case when goals are disallowed, the decision seemed overtly harsh. On this occasion it simply lit the touch paper and ignited mass hooliganism among the Leeds support. Sections found the refereeing decisions unbelievable and vented their frustration by throwing whatever they could get their hands on behind the Bayern goal. As Bremner observed:

'It went crazy, nobody could understand it, the referee seemed blind to everything we did and there was nothing we could do about it. I could see that as a team we were filled with anxiety. We needed a time-out but that clearly wasn't possible.'

Within five minutes of the restart that anxiety spilled back onto the terracing as Roth hit a right-foot shot past Stewart and into the Leeds net to give Bayern the lead. The referee pointed to the centre circle signalling a goal. It was the signal for Leeds fans to begin to rip out their seats and use them as missiles against anyone who didn't look like a Leeds supporter. Another angry group made a concerted effort to get over a wall and across a moat that separated them from the pitch. The French police tried to intervene and the fighting escalated:

'We were aware of what was happening on the terraces but we were concentrating on trying to get ourselves back into the game and get an equaliser. With a few minutes left another of our attacks broke down and Bayern broke away down the wing. We were caught out and tried desperately to get back to defend, but

Kapellman centred a ball that fell to Gerd Muller who scored at the near post. It was game over for us. The referee was smiling and that was like showing a red rag to a bull. I got near him and really let him have my thoughts and opinions as to how he had managed the game. I don't think he heard a word of it as he seemed totally unfazed by it all and carried on. In hindsight I was wrong to do it but then again he deserved it.'

As was the case in the European Cup Winners Cup of 1973, the winners of the competition were prevented from doing a lap of honour through poor crowd behaviour. It was behaviour that was again to cost Leeds United dearly. There was thousands of pounds worth of damage done to the stadium, which shamed the club and would be punished by a lengthy ban from competing in all European football.

It's still my opinion that the law enforcement authorities got it all wrong, and provoked and instigated the violence. Not that Leeds fans should have responded so defiantly but, if you treat people like animals, then ultimately they will behave like animals. I recall being treated very poorly by the authorities and felt intimidated by the police. Police still seem to believe that by saturating potential public order incidents, they will ultimately overcome. Sadly, the commonsense approach to policing football has long since disappeared, and with it went the absolute respect a police officer once held.

13

OVER THE HILL AND
NOT FAR AWAY

The following season was very much a non-event on all fronts for both Leeds United and Billy Bremner:

'Our league form was all over the place – win one, draw one, lose one. We did enough to stay close to the sides at the top but we were never challenging for the league title. So many key players from that original and great Leeds team built by Don Revie had now gone, the heart had been ripped out of the team, and fresh talent introduced. John Giles was the latest to move to pastures new.

'I was beginning to feel very aware that my days at the club may be numbered. I was also feeling a little weary. I recognised that my pace and stamina were dropping off, though I don't think the fags helped too much in that area, but I opted to train and work harder in order to keep my place in the side being built by Jimmy Armfield.'

Leeds finished the season in ninth and were knocked out of both Cup competitions in the early rounds:

'It was a bit embarrassing at times. In the League Cup Notts County, who were in the Second Division, beat us 1-0 at Elland Road and in the FA Cup Crystal Palace, who were in the Third Division, beat us by the same scoreline in front of our own fans.

'There comes a time in everyone's life that you have got to be honest with yourself. For me that time arrived towards the end of the 1975-76 season. I felt that Leeds needed to move on and that I had become a dinosaur and was hampering the club's progress. I had a chat with Don Revie and then with Jimmy Armfield, hoping that the latter may offer me some words of comfort or even a coaching position, but there was nothing. Jimmy still wanted me to play as I was more influential on the pitch than he was in the dugout. Sadly he all but told me what I already knew, that my days of playing regular football at the highest level were numbered. I asked him to let me know if any club showed interest, or if he heard of any management positions that came up that may suit me. Jimmy is an honest and fair man and I trusted him.

'September 1975 isn't a month I will remember with any great fondness. It was the month when I won my last full international cap for Scotland, and with it, a lifetime ban from playing for them again. All over a lot of nonsense. We were staying in Copenhagen after playing Denmark and a few of us decided to go out and have a few beers. We didn't do anything bad or really wrong, we went out for a few beers and to a nightclub in search of late-night drinking. We got a bit boisterous and loud and the management of the club asked us to leave, which we did. The worst thing we did was to break the 1am curfew set by the Scottish Football Association. The outcome of that was a lifetime ban from Scottish international football for several of us. I was embarrassed about what had happened but it wasn't a heinous crime.

'Again the punishment outweighed the reality of the matter. I felt like telling them to go and f—— themselves but somehow managed to keep my calm about it all. The five of us who were banned became known as the "Copenhagen Five". How embarrassing. The ban was eventually lifted in 1976, when I was past playing international football so I never played for my country again.

'I remember my last game for Leeds United. It was on 18 September 1976, against Newcastle United at Elland Road, in front of 35,089 spectators. It was a very emotional time. I knew my body couldn't sustain the rigours of regular First Division football and I was getting caught by lesser opponents a little too often for my liking. As ridiculous as it may sound, I felt I was losing my dignity, getting caught in possession by "Johnny come lately" players, that in my younger days I would have left in my wake. My trademark reverse pass was getting to be a rarity too, and I didn't fancy the thought of putting my back or knees out for the sake of one pass. I can laugh about it now, but I was genuinely sad that it was coming to an end. I loved that place, Elland Road was my second home and I loved doing my stuff for the people who watched us every week. During my time at Leeds, some supporters had grown from being children into young men and women. I felt partly responsible for teaching them positives, self-discipline, respect, never to give up on anything – keep fighting for what you want and believe in. Now it was all coming to an end, I was a little apprehensive about my future, if not scared.

'It wasn't long before the inevitable happened. Jimmy told me of Hull City's interest. I was honoured, but I so wanted someone at Leeds United to ask me to stay. I would have done anything and even if it was in a different capacity from playing it would still be part of Leeds United and therefore a major part of my life.

'Sadly, nobody at Leeds did say they wanted me to stay so I was forced to look at the Hull offer. It was easily accessible from Leeds and they were regarded as a decent side who liked to play football as opposed to just hoofing the ball forward and chasing it. So I decided to speak with their manager, an old adversary of mine, John Kaye. Somehow, the press got hold of the story and ran it in the local papers before I had actually signed. I had talked it through with my family, relatives and friends. I still had a few years play left in me so I agreed to join them. They paid a £35,000 transfer fee – that's a full £10,000 more than Hibernian valued me at all those years before. Inflation I expect.'

Starting a new career away from Elland Road wasn't as difficult a transition as Billy had anticipated:

'I had talked to some of the other players who had moved on and they told me of some nightmare experiences they had encountered at lower league clubs. Inferior quality players were virtually bullying them, making derisory comments and remarks about "dirty Leeds" and being more like wrestlers than footballers. Not that I would take or accept any of that sort of crap. I would rather flatten someone than put up with shit like that. Big Jack was great, he told me how it wasn't that bad and how it was all about attitude.

'To be perfectly honest, Hull City were great to me, the players were decent lads, the manager was good, and the fans were right behind us and me. I got no preferential treatment and got stick if I messed up. John Kaye insisted that I was given the number four shirt for the entire time I was there, and naturally I accepted it. I got off to a good start scoring the winning goal against Nottingham Forest on my debut. We had some decent young footballers in the side and one player I rated highly was a kid called Paul Haigh. He had the strength of a bull, and talk about quick! The one thing he lacked was on-the-pitch vision and awareness, that special, almost psychic thing that tells you precisely what your team mates are up to and where they are at any one time. I thought Paul would go on to bigger and better things – he had represented England at under-21 level – yet he never lived up to expectations and he was sold for a big-money fee (around £100,000) to Carlisle.

'It was something of an eye opener visiting grounds that were near empty, and places I had only heard of week in, week out. Everywhere I played, supporters were always decent to me, asking for autographs or just having a chat. Of course you got the odd one who would be abusive but they got the shock of their lives when I would laugh at them and return the stick or abuse. One lad offered me a scrap because I played for Leeds and he hated Leeds. A club official wanted to call the police but I told him to hang fire and let me talk to the lad. I talked him down and had him laughing and joking. After a few minutes he shook my hand and apologised for being such a prick and walked off. I'd never walk away from confrontation or my critics.

'Perhaps the worst thing I had to endure during my Hull City days was the abuse from fellow colleagues, those who we were playing against. Every so often, and in almost every game I

112

played, I would receive a threat of physical injury or violence. It was bang out of order but the lower leagues were full of it. At first I thought it was a one-off and I had to give the player in question a gentle reminder that I wasn't some dithering old git who could hardly stand up or support himself. One occasion, I thought the lad needed reminding that I was Billy Bremner, *the* Billy Bremner, so I gave him a bit of knock and, sure enough, down he went like a sack of spuds, rolling about on the floor crying. I bent over him, gave him a wink and a nod of the head and offered my hand to lift him up. He declined my kind offer of help, so I stared at him and told him that if he came anywhere near me for the duration of the game I would give him something to really cry about. He apologised and carried on rolling about on the floor.

'Another player, without any provocation whatsoever, tried to kick me into the stand, but he completely mistimed everything and did himself an injury. I nearly pissed myself laughing at him. Then there was the manager who should have known better, who informed me that he had told his players to "hurt me" before I "hurt them" – how nice and respectful was that?

'Whenever I talked these things through with other ex-Leeds players they had similar experiences to tell. I was told it was a backhanded compliment, that they still saw me as a threat, yet I always found it alarming and unnerving, that people should automatically think about me in a violent way. I was tough, firm and always fair. If I kicked or lumped somebody, then they must have deserved it.

'I think the highlight of my career at Hull has to be the Football League Cup game against Arsenal at Highbury in January 1978. We were woefully inadequate and no match for the Gunners, eventually losing the game 5-1. The whole atmosphere of the night took me back to my years with Leeds, as did meeting up with many football friends who had come along to watch the game solely because I was playing. It was a real honour to be told that. Oh, how we reminisced. The Arsenal game showed me how slow and ineffective I had become in midfield. I was once regarded as a terrier of a player, now I was more like a basset hound, reliable, yet slow and predictable. I feared the worst, that my days as a player who covered every blade of grass had long gone and, in fact, one hack said I had a sedentary pace. If I could ever catch him I would show him what sedentary pace really was, the cheeky bastard.

'Gradually my legs began to ache more and more after games and training sessions. The little knocks that I had always dismissed and ignored now seemed to be very painful and took longer to heal. Whilst my mind was still that of a sixteen-year-old, my body was that of a man in his thirties. Whilst I was still fit and able to, I wanted to continue playing, but it was getting more difficult with each game.

'One evening I got a telephone call from Don Revie. It was lovely speaking to him, and we had a long chat about the game and the respective things we were both doing at the time. I told him how I was feeling as a player, competing in Division Two having spent the majority of my career in the top flight. He reminded me that my club career in some ways mirrored his own, he had found himself slowing down at Leeds then came management, which reinvigorated him and gave him a new and fresh focus. He advised me to consider going into football management, starting in the lower leagues, making a good name and building a decent reputation for myself that way. That was just what I needed. The boss, after all those years, was still looking after me and giving me good sound advice. I took everything the boss said seriously so if he told me I would make a good manager then I believed him. The following day, unbeknown to anyone outside my family, I put the feelers out for potential management opportunities. I was honest and open about my aspirations with Hull City and talked it through with the management team there. I was pleased when they said they would support me and not stand in my way if an opportunity came along. Hull at that time was full of very decent people and I really did respect them for being so open and honest.

'There was a whisper that a position may become available at

Grimsby Town but, not knowing much about them at that time, I sought other people's opinion and was firmly put off by them. I now know that was the wrong thing to do. I had always been my own man, making my own decisions, yet here I was acting all insecure and seeking guidance from others, some of whom were in no better position than I was to know about Grimsby Town or anything about them. Since then I have tended to rely on my family and gut instinct about many matters – it doesn't often get it wrong.

'When Doncaster Rovers were first mentioned, I got myself over to Belle Vue sharpish and introduced myself to the board of directors. I was honest and asked what their short- and long-term plans and vision for the football club consisted of. If they matched my ambition then I would be interested. I didn't have to think twice. As soon as I was inside Belle Vue my gut feeling was very positive and the directors were open about limited playing budgets, player quality, how the job would be hands-on and in many different guises, not the usual sitting behind a desk, or out on the training pitch. This included everything from writing programme notes, radio interviews, commercial activity to bring in sponsorship, community work, and visiting schools and colleges in the name of Doncaster Rovers, even helping to paint the crush barriers on the terracing. I was sold on it, I wanted the job there and then.

'My enthusiasm waned slightly when I was told that I was not the only candidate they were interested in. I was reminded that, in the world of lower league management, Billy Bremner and other ex-players like him were nothing but a name. "Player reputation has no authority with directors here. Clubs want achievers, proven winners, ambitious people who will work twelve hours a day for seven days a week, just for a regular wage." I wanted to be such a person and had my wish granted in November 1979, when Doncaster Rovers offered me the manager's position and I accepted.'

14

THE MANAGEMENT GAME

The first murmurings that Billy was about to take his first step into football management came to me via the Leeds United ex-players association. As an associate member, I had wanted to sort out diary dates for future functions and during a conversation I got the heads up that Billy was about to move to Doncaster Rovers to replace Stan Anderson. Coincidentally, I had interviewed Anderson just a month earlier and we had discussed his time as boss of Middlesbrough. Stan struck me as a determined and understanding man who was attempting to resurrect his managerial career at Rovers but had lost both impetus and know-how, and was struggling to provide solutions to Rovers' inconsistent form. He was a likeable man and was clearly something of a disciplinarian, and importantly for me, he could tell a good football story. Stan also had a book of contacts that many top division managers would be envious of.

The news that he had left the club was sad, particularly as he had clearly failed with his long-term vision for Doncaster. He had moved to an assistant manager position under Ian Greaves at Bolton Wanderers. There he replaced another footballing great, George Mulhall, who had taken over as manager of Bradford City as part of the merry-go-round. The managerial jigsaw was missing one final piece, the formal announcement as to who was to be the new manager of Doncaster Rovers.

Billy was officially appointed Saturday, 25 November 1978, and I was fortunate enough to get one of the first interviews with the new Doncaster Rovers boss. The Monday following the announcement I made an early morning telephone call to Belle Vue and requested an appointment with Billy, leaving my contact details with the receptionist, who politely advised me that Mr Bremner was screening his own interviews. Within an hour my call was returned and I was told to come to the ground for 11am when Mr Bremner would see me. I always liked the Belle Vue football stadium, a typical northern English ground with its own unique identity and character. In need of a complete overhaul, it was the sort of ground where annual maintenance consisted of a lick of paint on the dugouts and perimeter wall, followed by a thorough weeding of the terraces. It was a proper football ground and it smelled like football grounds used to – grass, Oxo and fags. For me it was a privilege to get access to the club's latest acquisition and integral part of the infrastructure – the new manager.

I waited nervously in the reception area at Belle Vue, and after a few moments Billy walked through, smiling and winking at me and holding out his hand in welcome.

'Hello there, big man,' he said, with the appearance of a small child being let loose for the first time in a sweetie shop. He was excited. He proceeded to introduce me to every member of the club back-office staff, describing me as the 'best up and coming journalist in the country'. Billy was a master of motivation and put me at ease. It felt good that he was comfortable and trusting of me. Guiding me through the corridors of power within Belle Vue, we walked out onto the playing area where he took me to the dugout and immediately lit up a cigarette: 'We can have a good chat here if you like, if you are not too cold that is?' I wasn't about to let the weather get in the way of an interview with one of the game's greatest characters. We talked of Leeds United, his time at Hull City, and some of the personalities and incidents he encountered there, before moving onto a subject of great importance to him – what he hoped to achieve for Doncaster Rovers. It was illuminating to hear him expounding his positive commitment and enthusiasm for the challenge that awaited him at Doncaster. He looked well, and was very much talking in 'manager speak'. I had to ask him to stop it as he was making me laugh with it all.

Billy was talking of Doncaster Rovers as though they were his be all and end all, and it was clear to me that Leeds United were now a thing of the past for him. Billy lived for the present and the future, he never liked discussing his personal success on the field and always seemed a little embarrassed by the thought that tens of thousands of football fans actively followed his career because he was their idol. What genuinely struck me at this interview was something I had never seen in him before: he was like every other working man, his ultimate aim was to provide for his family, and financial security would be of great help in achieving that. He worshipped and adored his family and always talked affectionately of the true love of his life, his wife Vicki.

I asked him about his professional ambitions. He responded with two immediate aims:

'I want to take Doncaster Rovers as far as I can, the supporters here are first class you know, they are devoutly loyal and above all else, honest. I want to give them a team that they can be proud of. It's my first managerial position and I think I can draw upon a lot of experience from some of the greatest football managers I have worked with and know. If I do well here, then who knows what awaits, it would really suit me to one day have a crack at managing Scotland, but that's a long way off. My first goal is to get Rovers moving in the right direction, up through the leagues.'

I asked the obvious question: 'Would you like to manage Leeds United one day?'

I knew there could only ever be one reply. His face lit up and he began to laugh: 'For crying out loud Paul, I've only just started my job at Doncaster and f—— hell you're asking me about moving to Leeds United. Dream on, my boy.' Then with more than a hint of seriousness he looked straight at me and said: 'It would be a dream come true right enough, Leeds United is in the blood. That's a long way ahead though, Paul. My main objective is to get Doncaster promoted through the leagues and maybe play at the same level as Leeds.'

Tempting fate, I asked if he would base his management style upon Don Revie: 'As a new and untested manager, I don't think I qualify to clean the boss's boots just yet, but I did learn a lot from him. No one could ever emulate him or even come close to it. Yes, I would like to make as big an impact as a manager as he did. I think I have it in me to succeed, but not all footballers make good managers; no matter how good they are as a player, management is a different game altogether. It's fine being a captain on the pitch, you can get round each and every one of your players and help them. Lead by example if you like, but in the dugout it's a different game altogether. You have to instil your will and desire into those players in the dressing room before they cross that white line and get into the game.

'It's all about getting the players to believe in you and themselves, and transmitting desire into reality through practice. I want my players to give me everything they have got, anything less and they have me to answer to. This team are currently sitting in the wrong half of the Fourth Division and slipping backwards. We are twenty-first – that's the third worst team in the country. Third from bottom of the football league. That's a f—— awful place to be and to play your football. What I first need to do is to stop the decline, address the weaknesses and build upon the strengths, if there are any. I don't want Doncaster to finish bottom, or anywhere close to it. I need fighters, players who will give their all seven days a week to improve the team and themselves.

'I like some of what I see, we've got Joe Laidlaw here, he is a player with vast experience, a goalscorer. I have played against him in the First Division, the flying pig they called him. Players like Joe are dependable and reliable, they know how to play the simple but effective game. I've also got Bobby Owen, he played for Manchester City and Carlisle in the First Division; Bobby knows where the goal is, and scores a few goals. What I really lack are midfield battlers who will run themselves into the ground, I need some of those. F—— Stan Anderson has left me a bit of a mess here; he had the audacity to say that the basis of a strong side is here for [a new manager] me to work with.'

My time was almost up. Billy took to his feet and beckoned me to follow him onto the pitch. We wandered silently to the centre circle where we stopped and he looked around the playing surface:

'This used to be the biggest pitch in football, you know, I think it still could be. We are away from prying ears out here. There is plenty of room to play good football on this, not a good place for old football crocks to be. I intend to move on anyone who won't, or physically can't, give me 100 per cent. I have got some crocks here, I want to introduce young blood, local talent, players with passion and desire. I don't want a team full of has-beens – so expect transfer activity.'

As we walked off the pitch, back down the tunnel and back out into reception, I felt proud and fortunate to spend time with Billy Bremner the manager. I bid him farewell and wished him luck in his new challenge. He was still smiling, that was a good sign. As he walked me out to my car he offered an open invitation to attend any Doncaster game I liked, courtesy of him, adding: 'Paul, you better get your f—— arse down here, to Belle Vue, on a regular basis or else. Okay?' I assured him that I would keep one eye firmly fixed on the fortunes of Doncaster Rovers and would stay in touch.

Within weeks the Bremner football magic appeared to be having a positive impact on Rovers' form. In his first game in charge, his side beat Rochdale 1-0 at Belle Vue – courtesy of a Bobby Owen goal. The team moved up into nineteenth position in the Fourth Division table. There were obvious signs of self-belief within the team, and in the club itself as media interest soared, primarily through interest in the new manager. The fortunes of Doncaster Rovers looked much brighter than they had done for some time.

Commercially, local industry and businesses were keen to get involved with sponsorship, many on the sole proviso that the manager would be photographed or be seen with their brand. It was a marketing dream for many businesses to have the legend that is Billy Bremner associated with their company:

'I never really bothered about marketing and commercial aspects of football life before coming to Doncaster. Now I realise how important it is to have the Rovers brand known and out there. I suppose at Leeds it was much easier, because across the world everyone knew who we were and it sold itself. Here it's a much more hands-on affair, and if it brings positive funds and publicity into the football club then I will help in any way I can. I would love to have the time to call into every shop and business in the town, and ask them to get behind us and what we want to achieve. Hopefully, with an improvement in publicity, form and results, they will all take note and want to get involved.'

Bremner's charges won three of their first half-dozen games under his command, conceding six and scoring eight goals during that spell:

'We look okay up front but it's the back end, the defence, that is my real concern. It always looks shaky and nervous and vulnerable. I hold none of the blame on our goalkeeper Dennis Peacock, he is as reliable as they come at this level, better than Gary Sprake any day of the week, and we are fortunate to have him here. I need to sort it out, otherwise we are going to get a right spanking off somebody.'

An away trip to AFC Bournemouth in early February looked anything but spectacular on the fixture list but it was to become a game that Billy Bremner the manager never forgot:

'Christ, it was horrible, I wanted the ground to open up and swallow me. It brought memories back of when, as part of the Leeds team we destroyed Southampton 7-0 at Elland Road and the crowd cheered our every pass. AFC Bournemouth did that to my team, they hammered us 7-1 at Dean Court. We deserved it as well.

'That performance really hurt. Many of my players were gutless and anonymous. I am embarrassed to say that it is my team, players I picked and instructed before and during the game that let me, the fans and themselves down. Joe Laidlaw aside, I thought they were a f—— disgrace, they cheated me. How dare they think they can do that? I'll get rid of the lot of them if they do that again.

'I shall never forget the day I first arrived at the club and met some of our supporters in the car park. In the space of a few minutes, while I signed autographs, those supporters told me what the problems were in the team set-up and our weaknesses and strengths. They have been proved to be absolutely right in their perceptions.'

The mauling at Bournemouth was followed by three straight wins, two of which came on their travels, an excellent 4-2 victory at Crewe Alexandra and a determined and gritty performance earning a 1-0 win at Stockport County. I dropped in at Belle Vue, wanting to congratulate the manager on turning things around so quickly. His response was not what I expected:

'Turned things around? Like shit I have. Those results are papering over the cracks, the older players in this team aren't able to keep up with the pace of the game for the full ninety minutes, the inexperienced players give the ball away too easily and there are a couple of dressing-room dissenters and agitators that I need to get rid of as soon as possible.

'This team are going to be regularly beaten, unless we can develop some kind of understanding and belief amongst the squad. Some of the players I have inherited here are far too comfortable, they believe they are untouchable. Well, they have a shock coming. As far as I'm concerned they can go and get comfortable elsewhere and not at this club. Doncaster Rovers don't want them, and I don't need them.

'I have told the players that if any of them are unhappy here, or with me, or what I am doing and trying to achieve, and they don't want to be part of that, then all they have to do is put it in writing and I will support getting rid of them. I have received just one request so far, with no interest being shown in that player by any other clubs. Not even a pub team would want him, and I think that speaks volumes about how he is perceived elsewhere in the game. He won't play for me again, that's for sure!'

Sadly, Billy's forecast was right, Rovers won just three more games that season and finished in twenty-second place in the Fourth Division standings:

'It is appalling. I feel like I am letting everyone down. The team just aren't playing as a unit. There are pockets of decent football, but nothing I can positively shout about. There is no doubt about it, I am going to have to register as a non-contract player next season, to cover for emergencies. I have missed the activity on the pitch, but at least if I play myself as a substitute I can not only change things round tactically but get out onto the pitch and get the players moving when I deliver a swift kick up the backside.'

The following season saw some much-needed transfer activity at Belle Vue. Over half a dozen players were moved on, replaced by Bremner's own players:

'The time had come for a complete clear-out, some of the players needed to be put out to graze and take their place in the dole queue. I couldn't see many clubs lining up to take on some of those being released. The one thing I won't take is a footballer with no passion or desire; a club man with no ambition is of no use to me.'

Coming in was a new strike force, the vastly experienced Alan Warboys, who had played alongside Bremner at Hull City, and Ian Nimmo arrived from Sheffield Wednesday. Both proved to be very astute and influential acquisitions. Meanwhile, a newly formed network of scouting contacts across Scotland pointed Bremner to Glasgow Celtic, and the skilful midfielder John Dowie. Dowie had made twelve senior appearances for the Bhoys, and was soon persuaded to join the Rovers revolution, as was his Celtic team mate, the influential defender Billy Russell. More importantly, Billy gave an opportunity to youngster Ian Snodin, brother of Rovers forward, Glynn Snodin:

'I have really unearthed a raw talent in Ian Snodin; the first time I saw him play it was clear that he was in the same mould as me, a youngster too. Just sixteen when I gave him his chance. He has grasped the opportunity and proved to me and the supporters that he has real commitment and talent.'

123

Snodin later recalled his time at Doncaster under Billy Bremner's management: 'Billy Bremner was the greatest, most complete manager I have played under. He was totally convinced that I was capable of achieving and would do well for Doncaster Rovers. He gave me my debut when I was just sixteen years old and, two years on, at eighteen, he promoted me to team captain. That was a real honour. When someone shows that level of belief in you, then respect for that person comes naturally.

'I knew I was an aggressive kind of player, I always wanted to win every challenge, every loose ball, every game and every trophy we competed in. My father said that Billy had once told him that as soon as he saw me play he saw something of himself in my style and demeanour. Billy was such a great man and football person, I would have followed him to the end of the earth if he wanted me to play football there. I would never let him down and played through some painful injuries so that I was there on the pitch leading by example and pushing players to give all they could for the boss.'

Performances significantly improved as Rovers started to show a winning determination and were transformed from relegation battlers of the previous season to potential promotion challengers. Reviewing it some years later, Bremner recalled:

'We finished my first full season in charge in twelfth place. I was relatively pleased with that considering what I had inherited the year before, and where we finished then. It was more pleasing that I only had to include myself in the starting eleven once, which, by pure coincidence, was against AFC Bournemouth. I wasn't paranoid about Bournemouth. We had taken a point at Dean Court earlier in the season and laid the ghost of the previous season to rest, but going into the home game against them, we had lost three games on the trot and had dropped into the lower half of the league. I didn't want player confidence dropping off so I played myself. It worked as we won 1-0. Bloody hell, my legs were aching when I came off, my appearance on the pitch seemed to give everyone a lift, including some of the Bournemouth players, who took it upon themselves to try to prove they were tougher in the challenge than me. They never got near but I felt it my responsibility to serve my wrath upon them anyway!

'We had come a long way from being the team everyone looked forward to playing to being worthy and feared opponents. We finished the season in a respectable twelfth place. It had taken a full season to partially get to grips with it but I was beginning to enjoy the management game and believed we were creating a decent team and infrastructure at the club.

'The following season I targeted promotion and was laughed at by the directors of the football club, who said they admired my positivity but that to expect the team to win promotion I must be living in dreamland. That was it, they had thrown down the gauntlet and I wanted to show them how influential Billy Bremner the manager actually was.'

With the hugely influential Dave Bentley becoming full-time coach, replacing the outgoing Cyril Knowles, who was moving to Middlesbrough as assistant manager, Bremner was appointing from within and displaying similar ethics to those of his great mentor Don Revie. He realised the importance of a close-knit team spirit and the togetherness that had so influenced his game and time at Leeds:

'Cyril Knowles (yes, he of "Nice One, Cyril" fame) was a solid player and a very good coach, too. He was never going to be a permanent fixture here, and was always going to move on. So in anticipation of that I prepared for his departure and had David Bentley working with us, initially as player-coach, but later as full-time coach. David knew the club, the area and the players as well as anyone; he was well respected by everyone within the football club and by the supporters, which was important. For me though, he understood the game so well and was fully behind what I was trying to achieve.'

By the end of the 1980-81 league season Billy Bremner's Doncaster Rovers proudly sat in third place in the Fourth Division league table, winning the promotion the manager had so wanted and anticipated:

'It was a great feeling to have turned it round so quickly and to see the joy that success bred amongst our supporters. The players had performed magnificently all season – I had no criticism of any of them for the effort they put in for me. I had the feeling we could win promotion, but didn't really start to believe it until the end of February, when we visited promotion rivals Southend and Lincoln City in consecutive away fixtures. We came away from Southend with a 0-0 draw, that was a really big result for us. Just over a week later we went to Sincil Bank, where Lincoln City were unbeaten, and we won 1-0. That really proved our credentials as genuine promotion contenders. We lost just two of our last sixteen games and lost less away games than champions Southend United. I felt very proud but was not yet content.'

The average home attendance had significantly increased too, and to Billy Bremner he hoped that meant more money coming into the club and to him for team strengthening:

'Of course it would have been great to have a couple of hundred thousand to spend on players, but we are talking about Doncaster Rovers here; the reality of life in the Third and Fourth Division of the football league is vastly different from that in the First Division. I managed to do a bit of wheeling and dealing, and to bring in a couple of players who I felt would do a good job for us in the Third Division and also become assets to the club. A big centre forward, Colin Douglas, arrived from Glasgow Celtic and a certain full back called Terry Cooper joined from Bristol Rovers. I knew the potential of both players and that they would do a good job for me. Terry may have lost a bit of pace but he still had an excellent football head on him and his timing in tackles was still impeccable.

'I didn't want it to be a Leeds Old Boys reunion. I wanted players who gave me total honesty. In fact, I had brought in Mick Bates the season before, but sadly Mick struggled with his fitness and by mutual consent we cancelled his contract before Christmas as we couldn't afford to carry players who didn't give us that additional strength. I signed another ex-Leeds player, Keith Parkinson, in the summer of 1981; that didn't work out either, and I cancelled his contract after five games – says it all I think. The situation with Terry was far different, he was a proven athlete and a footballer who maintained a desire to achieve and he genuinely wanted to help me and Doncaster Rovers to succeed.'

Early life in the Third Division wasn't proving too difficult for Bremner and his team, and at one stage, in September, they went on a six-game unbeaten run, actually winning five games in succession without conceding a solitary goal. Thereafter things got decidedly tougher, as the team dropped down the league table, not helped by a spell devoid of any victories that ran through all of November to mid-February, a total of eight defeats:

'I always had faith that we could avoid relegation but it was difficult keeping the players focused and believing in themselves, especially when the fans began to question some of our performances and my own abilities as manager.

'I have always believed that the best way to deal with your critics is to meet them head on, face to face. So I would get the players, along with myself, to meet and talk with supporters, and to talk and listen to them. I think we won a lot of respect for that and, ultimately, there were never any real problems between the fans and players. I wouldn't have prima donna type footballers in my club. They were all good-mannered working-class lads who had done well, or had aspiration to do well for themselves in the game, and saw it as a privilege to represent Doncaster Rovers Football Club.'

Relegation was avoided as the team finished sixth from bottom, and several points clear of the drop zone: 'It was a success, no matter what anyone may say about it. We survived that first season in a higher division and managed to hold our own against some very decent teams.'

Despite his success at Belle Vue, the media had him inextricably linked with issues involving one of his previous clubs, Leeds United. I met with him at a Doncaster Rovers club function at the end of the 1981-82 season. While he was basking in the relative glories of life at Doncaster, approximately fifty miles up the A1, Leeds United had suffered relegation to the old Second Division, finishing an ignominious twentieth in the then First Division, under the management of Allan Clarke.

Bremner talked about the Leeds situation:

'It's difficult at Leeds at present. Allan Clarke and I are close, I feel so sorry for him, he's done everything he could to save that team and the club from relegation. It is going to have to be a complete rebuild now and some of them players at Leeds won't want to play in the Second Division, they will see it as being beneath them. There are too many prima donnas in that side, I am afraid. I feel sorry for everyone connected with the club – management, players and supporters, it's a real shame. No one can blame Allan for what has happened. Off the field, you don't always know what you are getting when you sign new players. Dressing-room agitators are damaging and de-motivating. They are the quickest route to a sudden drop in form, along with a heavy injury list, and in too many instances that has just one outcome, the sack for the manager.'

The phrase 'Leeds United' and 'relegation' simply weren't part of the Billy Bremner vocabulary. It was obvious to me that he felt much hurt and pain by the situation, but it was out of his control and he could do nothing about it but support his good friend through a tough time. Clarke was to suffer dismissal for not being able to replicate the glories of past years and, sadly, he was not to be the last ex-Leeds player to meet such an ignominious fate at Elland Road.

Unfortunately, at the end of the 1982-83 season, Doncaster Rovers suffered relegation too:

'We had an incredible amount of genuine and crippling injuries that affected the first team and really rattled our consistency. That whole season we just didn't get things going for us and disappointingly we were relegated back down to the Fourth Division. I wasn't about to hide nor was I going to allow my players to run away. During the summer we took stock of what we had, reviewed where it had all gone wrong and assessed our options to strengthen and improve the team, mainly through free transfers.'

By the end of the following season, and typical of the man, his side bounced back to win promotion back to the Third Division. They eventually finished as runners-up to York City, attaining their highest points total for thirty-seven years – eighty-five points. Belle Vue became a fortress and incredibly Rovers did not lose a game at home until the end of that season in May 1984:

'It was a good feeling to get back to winning ways and achieve honours. I did strengthen the team and got much in the way of backing and support from the boardroom. I made sure we got the right players in.'

Billy was alluding to people like John Philliben, who signed for a then club record fee of £70,000 from Stirling Albion. A Scotland youth defender, he arrived in March 1984 and added extra defensive strength. Also joining was midfielder Jim Dobbin, a Scottish schoolboy international signed from Celtic. A lumbering centre forward, Ernie Moss, was also signed from Lincoln City in the summer of 1983. Moss was a proven goal scorer at every club he joined and was joint-top scorer with fifteen goals in his solitary, promotion-winning season at Belle Vue.

Bremner knew the size of the task he faced at Belle Vue:

'Getting promoted back to the Third Division, with essentially the same nucleus of players, was an achievement in itself and I new we were all better prepared for the challenge at the second time of asking. The Snodin boys were both looking very sharp in pre-season, and I had high hopes that they would really impact and settle to life in the Third Division.'

It was another season of achievement as Rovers quickly settled into life in the higher league, and at one point sat in fourth place, before finally settling for a mid-table finish of fourteenth: 'We were a big strong side but lacked that little bit of extra class that would have made us consistent. Young Ian Snodin had a terrific season and Glynn weighed in with twenty-one goals. Aiden Butterworth, a youngster who once left a first-team place at Leeds in order to pursue his education, joined us and did a workmanlike job up front. There was a good mix of youth and experience, and again I was looking at a promotion push for the following season.'

In the summer of that year, Ian Snodin was sold to Leeds United for a transfer fee of £200,000:

'It was a great piece of business for the boy and for Doncaster Rovers. The boy had cost us nothing and had been an integral part to a previous promotion. He had been impressive to say the least and was too good a footballer to stay in the Third Division. The move to Leeds would suit him well, it wasn't too far from his home and was commutable. I was confident that he would do well at Leeds and told their manager, Eddie Gray, that he had got a real gem, and to look after him.'

15

MANAGERIAL MERRY-GO-ROUND
AT LEEDS

In October 1985, completely out of the blue, I received a telephone call from someone at Doncaster Rovers who informed me that Billy had asked them to call me, and I was to listen to the BBC Radio Leeds news. There was no intimation as to what I was listening for, or at what time. I knew it had to be something of importance for Billy to get a member of the Doncaster Rovers staff to call me, so naturally I tuned in. I was immediately greeted by speculation about Eddie Gray's future as Leeds manager. Rumours were rife as to what was happening at Elland Road but nothing was confirmed. I got back onto Doncaster in a flash, and asked to speak with Billy. I was told that he was busy. I tried every fifteen minutes thereafter, but was knocked back on each occasion. It was mid-afternoon before I finally got through to him, and asked for his take on the news story. Billy told me to come to the ground where he would talk to me.

Without hesitation, I jumped in the car and drove down the A1 from my Leeds home, to Belle Vue. Billy looked stressed and was puffing on one cigarette after another. I was first sworn to secrecy, and he then went on to tell me that the directors of Leeds United had been in touch with him and asked if he would be interested – should the manager's position become vacant – in taking over as manager of the football club. Like Allan Clarke before him, Eddie Gray was struggling to take the team forward. The words Billy next uttered remain with me as testimony to his loyalty and honesty to his friends:

'It's all wrong. Eddie, like Allan before him, has done

brilliantly since he took over and I don't really want to go in there to replace him. I would far rather he stayed on and turned it around. He's not getting the full support of senior people at boardroom level. The thing that concerns me is that if they can act like this behind Allan and Eddie's back, they could do it to me too.'

The reason Billy had asked me to Belle Vue, as I was to quickly find out, was to ask if I had heard of any circulating rumours in the media as to other potential managerial contenders should the role became vacant. I could offer Billy no advice. Selfishly, I wanted him to take the Leeds job, but it was a decision for him and his family to make.

I made a few telephone calls but the only information I could obtain was anecdotal and of no real use. The rumour was that the Leeds board, Leslie Silver in particular, had already talked to Keith Mincher, who was the youth team coach at Leeds. Apparently Mincher had watched the first team in League Cup action at Walsall on 8 October, with a view to taking over.

Within twenty-four hours of my conversation with Billy, Eddie Gray was dismissed from the player-manager role at Leeds United. Rumours were rife, and once again I heard the name Keith Mincher mentioned. It was claimed that shortly after Gray's departure, Leslie Silver took Keith Mincher into the Leeds dressing room after a training session, announced the dismissal of Eddie Gray and introduced the players to the manager elect. There was uproar as players unanimously refused to play for Mincher and expressed their concerns as to what was happening to the football side of matters at the club. It was alleged that the Leeds chairman had no option but to withdraw the appointment, and Mincher moved on. Worse still, there was dissent in the boardroom, where several board members disagreed with the sacking of Eddie Gray, and how the entire situation had been handled. One director resigned in disgust. The club placed coach Peter Gumby in temporary charge for the following day's Elland Road fixture against Middlesbrough.

On the day, there were angry protests inside and outside the ground. Eddie Gray's name was constantly chanted on the terraces during the game. Afterwards, in the main club car park, groups of Leeds supporters staged further demonstrations, demanding the reinstatement of Eddie Gray and the resignation of chairman Leslie Silver. The demonstrators were eventually moved on by police and club stewards. As a marketing exercise, it was devastating to the overall image of Leeds United as a brand. There was a clear need for calm and positive judgement from the Elland Road hierarchy. To be fair to him, Leslie Silver was doing what he believed to be the right thing but what people objected to was the manner in which it had been handled.

Throughout it all, Eddie Gray was the only one who came out of the situation with any respect. He remained dignified and said not a negative or bad word about the matter or about the individuals involved. The players were sworn to secrecy and were told not to discuss club affairs with the media or in public. It wasn't long before I received a telephone call from Leeds United inviting me, as a freelance journalist and writer, to a press conference at Elland Road. I hoped the resultant press conference was going to be the unveiling of the new manager and I rang Doncaster Rovers in an attempt to find out if Billy had left there. Confusingly, I was told he would call me back.

The drive to Elland Road was eventful. On the radio all the talk was about Billy Bremner and the sacking of Eddie Gray. The anti-Leslie Silver campaign was temporarily forgotten as Billy Bremner mania hit the streets of Leeds and West Yorkshire. As I drew up outside the ground I was forced to park in a street opposite and walk down to the main reception area by the sheer quantity of gathered media. Virtually every country in the world was represented within the gathered press pack. It was bedlam, and more like a rugby scrum commonly seen at Headingley.

Despite my protestations, I was refused access to the press conference, so had to wait for things to calm down. But it gave me time to plan my next course of action. Eventually, after a wait of an hour or so, I managed to get in to see Billy. The media scrum, through no choice or fault of his, had meant restrictions on most reporters, with one initial group interview session as opposed to one-to-ones. On Billy's authority, I was given a private fifteen-minute interview slot in a separate office. I sat waiting, not knowing what to say. I wanted to hug him and welcome him back, but I knew that could never happen. Behind a closed door, I could hear his unmistakable Scottish accent. He was clearly bubbly and very excited, and once again I became a little nervous. I wondered if everything would be different now he was at a big club. For me, it already was. External access to Billy was severely restricted and he was seemingly surrounded by an army of assistants, each one expertly trained in rebuffing all requests for interviews or contact with the Leeds boss. Unless your name appeared on their list, you were denied access. There was no provision for getting your name onto such a list, and I knew several members of the National Union of Journalists who couldn't get themselves onto the list.

Back in the office I was further deliberating when suddenly the door flew open and in he walked. He was smiling from ear to ear and literally bouncing with joy. He greeted me with the usual 'Hello there, big man'. He threw his arms wide apart at shoulder height and exclaimed: 'Can you believe it? I'm back! Billy Bremner has come home!'

Without further ado, he grabbed hold of my arm and walked me through the Elland Road corridors. It took me back to my childhood and the unforgettable day he took me to meet all the players and the great Don Revie. This time we briefly stopped to look at the trophy cabinets: 'I want those filled with new trophies and awards. A personal ambition has been fulfilled today, and funnily enough it's as though I have never been away. What I want to achieve for this club and its supporters is unadulterated success. We were once a great club but look at us now, back in Division Two and struggling to string two good results together. But do you know what? This is still a bloody great club. The boys [Allan Clarke and Eddie Gray] have done great in their own way and style, and it's now up to me to complete the task they started.

It's going to be f—— hard, but I know that everyone here and on the terraces and in the stand wants me to succeed. I want to do it for all of them, not just me. And before anything is said, as far as I am concerned, Allan and Eddie have an open invite to Elland Road and are very welcome to come to see me any time. They are my pals and you don't ever turn your back on your pals.'

As we walked through some swing doors we arrived at the players' tunnel. It felt brilliant to be standing there like all those legends and great players that had previously traversed this same route – the tunnel that led out onto the promised land, the pitch. There I stood in the Elland Road players' tunnel, just me and Billy Bremner. It was sublimely surreal, my emotions got the better of me, and I cried. Billy asked what was wrong, I explained that I had been overwhelmed by the moment, and he laughed. We made our way down the tunnel and out onto the perimeter of the pitch. It was as though he was looking at every seat, every square inch of terracing, dreaming of those glorious days of old when Elland Road would be packed to the rafters. In his mind he was recollecting images of the sea of excited faces that greeted him as a player at each and every home game. It was indeed a homecoming. Billy knew it, and so did I.

It was a privilege to have been present at that precise moment in time, for I honestly believe that it was at that very moment that William John Bremner truly realised he actually was the first-team manager of Leeds United AFC. I wasn't the first to interview him, nor would I be the last that day; however, I think I saw something that others didn't, the sheer pleasure, ecstasy and pride in the fact that he was at the football club he so loved. The fifteen minutes lasted well over an hour and I was pleased, very pleased. It was perhaps the most poignant moment I have ever witnessed in football. Billy Bremner had finally come home and Elland Road stadium would soon be rocking at its seams, with tens of thousands of loyal Leeds supporters celebrating the return of the club's favourite son.

16

THE KING RETURNS

After the euphoria of Billy's appointment came the reality of life
in football management. Despite a dramatic upturn in the club's
fortunes, a place in the 1987 FA Cup semi-finals, losing out to
Coventry City in extra time, and a sickening promotion play-off
defeat to Charlton Athletic, Leeds and Billy Bremner were left
with nothing to show for their positive endeavours.

Through it all Billy had remained defiant:

'We were so close to promotion and a Wembley Cup final. I
feel sad for the players and the supporters, but at the very least,
the good name of Leeds United has been highlighted for all the
right football reasons, very positive football reasons. We must
now all pull together and build on the achievements we have
made and use that to our advantage. If the fans get down to
Elland Road in their numbers and get behind us they are as a
good as a twelfth man to the team.'

The following season it was all over after just six games. Billy
Bremner was unceremoniously sacked. A formal statement from
the club read:

'The board felt it was time for a change . . . I don't think there
are many people with as much feeling for this club as Billy . . .
under Billy we came within a whisker of promotion and also
reached the semi-final stages of the FA Cup, and we all had
hopes of building on those near misses. Unfortunately, we again
missed out and we must again find the right man to arouse the
"sleeping giant" and take the club back to its rightful place
among the game's elite.'

Getting the sack, in anyone's terms, is a devastating matter. The high-profile position Billy enjoyed at Leeds ensured that his every move came under the closest scrutiny. I was there when he arrived, and sadly, I was there when he left. Both days were emotional in the extreme. Without doubt, the Billy Bremner I saw leaving Leeds United was a distraught man. Once again crowds of journalists and photographers had gathered, like vultures circling their prey, outside the club's main entrance. For me and many others, it was a dreadful scene. Inside Elland Road, Billy puffed away on cigarettes, impatiently pacing up and down and saying his farewells to everyone, including the laundry women, the tea-room staff and the receptionists. Tears flowed everywhere. Then he appeared, stepping out into the club's main car park from the back of the West Stand. Head down and deep in thought, he made his way to his trusted Jaguar that was parked nearby. With a great deal of dignity, as so many of his predecessors had done before him, he walked the journey of the condemned manager. Within moments he was gone, exiting the club car park and turning out onto Elland Road, leaving dozens of despairing fans behind. Many were in tears and once again questions were asked of the people who pulled the strings at Leeds United.

The media, who had hoped to provoke some response from the departing manager, were bitterly disappointed. It was clear that some had wanted to taunt and wind him up in the hope of getting a response. It didn't happen. Billy was an absolute gentleman to the very end of his Leeds United career. As I stood amongst the tear-filled supporters, one consoled another:

'Billy always did his very best for us, I feel so sorry that it had to end this way. That lot in there [club directors] don't know what they are doing. They are tearing apart, piece by piece, player by player, our wonderful history, and they are turning players and ex-players and supporters against them. Billy knows he will always be welcome back here at Elland Road by us, the fans. We will always love him very dearly.'

Nearby, a reporter who had overheard the comment, added: 'Billy won't be out of football for long, he needs it and football needs him.'

17

ROVERS RETURN

Sure enough, on 3 July 1989, Billy walked back into football management with Doncaster Rovers. I couldn't be there but was pleasantly surprised at his return. A quick phone call to the friendly Rovers staff, and once again I had arranged a meeting with the great man himself. Driving to Doncaster I was again thoughtful. I felt it best not mention his departure from Leeds United. It was still painful for me so it must have been a damn site worse for him. I wondered how the affair might have affected him and whether he would still be as motivated and focused. I parked my car in the Belle Vue car park and meandered into the office area where I was directed out to the pitch area. I wandered down through the player's tunnel, my footsteps echoing, until I emerged out onto the pitch. It looked resplendent, green and lush. In the distance, on the far side of the ground, I saw Billy chatting to the groundsman. His back towards me, he was oblivious of my presence. 'Mr Bremner,' I shouted out. He turned to look to see who called him and, on recognising me, waved and smiled: 'Back for more are you? What do you think of this pitch? I reckon it needs sorting out, don't you?' This was accompanied by a quick wink – he was evidently winding up the groundsman as the pitch to me looked to be in perfect condition.

Billy was laughing and ushered me to the Rovers dugout where, like before, he lit up a cigarette, and perhaps sensing my unease at what had happened at Leeds, immediately put me at ease:

'You know, things are okay with me. I have my family, I have all this and I am happy with my lot. Not many people can say that, can they? It was a bloody awful and bitter blow to me leaving Leeds the way I did, but the club have profited from my departure so it must have been right. The board must have found it a difficult decision to make, but we are all faced with such decisions at some time in our lives, and we do what we think is right at the time.

'I don't hold any malice towards Leeds United – in fact I don't think anything could make me feel animosity towards the club. As for those who run the football club, well, they know how I feel about them and their actions towards not only me, but Allan and Eddie also. Someone once said that you should never return to the scene of former glories. I don't hold with that – if you feel it's right then go for it. I always gave my all for Leeds United, I don't think I was a bad manager, but circumstances and personalities dictated what I was able to achieve. We very nearly achieved promotion, I think I helped build the platform for future success, and showed football that the Leeds fans are loyal and still behind the team despite the current position. I will forever love Leeds United, but perhaps not in its present form, and with those idiots in charge. I've come back here because this is a good honest club with plenty of potential and the people of Doncaster are enthusiastic about their football club and everything it stands for. It's part of the community and I want to help the people of Doncaster as much as I can. I want the supporters of Doncaster Rovers to feel wanted by the club, its players and officials. Managers and players have become too remote from the general public, particularly at the higher level of the game. This is a people's game and the comradeship between the players and the fans is all-important.'

We chatted about the general state of football and with great foresight he told me: 'I do believe that there will come a day when football supporters of the future attend games in support of one player who they will follow no matter which team's colours he wears. Obviously, the true supporters will remain devoutly loyal to their individual club. The powers that run the game are definitely encouraging a certain type of spectator, middle class, almost affluent. When the day comes that the average working man in the street is priced out of watching football then it will be a sad day for football. I can see that happening.

'Likewise, players cannot be allowed to become bigger than the football clubs themselves or they will have the power and hold clubs to ransom. These things will happen in the future but football, with all its commercial future, needs to keep it as the game of the people and not simply follow the money. Football is facing some difficult times, especially the smaller, lower-profile clubs with smaller catchment areas and lower turnover. The bigger, more prominent clubs will continually chase the honours and the trappings that go with success, forcing lesser clubs to suffer as a consequence of no longer being able to compete.'

Less than a decade later and the prophecy of Billy Bremner was coming true. Some players receive far more recognition than the respective clubs they represent. Lower down the league chain more clubs are feeling the financial strain of supporting the superstars' wage demands. One needs to look no further than Leeds United for a good example of how such issues can negatively impact upon an entire community. With the best of intentions, the club took a financial gamble and spent money they did not have, in order to compete and remain amongst a handful of elite clubs who are able to win major trophies and bring in greater revenue to feed the debt. Despite all the mega and wasteful spending, success didn't happen and Leeds United spiralled out of control. Some of the so-called 'loyal' players, now that the cash cow had dried up, abandoned the club, seeking personal wealth and fortune elsewhere, before matters were finally stabilised with the team in League One [the old Division Three].

As I left the Belle Vue ground for the last time, I asked staff members what they felt about the appointment of Billy Bremner as manager. I was informed that since the announcement of his appointment, season ticket sales had doubled and club merchandise sales trebled. There had also been a marked interest in commercial support and ground advertising. The Doncaster board of directors received dozens of letters of appreciation from supporters and businesses for making what they believe was an outstanding appointment in bringing Billy Bremner back as team manager. The Billy Bremner brand remains to this very day, a respected one.

Unfortunately, Billy's reign at Doncaster lasted just twenty-nine months. Despite making a profit in excess of £400,000 for the club, mainly from transfer fees, he resigned from his position on the evening of Friday, 1 November 1991, with Rovers sitting bottom of Division Four. The Doncaster fans, despite the club's league position, maintained wholehearted support for the manager and never once protested against him or stopped believing in him. In fact the opposite occurred. When news of his resignation broke and spread through the town, many made their way to the Belle Vue ground and expressed their disdain towards the board for allowing him to leave. In response to this, Bremner expressed his own disappointment at being forced into making such a decision:

'My main regret is that I could not do something for the fans, to give them a team they could be proud of. The fans of Doncaster Rovers have been bloody marvellous to me and the club. I wish each and every one of them good luck for the future.'

That he was no longer professionally involved in the game of football seemed almost criminal. He had so much to offer the sport: experience, desire and down-to-earth humility and common sense. He was a capable manager, who was unfortunate to take up the trade during a time when boards of directors demanded instant success and interfered in team matters. Money was more influential to them than supporters' passion. Outside the top half of the first division, financial support was not readily available, and to be honest, neither Leeds United nor Doncaster Rovers were clubs in a healthy financial position. Bremner was constantly juggling club finances in order to meet demands, selling valuable commodities like players, even stadiums, in the vain hope that it would satisfy the directors' demands.

His managerial career over, Billy Bremner continued to spread the football gospel to the people who he knew cared, the supporters. A good career in after-dinner speaking was a natural progression for someone who had so much to say, and had thousands of anecdotes to tell. Having attended many such events, I can confirm that he maintained his charisma and was an undoubted success. At Spalding in 1994 he signed autographs for well over an hour, he answered every question thrown at him from the audience in his usual honest and open manner. He visited every table in the room and spoke to everyone, making sure that each and every person had enjoyed themselves and had a good memory to take away from the evening. He told me:

'I still get a buzz out of this. Footballers earn a living the same as everyone else, so I think it's a great honour to be able to recount some of the great and not so great times, and the anecdotes that accompany being part of the game. As for being a manager again, well perhaps if the right offer came along I would consider it, but it would have to be the right club with the right people in charge. People I trusted and the fans trusted. If the Football Association of Scotland were to ask me to manage the national team, I would gladly walk to Glasgow to accept the position, but that isn't going to happen. I have too many opinions for them to see me as a likely candidate. It's time that football clubs, and the people who own football clubs, realised that the fans are the real life blood of the game and without them there would be no football.'

When I was told in 1997 that Billy Bremner had passed away, I was speaking at a public conference in Scotland. I received the telephone call informing me of the sad news during a break. When the conference delegates reconvened in the main hall, I returned to the podium but I couldn't hide my sadness as tears ran down my cheeks. I made an impromptu announcement:

'Ladies and gentleman, I have just been told that my childhood idol and perhaps the greatest footballer to walk this planet, Billy

Bremner of Leeds United and Scotland has passed away. Can we please have one minute's silence as a mark of respect.'

Over 300 people rose as one to their feet, bowed their heads and displayed the dignity and respect I had hoped they would. As the minute ended, a chant spread from the back of the hall, passing right through the crowd, until everyone was singing. For fully three minutes, the professional audience voluntarily chanted his name: 'Billy Bremner, Billy Bremner'. It was one of the most moving moments I have had in my entire life. Billy Bremner may be gone, but he will never ever be forgotten.

I was in Edlington on Thursday, 11 December 1997, stood alongside hundreds of other football supporters, mainly of Leeds United, at the funeral of my idol, Billy Bremner. It was a truly incredible turnout, as dozens of football legends and respected guests attended the ceremony at St Mary's Church. Alex Ferguson made a special journey from Europe, flying out immediately after a European Cup tie against Juventus. The funeral was like a 'who's who' of Scotland and Leeds United. The Mass was conducted by Father Gerry Harney, and as he and others delivered personal eulogies, there wasn't a dry eye in the gathered crowds that lined the village. The magic of Billy Bremner truly touched many different people across football and beyond.

I felt privileged and honoured to have known him and to be there paying my respects, yet deep inside there was a feeling of emptiness, a void that could never be filled. A man who I had admired since I was but a child, a footballer as loyal as they come, was gone. I knew deep inside that it was the end of an era, not only in my life, but in football also. No one could ever replace Billy Bremner.

18

BILLY'S MOST MEMORABLE GAMES

ENGLAND v SCOTLAND
Home International Championship
Saturday, 15 April 1967
Wembley Stadium

Games between these two countries are always passionate encounters, not only to the fans but also to the players. This classic took on even greater importance to the Scotland side, as the previous year England had been crowned World champions, winning a dramatic Wembley final 4-2 against West Germany. The home nation had achieved an unbeaten run of nineteen games prior to taking on Scotland, making the task facing Billy Bremner and his troops an enormous one.

A packed Wembley stadium, filled with 100,000 passionate and vocal supporters, covered every piece of the terracing, the majority anticipating a comfortable England victory. Both sets of support were well behaved with much good-natured patriotic banter taking place. Inside the Wembley tunnel the tension was much more obvious, and as both sides lined up alongside each other the anxiety could be cut with a knife. The Scottish midfield, consisting of Jim Baxter, Willie Wallace and Billy Bremner appeared to be unfazed by the occasion. Bremner and Baxter utilised the time to wind up their opponents by making comical quips to them:

'I loved wearing that jersey, playing for Scotland meant everything to me, I always wore it with pride and passion.

We were well up for the fight and the game. Some of the England boys were full of themselves, believing in their own hype about being the best World champions of all time, and all that kind of thing. Jim Baxter reminded them that two of their goals should not have been allowed – the ball never crossed the line on one, and the Germany players thought the final whistle had gone for another, and had therefore stopped playing. It was all part of the wind-up and nothing nasty or serious, well not too much anyway.

'The next thing, some of the England players began throwing personal insults at us, so we reciprocated. I kept calling Alan Ball a puff and a softie. He hated it and told me to f—— off out of his sight before he hurt me. I laughed at such a preposterous thought so he began to call me Brillo pad hair! So I laughed even more. He was almost in tears. The tension before we walked out onto the pitch was there for all to sense and I was loving it.'

With their opponents rattled before a ball was kicked, it could be said that Scotland had won the first battle. When the game kicked off, the England players seemed nervous on the ball, not fully controlling it, and kicking it away as though it was a hot potato burning their feet. Scotland settled far quicker, with Bremner and Baxter dominating the midfield and managing the game with relative ease. The World champions were un-nerved and lacking in composure. On the terraces, it was the Scotland fans who sang louder and longer as they sensed the confidence brimming through their team.

'I never really thought a great deal about it at the time, but as I am a passionate Scotsman, I could never accept that as a nation we were inferior to anyone else at anything, let alone football. Each time I went close to an English player I was making comments like "Call yourself World champions – lucky bastards more like, you'll never rule over Scotland." There was an element of grudge between the players – no one in our dressing room wanted to consider losing to the "auld enemy".'

On twenty-eight minutes, Scotland forward Denis Law broke the deadlock with a shot which caught out the usually reliable

Gordon Banks in the England goal to give Scotland a 1-0 lead, a lead they held up to half time:

'We went mad when Denis scored, you could see the English hearts sink. We knew that if we could take it to half time and still be leading, then the England crowd would turn on their players, putting even more pressure on them. We were cock-a-hoop at half time in the dressing room and I couldn't wait to get out and at them again in the second half.'

When the game resumed, it was Bremner who orchestrated much of the football in midfield, stroking the ball in every direction and finding a fellow Scot with every pass. His influence on the flow of the game was incredible. To exacerbate matters even further, when he was on the ball, every so often he would stop, place his foot on it, drag it back a few inches, and look around for a blue-shirted colleague before laying off a pin-point pass. He made it all look very easy. England were getting more wound up by his arrogance on the ball but could do little to stop him. As the game drifted on, and with some England fans streaming out of the stadium, it looked as though the solitary Denis Law goal was to be sufficient to win the game. Then in the eightieth minute, the game again burst into life when Bobby Lennox scored a dramatic second goal for the visitors, latching onto a clever Tommy Gemmell lob, and firing past the helpless Banks.

The second goal forced England to push forward and attack and in the eighty-fifth minute, Jack Charlton managed to prod home from close range. Incredibly, more goals were to come, but any hope of a dramatic England come-back was destroyed as International debutant Jim McCalliog comfortably slotted home Scotland's third goal of the game. The Tartan Army's celebratory chants echoed around a fast emptying Wembley and the partying began. A late headed goal courtesy of Geoff Hurst couldn't silence the dancing Scots on the terraces. They knew, as did each and every Scottish player on the pitch, that they had done more than enough to win the game.

As the final whistle sounded, the Scots celebrated their famous victory with conquering hugs and smiles broad enough to span the Firth of Forth. Bremner did not hesitate to remind the English players that Scotland had beaten the World champions, which therefore made them World champions:

'It wasn't the fact that we had beaten them, but we had done it on their own territory and in such an emphatic fashion. Some people have tried to justify the result by claiming that Jack Charlton and Jimmy Greaves were both carrying knocks, but I will have none of that – we won the game fair and square. We beat the World champions in their own backyard. If it wasn't that important a result then why is it so often recalled by writers and football supporters alike? The final score that will be forever shown in the history books was England 2, Scotland 3. It still makes me smile and feel very proud all these years later.'

LEEDS UNITED v CHELSEA
Division One
Saturday, 7 October 1967
Elland Road

In their previous game, Leeds had held West Ham in an uninspiring 0-0 draw at Upton Park. Much of the newspaper talk prior to the Chelsea fixture surrounded the Leeds captain Billy Bremner, who was about to play his last game for Leeds before starting a twenty-eight day suspension imposed for a sending-off at a league game with Fulham on 2 September 1967:

'I was made a scapegoat for the incidents at Fulham. The whole game had been bad tempered and I was telling the referee to sort it out and to stop hiding from it. He lost his rag with me and told me to stop interfering and to get on with my own game and not his. A couple of challenges, more like desperate lunges, on our players went without so much as a warning for Fulham. I could feel myself losing it, not only with the Fulham players but with the f—— useless referee.

'The Fulham manager was a man by the name of Vic

Buckingham. I wasn't aware of anyone mentioning this at the time but he later said we had been winding his players up by taunting them about fixing games and that's why it had deteriorated so badly. Whatever, the whole situation could have been better managed by the referee. I admit I clattered into a few players, but all I was doing was sending out a message to them not to f—— with us. It backfired big style and I got myself sent off and suffered that ridiculous punishment. I wrote a letter of apology to Fulham right after the game but they sent it back to the club, torn up.'

A few months before the Chelsea game, the Pensioners (as they were then known) had scraped through an FA Cup semi-final against Leeds, 1-0. The result had come about in controversial circumstances. First, an eighty-third minute Terry Cooper goal had been adjudged to have been 'marginally offside' and disallowed, then incredibly, in the final minute, Peter Lorimer flashed a long-range free kick past the despairing Bonetti, only to have the goal ruled out. Experienced television commentator Kenneth Wolstenholme said of the incident: 'You would have to turn the rule book inside out to find out why the referee has disallowed that goal.'

Bremner recalled:

'I could not understand why the goal was not given – it was hard to accept at the time. We won the advantage with the foul being awarded to us, yet we were punished. It wasn't the first time something like that happened either, and it certainly wasn't to be the last. We felt much cheated. It was an accepted part of the game at that time that referees were not consistent and could easily be influenced by players and the crowd. Ken [Burns] was one of the better referees but he wouldn't be moved from his decision. Even years later he stood by it as being correct, albeit he did admit that we are all human and therefore make mistakes, so maybe that was him admitting it. The referee's decision is final and we had to accept that, but knowing they were human and could err more than most it didn't make it any easier to accept at the time, or now. I had issues with Chelsea all my playing career.

If we were dirty then they were savages. There was nothing they wouldn't resort to.'

The stage was set for another closely fought encounter. Chelsea's preparation hadn't been good and they had been rocked by the resignation of manager Tommy Docherty the day before the game. Docherty was a class act and a huge loss to the football club and the team's morale. Many of the London-based journalists and reporters categorically stated that the loss of Docherty would not particularly upset the professional Chelsea style – they would pull together and fight for victory for the sake of Chelsea FC.

That day Bremner ran the Londoners ragged. Nowhere to be seen was the arrogant swagger of the Chelsea superstars, and even when they threw themselves to the ground feigning injury, they looked distinctly amateur. The *Yorkshire Post* reported: 'Bremner teased and tormented them [Chelsea] with dexterity of foot . . . he could twist and turn on the proverbial sixpence.' The Leeds captain turned in a truly world-class performance as Leeds not only beat Chelsea but demolished them with a scintillating display of pure football. Bremner crowned his own performance with a tremendously executed overhead-kick goal which today would still have the pundits raving about its quality and glory in true Brazilian style.

The other Leeds goals, and there were plenty of them, that afternoon came from Albert Johanneson, Jimmy Greenhoff, Jack Charlton, Peter Lorimer, Eddie Gray and a Marvin Hinton own goal as Leeds ran out very comfortable 7-0 winners. The Bremner goal ensured that Leeds entered the football record books as the first side to win 7-0 with seven individual goal scorers.

'At the time we did not know anything about that record, and to be honest we didn't really care. It was a great all-round performance from the whole team, everything we tried seemed to come off for us. You get games like that every so often. Chelsea caught us on the wrong day, although some may say we caught them on the right day and blame the Tommy Docherty situation on their abysmal display. I believe that whatever the situation that day we would have still turned them over and they would have suffered the same fate. As for my goal, well that was a bit special, more so because I scored it in front of the kop at Elland Road. My back was sore for days afterwards, not from the acrobatics or athleticism used to strike the ball, but from players slapping me on it to congratulate me afterwards!'

ARSENAL v LEEDS UNITED
Football League Cup Final
Saturday, 2 March 1968
Wembley Stadium

The route to Wembley for a final is never an easy one to successfully traverse. At times pundits and supporters belittle a team's appearance in a national final, claiming they have got there via an easy route. Such was the accusation levelled at Leeds when they reached Wembley in 1968, by virtue of victories over Luton Town (3-1), Bury (3-0), Sunderland (2-0), Stoke City (2-0) and Derby County in a two-legged semi-final, who were dispatched 4-2 on aggregate. In the final their opponents were Arsenal, a north London-based club with a true armoury of firepower and a battling defence and midfield. The Arsenal side was filled with internationals and experienced professionals and were as tough opponents any team could face in a Wembley final.

'After losing the FA Cup final to Liverpool at Wembley in 1965, I didn't relish the thought of suffering the same emotional despair caused by defeat. I loved the feeling of winning at Wembley, beating England there in 1967 gave me an emotional high, and I wanted to replicate that success for my club. That aside, we really needed to win a major trophy to prove to ourselves and the manager that we had the ability to achieve and progress as a unit. In the build-up to the game there was a lot of talk about consistency and finishing. The boss told us that we would get very few goal scoring opportunities and to make sure we finished and made the goalkeeper work when the chances came along. On the pitch I told the lads to stay calm in the early stages and not to give Arsenal any space, and when we got the chance to shoot at every opportunity.'

The game opened with the initial sparring and tentative pressure from both sides, as gradually Leeds began to assert themselves on the Arsenal defence. In the seventeenth minute Leeds won a corner. The kick was exquisitely curled into the Arsenal penalty area by Eddie Gray and was headed clear of the goal line by George Graham. The ball dropped to Terry Cooper at the edge of the Arsenal penalty area and, doing as his captain had instructed, without further ado the left back thrashed the ball back towards the Arsenal goal and into the back of the net: 'It was a great moment for the team and for Terry Cooper. He was such an honest player and deserved that goal. His performance that day was as good as any full back ever produced in a Wembley final.'

However, the goal and the game were not without further incident and controversy. The ball had hardly struck the net when the Arsenal players began to remonstrate with match referee Mr Hamer. They furiously claimed that there had been an initial foul on their keeper Jim Furnell by Leeds centre half Jack Charlton. The referee remained firm and would have none of it; he dismissed all Arsenal protestations and correctly allowed the goal to stand.

From the scoring of the opening goal onwards, Arsenal had essentially controlled affairs and pushed Leeds back into defensive mode. So committed and serious were the Leeds outfield that goalkeeper Gary Sprake had just one serious save to make during the entire game. As the final whistle blew, signalling a Leeds victory and the winning of their first major domestic trophy, Wembley erupted into choruses of Leeds songs and the stadium was a sea of white, blue and gold. The late Don Revie was ecstatic about the victory and at last winning a domestic trophy: 'My lads have done me and the city of Leeds proud today. Every one of them gave me 110 per cent. At times it wasn't pretty but we worked hard and rightly lifted the trophy.' Revie looked on with much pride as his skipper raised the Football League trophy above his head to the sound of 40,000 enthused Leeds supporters.

'I shall never forget the final few minutes,' Bremner recalled. 'The crowd were whistling so loudly that I could hardly hear the referee's whistle blowing for fouls and throw-ins. I kept my eyes firmly fixed on him when our defenders had the ball; I think all our players stared at him, anticipating him blowing the final whistle. It seemed an eternity before he did. When I heard it go I couldn't take it all in and I kept asking other players if it was all over. It was as though I felt it was going to be taken away from us at the last moment. My relief was truly great. Marching round Wembley stadium with that trophy was, I have to say, an awful nice feeling. The support was fantastic, people were crying with tears of joy, I wanted to take them all by the hand and thank them individually. That first trophy was won in honour of them.

'When we arrived back in Leeds thousands of supporters filled the streets. The last time I had seen this was after our FA Cup final defeat to Liverpool back in 1965 but the mood had been a little more sombre then. This time it was one massive party, people dancing and shouting and singing. Every player had a lump in their throat that day when we saw how happy we had made so many people. I like to think we gave every Leeds supporter a great deal of pleasure in what we achieved. Without our supporters, we as footballers would have been nothing and today's players should really bear that in mind.'

Afterwards, the Leeds match winner Terry Cooper told colleagues and reporters that he had dreamed he was going to score in the game, a self-fulfilling prophecy!

FERENCVAROS v LEEDS UNITED
Inter Cities Fairs Cup Final (Second Leg)
11 September 1968
Nepstadion

Ferencvaros, Hungary's most successful club side, had been previous winners of the Inter Cities Fair Cup in 1965. Nicknamed 'the Fradi' or 'the Green and Whites' they were founded in Budapest in 1899 and were deemed 'formidable opponents' by Leeds boss Don Revie. Bremner and his troops went into this game eager to protect a 1-0 lead they had managed to secure at Elland Road in the first leg. There, before just 25,268 spectators, Leeds had successfully breached the Hungarian side's defence in the fortieth minute with a less than pretty Mick Jones goal that typified his penalty area prowess. On the night, Ferencvaros had proven themselves to be equal foes and had created a number of opportunities to score. However, some heroic defending and some fine goalkeeping from Gary Sprake had kept the intruders at bay.

The Nepstadion, 'The People's Stadium', was first opened in 1953 and constructed with the voluntary assistance of a mass of people, allegedly including Ferenc Puskas. On the night in question, when Leeds were the opposition it was a cauldron of tension and noise. Some 76,000 people filled the terraces, the majority believing that the hosts would be victors. Leeds had suffered defeat in the final of the same competition in the previous season and were not about to submit so easily this time. Experience had taught these Leeds players well.

Revie told his players to defend in numbers and to break with pace and with support from the midfield.

'I remember the boss telling me to play my usual game, get close to the man with the ball and to intimidate with my physical and vocal presence. I knew that very few of the Hungarians would understand my Scottish dialect. Yet most footballers, despite their background, nationality and the language barrier can understand a fellow player's desire and tenacity. I was really fired up for this game and wanted to show everyone that I was fully committed to every tackle and challenge.'

The Hungarian supporters booed every Leeds player and every pass in a desperate attempt to knock their confidence. Undeterred, the Leeds stars battled on, ignoring the hostility of the whole affair. Ferencvaros ran at the Leeds defence each time they won the ball, and playing neat interchanging passing moves they came close to scoring several times in the opening half hour. Gradually Leeds rose in confidence and began to realise that they needed to, and could take control of the game. Cooper and Reaney were magnificent in the timing of their tackles. Bremner and Giles were at their industrious best, utilising every ball they played to maximum effect. A floated free kick from Mike O'Grady found Mick Jones in the Ferencvaros penalty area and the striker met the ball with his head and directed it goalwards only for the ball to thump against the Hungarian team's crossbar and be kicked to safety. The Ferencvaros support began to turn against their own team for not scoring as freely as they had anticipated which worked in Leeds' favour.

'We always knew that our backs would be against the wall in Hungary. Ferencvaros needed an early goal really. That would have settled them and the supporters down but it didn't happen and we slowly grew in confidence. We gave as gritty a performance in that game as I can ever remember. It became clear to us that as a unit in order to compete at the top of the game we had to consistently work for and support one another throughout the full ninety minutes and more. There was enough quality in our team for individuals to produce their own moment of brilliance in any game.

'That night in Hungary we proved we were able to compete with the very best Europe had to offer. It was a real milestone in my career and that of Leeds United and our second trophy in six months. We could now force our critics to recognise that we had the capability to progress to even greater achievements, and that we were not too bad a team in the process. The boss was ecstatic about winning the trophy. To him the desire to make Leeds

154

United a major football force was not only limited to British shores, he wanted us to be regarded as the best in Europe and we had now achieved a very small portion of that goal. We were the first British side to win the Inter Cities Fairs Cup; we had achieved a lot in a relatively short space of time, now it was up to us to maintain that momentum with even more success.'

LIVERPOOL v LEEDS UNITED
Division One
Monday, 28 April 1969
Anfield

Anfield, home of Liverpool FC, has never been a welcoming place for visiting teams to play their football. The Liverpool side of 1969 were as good as any club side in the world, especially at Anfield. They had strength in every department, and that season had lost just one game at their home ground. This game took on additional major importance by virtue of the fact that the First Division championship would be decided by the result. It was a two-horse race between Liverpool and Leeds. United needed just one point to secure the championship, Liverpool needed a win to keep their hopes alive. The tiny terraced-house-lined streets surrounding much of Anfield stadium were packed almost three hours before the 7.30pm kick off. Street parking was a virtual impossibility and the flow of traffic around all routes close to the ground was at a virtual standstill. The Stanley Park car parking areas were crammed to capacity resulting in cars being abandoned wherever any space to stop and park was found. This included on complete strangers' driveways, pavements and garage forecourts. An estimated 10,000 loyal Leeds fans were in a partying mood as they filled much of the Anfield Road end of the stadium. Loud and raucous, they were there for one reason: to cheer their team on to success and to celebrate the occasion.

Meanwhile, Liverpool's famous Kop was typically filled to the rafters an hour before kick-off, with fans chanting their usual anthems. The Anfield stadium was bursting at the seams and crackling with tension and anticipation as early as 7pm with thousands of fans being locked outside.

In the Leeds dressing room the importance of the occasion was not lost, but was somewhat dismissed by Don Revie. Bremner recalled:

'A season was over forty-two league games and we were continually reminded by the boss that this game was no different from any other game we had played. We all knew the rewards that one more good performance would bring, yet none of us dared to mention it. The usual pre-match routines were being carried out, players and staff wandering round talking to themselves or having a chat with other players. This was to psych themselves up in preparation for the final push on the pitch. Looking back, it was an incredibly tense time; everything we had competed for all season was now potentially going to be determined by this one game.

'An official popped his head round the dressing-room door and told us to make ourselves ready to go out onto the pitch. The strange-looking little man was greeted with comical abuse from us all. This was our signal that it was time for us all to come together and to fight for the cause of Leeds United. As I walked down the passageway and steps and out onto the pitch, the noise the spectators were making inside the stadium was incredible, it was easily the loudest I have ever heard. I couldn't hear our players or my own voice. It was intimidating and quite scary.'

As the game kicked off, Liverpool surged forward towards the Leeds goal. Time and again they attacked, wave after wave of intense pressure. Gary Sprake played one of his finest games that evening, impeccable in his handling and awareness of the Liverpool threat. One save in particular from Ian Callaghan was spectacular, as the Welshman somehow changed direction mid-dive, spun backwards and managed to tip a wicked spinning shot over the bar. The Liverpool front line swarmed round the Leeds goal like bees round a honey pot. Bremner marshalled and rallied his troops magnificently, throwing himself into challenges and acting as a human shield, repelling shots from reaching their intended target.

It has been said that Billy Bremner worked as hard that night as he ever did for Leeds United. Every so often he would slow play down, controlling the ball, putting his foot on it and allowing his team mates to regroup and push up towards the Liverpool goal. Liverpool, eager to get a goal, were not about to stand on ceremony and thumped into Bremner with strong challenges time and again. They should in fact have taken the lead through young striker Alun Evans who somehow contrived to miss two easy chances.

The longer the game went on, the stronger the Leeds rearguard became. Each man gave his all, continually roared on by the tigerish Bremner and the Leeds supporters: 'There can be no doubt that it was an almighty battle we found ourselves engaged in that evening. I kept encouraging the players to use the ball wisely, make easy passes and make movement off the ball. It was all about keeping possession. Liverpool kept at us and big Tommy Smith, the Liverpool defender, seemed to be urging his players to kick us off the park if needs be. Emlyn Hughes, a good friend of mine, worked really hard and was his usual playing self, a pain in the arse – he was continually moaning.

'At one point he said to me: "Come on Billy, you are not being fair mate, give me a chance to get close enough to kick you into the stand." I always had a lot of respect for Liverpool and their style of football, but that night in April 1969 I don't ever recall seeing them chasing a game as much as they did that evening against us. Liverpool's game is all about possession and patience, but that night they were different. Bill Shankly, God bless him, really had them going for it. Eventually we had them covered in all areas and displayed patience and control.'

As the ninety minutes mark came and went, the referee Mr Dimond played out injury time but for Leeds it seemed like an eternity. On the touchline, Don Revie paced up and down like a man possessed, continually looking at his watch, nervous, irritated, excited. In the space of a few seconds just about every emotion was expressed upon his face. Eventually the referee blew the full-time whistle, some Leeds players sank to their knees, tears streaming down their cheeks, and it was all over. For the first time in the club's history Leeds United were the League Champions. The players at once saluted the Leeds support. Revie, who was not a man to outwardly express emotion in public, had the smile of a Cheshire cat. Bill Shankly, the Liverpool supremo, congratulated him on a marvellous season, shaking his hand whilst bearing a somewhat disconsolate smile.

Bremner meanwhile was being congratulated by members of the Liverpool team: 'Ron Yeats gave me a pat on the back and told me that we deserved to be champions. Most of the Liverpool players did the same. I went over to congratulate the boss and I didn't know whether to laugh, cry, scream or sing. As I ran to him he typically gave me a greater challenge when he said to me: "Bill, take the team round the pitch, round the ground. You are Champions Bill, the best team in England. Celebrate it in style."

'As we made our way round the Anfield pitch I looked into the sea of red and white Liverpool support wherever we went. The Merseyside supporters were reciprocating our gesture and openly applauding us. I admit, all the time I kept one eye fixed firmly on the Kop. I didn't think it would be right to go to them and rub salt into their wounds. I was more nervous about that than through any footballing reason – everybody had respect for those supporters who stood in the Liverpool Kop. It was strange because as we got closer to that end suddenly their supporters started singing "Champions, Champions" and they were singing it in honour of us. It was one of the most amazing and humbling experiences I have ever encountered in football. Those supporters are superb. I never feel sorry for losing opponents, but I remember apologising to some of the Liverpool supporters stood at the front of the Kop, for winning the Championship on their soil. I cried, the emotion and relief was all too much for me and some of them on witnessing this sang my name. The memories of that night will never be far from my mind, I didn't want to leave the pitch.'

'In the dressing room the celebrations continued but they were though, momentarily, brought to a halt when Bill Shankly walked in. He simply said: "Well done boys, worthy Champions, good luck for next season." Champagne was produced courtesy of Liverpool FC and we all gladly accepted this kind gift – why not, and it would rude to waste it! While we were all celebrating in some style the boss came over to me and whispered: "Bill, there is the little matter of Nottingham Forest for us to beat in Leeds next Wednesday. Let's save our full celebrations till then." Typical of the boss really, forever the professional.'

LEEDS UNITED v SK LYN OSLO
European Cup, First Round (First Leg)
Wednesday 17 September 1969
Elland Road

With the English League Championship under their belt, United entered the European Cup competition for the first time in their history. The first-round draw had been somewhat fortunate to them, providing opposition in the form of Norwegian part-timers SK Lyn Oslo. The Norwegians had an outstanding record in their own country where they were League Champions and Cup winners in 1968. Indeed, they had been crowned League Champions four years previously and had also won the Norwegian Cup on no less than seven occasions. In 1969 they reached the quarter-final stage of the European Cup Winners Cup, narrowly going out 5-4 to Barcelona.

Leeds' preparations for the tie had gone well. Four days earlier they had defeated Sheffield Wednesday 2-1 at Hillsborough and, in fact, the team had suffered just one defeat in its first ten competitive first-team fixtures of that season.

'To be fair to Oslo, we knew little about them; the papers said that their team consisted of office clerks, teachers, and students – in fact any occupation you could think of other than footballers. Knowing how reporters operate I don't think any of us really believed what we read of them, after all this was the European Cup, a competition in which only Europe's very best compete. Even if the reports were true, there is no side playing in the European Cup which deserves anything but complete respect. The boss had told us to ignore all the press speculation, Oslo would not lay down and die without a fight. He told us we had to be on top of our game from the start and, as usual, to fight for everything.'

The Norwegians arrived at Elland Road without Olsen their goalkeeper. Travel delays had held him up and he eventually arrived at the ground with less than half an hour to spare before kick off. By the end of ninety minutes one can only suspect that he wished he had missed the game completely. Leeds' precise football and determination to succeed saw them crush their opponents. After just thirty-five seconds Mike O'Grady shot United into a 1-0 lead, with what has commonly been agreed to be the quickest goal ever scored in the competition. Two minutes later, Mick Jones nodded the ball past the bewildered Olsen, and on nine minutes the same player added a third. The Oslo defence was in tatters as Leeds continued to force proceedings. Before half time two further goals were added to the home side's total, one from Allan Clarke and one from Giles, making the half time score an incredible 5-0 to Leeds:

'It was unbelievable; we went in at half time believing we could really thrash this team. It was obvious that more goals would come if we kept up the pressure in the second half. We threatened to score every time we attacked them. From my perspective it was a classic Leeds performance and although I don't like to scorn another club's misfortunes, this tie was a clear mismatch. We were head and shoulders above them in everything we did. The fans loved it and so did we. We were a team in every sense of the word. Performances like this really forge a close bond between the players, it is all about aspiring to achievement and that night we truly achieved.'

The second half provided no respite for the visitors as Leeds continued to plunder the Norwegian side's defence and, at times, it seemed as though they did this at leisure. Further goals from Clarke, Giles, Jones and two from Bremner himself completed the 10-0 rout:

'As we left the pitch to standing ovations everywhere, one of the players asked me how many goals we had scored! For the first time in my professional career I had to stop to think just how many goals we actually had scored. Just to be certain I asked the question in the dressing room and there was different scorelines offered. The boss told us it was ten and I sat there completely stunned by the result. It was an incredible team performance and achievement.

'To be fair their players took it really well, much better than I would have accepted it had it been the other way round. I still feel a great pride every time I consider that result.'

The 10-0 scoreline equalled the record score by any British club in Europe at that time. In the second leg, a further six goals were added to the aggregated total, without reply, producing an incredible overall victory of 16-0. It sent out a positive warning to the rest of Europe and football that Leeds United meant business. As for Lyn Oslo, they went on to suffer a nightmare season culminating in relegation and their demise as a major force in Norwegian football.

GLASGOW CELTIC v LEEDS UNITED
European Cup Semi-final (Second Leg)
15 April 1970
Hampden Park

The first leg of this tie, which the press had dubbed as 'The Battle of Britain', had been something of an anti-climax for everyone connected with Leeds United. Jock Stein's Celtic side had produced a clinical and defiant performance to earn a 1-0 away win over what looked like a weary Leeds side, who seemed on edge and lacking in confidence. The victory and the Scottish side's performance had everyone believing that the tie was over –

Leeds simply wouldn't be able to make any impact against them on their own soil.

'As a man I was extremely disappointed by our performance and Celtic's win at Elland Road. Throughout my formative years I had supported them, I still had more than a soft spot for them but I wanted so desperately to beat them. My heart was now with Leeds United and I wanted to go on to win the competition thereafter. I knew the entire Celtic team personally and the majority of us were good friends.

'Wee Jimmy Johnstone was winding me up throughout, it was all good-humoured stuff but deep down it hurt. I tried my best to kick "Jinky" into the stands but that night he was on magnificent form. Poor Terry Cooper couldn't get anywhere near him and the ball seemed to be glued to his feet as he weaved in and out and around our players. I do confess that Celtic did deserve to beat us at Elland Road, though I still believe that if we had met them earlier in the season it would have been a far different result and scoreline. We were tiring from an arduous fixture list and through our cup commitments. That's my excuse anyway.'

The second leg was played at Hampden Park, Glasgow, where a European Cup record attendance was created with 136,505 spectators crammed into the vast terracing and stands. Thousands were locked outside, and unconfirmed reports indicate that a couple of thousand more elected not to use the turnstiles as a means of entrance, clambering over walls and helping each other get inside Scotland's national stadium. It goes without saying that the actual amount of people inside the stadium was far greater than that officially registered.

The second leg kicked off amidst a frenzy of noise and screams as the Scottish side were willed on to further glory by their fanatical supporters. Hampden Park was ablaze with green and white and the stadium was truly rocking in an electric atmosphere. In the fourteenth minute it fell silent as Billy Bremner collected the ball, fully twenty-five yards from the Celtic goal and, moving forward, he unleashed a ferocious shot which flew high into the Celtic net to put Leeds level:

'It was a fantastic feeling, I just saw the gap opening up before me, the ball bounced just right for me to have a crack, it was one of the sweetest shots I have ever struck and as soon as it left my foot I knew it was a goal.'

Billy McNeill, one of the Celtic players that day, recalls the moment:

'I don't think there was anyone in the stadium who under-estimated the skill possessed by Billy Bremner. We knew that he was a real threat to us, and Jock told us not to allow him any time on the ball. We did and we were punished; the shot was unbelievable. I told him afterwards that he wouldn't get another kick the whole game.'

The goal shocked the Scottish side and Leeds looked far more determined and dangerous than they had in the first leg. They went in at half time leading 1-0. Sadly, shortly after the restart, John 'Yogi' Hughes sent the Celtic crowd into raptures with a header which went past Sprake and into the Leeds net. A short time later the Leeds keeper was stretchered off the pitch after a nasty-looking collision with the giant Hughes, receiving a standing ovation from the Celtic supporters as he was carried away to the dressing rooms. David Harvey replaced him in the goal and his first task was to pick the ball out of his net after Bobby Murdoch had shot Celtic in front before the replacement keeper could even touch the ball.

Celtic now led 3-1 on aggregate, a score line they maintained, earning them a place in the European Cup final. In that second-leg encounter, it has to be said that one player had stood out above all others, Jimmy Johnstone. The diminutive red-haired winger told me:

'It wasn't the greatest exhibition of football produced in Britain, but Leeds and Celtic were undoubtedly the top two sides of the time. Before the first game we had been written off as the losers and that really fired us up. Jock Stein used the media speculation as a motivator, it genuinely spurred us on and I believe we ran them ragged over both ties. Billy Bremner was his usual self. Being a close pal of his we were at each other the whole time, passing comments and insults, both red heads so we were also prone to the odd bit of ill-tempered confrontation. There was one confrontation in that game which I think really depicts Billy Bremner perfectly. He received a real clattering and fell head first on the pitch, enough to knock most players out of their stride – it looked an awful painful experience. Not the wee man, he would have none of it. Despite all the fuss being made around him he got up, shook himself down and trotted off, continuing to give everything he could for Leeds United. After the game he was the first one to congratulate every Celtic player and told us, "if we [Leeds] were to lose to anyone I prefer it to be Celtic," adding "now go on and win the f—— trophy." It wasn't that he wanted Celtic to beat Leeds, that would never do, but Celtic had always been a favourite side of his. He was magnanimous in defeat, a true gentleman of football.'

Bremner's wish was not fulfilled as Celtic lost the final against Dutch side Feyenoord by two goals to one. He recalled:

'I thought Celtic would win the trophy that year, it would take a special team to beat them, but they too seemed to suffer from tiredness in the final. It was disappointing to lose to them in the semi-final – we were so close to achieving personal ambitions but could not muster enough quality to get past Celtic. For me, it was a real experience playing in a competitive match against my other favourite side. I don't think I personally, nor any of our team, deserve any credit from either game against Celtic, it will always be one of my most memorable games, a really momentous occasion for me personally and professionally.'

LEEDS UNITED v SOUTHAMPTON
Division One
Saturday, 4 March 1972
Elland Road

The previous league match at Elland Road had seen Leeds demolish old rivals Manchester United in a 5-1 rout, a result which had caused soccer pundits the length and breadth of the country to sing Leeds' praise. There were those who believed the performance had been the most complete of any Leeds team in the club's history. Compliment indeed, but Don Revie's men were not the type to bask in such glory and rest on their laurels as Southampton, the next team to visit Elland Road, were to find out to their absolute horror.

To say that Leeds' performance on this day was exhilarating is perhaps something of an understatement. They quite simply wiped the floor with the Saints, who could muster no challenge or answer to the outstanding midfield leadership of Bremner and the clinical finishing of Mick Jones, Allan Clarke, Eddie Gray and Peter Lorimer.

The game itself burst into life on thirty-eight minutes when Clarke latched onto some clever passing between Jones and Gray to fire United into a 1-0 lead. Four minutes later, Lorimer shot home a second to give Leeds a 2-0 half-time lead.

'At half time there was not a thought that we would turn our possession into so many goals,' said Bremner. 'John Giles was playing out of his skin, every touch he made looked elegant and he was more like a ballet dancer that game so exquisite was his touch. As the game wore on I felt that my game moved to a new level, ball tricks I would normally only practise in training sessions appeared throughout the game. The boss was not one who enjoyed such antics from his players. He wanted more direct football, and finesse and trickery came after results as far as he was concerned. However, we enjoyed and milked every moment of it. It wasn't a deliberate attempt to make Southampton look inferior, it just happened that way. There are few football games in which any player can honestly say he thoroughly enjoyed it, but for me the Southampton game is one which will stand out in my memory for evermore. I don't want to put Southampton down but it was more like a training session for us. John Giles said afterwards that it was men versus boys and he was right.

'The Leeds support that day was as overwhelmed by our

performance as the Southampton players were, we just seemed to get better and better as the match went on. At one stage our fans were cheering every time a Leeds player touched the ball. I think we achieved around twenty-five passes in one move, before giving the ball away, then regaining control of it straight away. It was fantastic. If I had one disappointment from that game it was that I never scored; a goal would have capped it off nicely for me.'

The final score of Leeds United 7, Southampton 0, does not accurately reflect the manner of the victory. It could so easily have been double figures. Bremner and Giles rightly received glowing credit and were proclaimed as football geniuses for their dominant and controlled midfield performance. For the record, the goal scorers that day were Peter Lorimer (three), Allan Clarke (two), Mick Jones and Jack Charlton.

BRAZIL v SCOTLAND
World Cup Finals, Group Two
18 June 1974
Wald Stadium, Frankfurt

The 1974 World Cup finals presented Scotland with an ideal opening fixture, against Zaire who were expected to finish bottom of the group table. Scotland won the fixture 2-0 to head the group table. The press, though, were more perplexed by the fact that just two goals had been scored against what they regarded as being vastly inferior opposition. Bremner recalled the fixture: 'To score two goals against anyone in the World Cup finals is no minor achievement. I know we were expected to get more, in fact we should have scored more, but it just didn't happen for us. Kazadi, their keeper, was dropping the ball all over his area, but every time it fell to one of their players who lumped it upfield. He did make some decent stops as well – it wasn't as if he was completely hopeless. I tend to think that we paid them too much respect as a team, but nevertheless our failure to grab three or four goals cost us dearly in the end, and we as a team must take the brunt of the criticism.'

With Zaire successfully beaten, Scotland now faced the World Champions Brazil in their second group game. The Brazilian side – without the recently retired Pele – was filled with well-known superstars like Rivelino, Jairzinho and Levinha, and they were the clear favourites to again lift the trophy:

'To be playing against Brazil in the World Cup finals has to be every schoolboy's and man's dream. It certainly was mine. The travelling press pack typically had us well beaten before the game started, and that helped us to focus more on our strengths and put in a really determined showing. We didn't want to concede at all but we knew the early stages were important for us to defend as resolutely as we could.'

True to form, as the game kicked off Brazil pressed forward looking for the early goal, but Scotland defended well and managed to close down the South American side's attacks. Bremner, who was Scotland's captain, worked tirelessly and really showed his class as he controlled the midfield and continually broke down sweeping Brazilian attacks with some acute and brave tackling, all the time keeping a cool and level head, his leadership qualities evident for all to see. Pele, who was himself a spectator at the game, proclaimed Bremner's performance as that of 'the best midfielder in the World Cup'. The midfield dynamo played an outstanding game, perhaps his best ever for his country.

It is somewhat ironic that the best chance of the game should fall to Bremner, when a scramble in the Brazil goalmouth saw the ball cannon off a defender towards him. From just a few feet out he somehow put the ball wide of the goal and out for a goal kick:

'It was a truly dreadful moment. I knew as soon as the ball came up to me it wasn't going to be easy for me to make clean contact with it. It was spinning awkwardly and bounced, I tried to stab it home and got it all wrong. My heart was in my mouth and I honestly felt sick, I was regularly putting them chances away for Leeds every other week. The miss has haunted me but, as they say, it is history now and no matter how many times I watch it, the ball will never go in. Watching from the terracing or at home on television it looked an easy chance, but everyone who was close to me knew that the pace and spin of the ball made it hellishly difficult to control. The rest of the team and squad were great about it, especially when some British newspapers seriously criticised me for the miss. It is a real low spot of my football career, yet the game itself was a real highlight. After all is said and done, we held the World Champions to a nil-all draw in the World Cup finals. That Scotland side was a good one, and if we had progressed through past the group stages I believe we would have done very well.

'The other thing that will always stick with me about that game was Rivelino. Remember him? He was the one that could bend a free kick round a defensive wall. The press loved the way he did it, and gleefully reported his every kick and dead-ball strike. It's a pity they didn't notice the other strike he could make, like the one he committed on me in that game. It was crude and deliberate and he tried to take me out. He'd already been booked and should have walked for this offence. He later said that he held his fist up to me because I rabbit-punched him on the back of the neck, and that I had moved towards his fist pretending he had struck me! He thumped me good and proper and he knew it.

'The referee would have none of it though. Send a Brazilian off for taking Billy Bremner out? Unthinkable! "Bremner probably asked for it," was the comment one English hack made. And you wonder why football people in general have no trust of them! I kept in contact with Rivelino for many years after, and we did battle in a challenge game held in Paris in the mid 1970s and again he was like a whippet, quick and fleet of foot. This was the first time I noticed that I couldn't keep up with him, my pace was just beginning to drop off. So I kicked him all over the place, with a smile on my face of course. We shook hands afterwards, there was mutual respect between us.'

Unfortunately for Scotland, a 1-1 draw with Yugoslavia in their final group game ensured that they were eliminated by virtue of goal difference; scoring fewer goals against Zaire (Brazil had beaten them 3-0 and Yugoslavia put nine past them without return) had knocked them out.

'I think the worst moment came after our 1-1 draw with Yugoslavia. We were left to wait for the Brazil-Zaire result, and they had to win by three clear goals to go through and knock us out. We had to sit it out in the Frankfurt dressing rooms until the score line came through, which was about five minutes after our game had finished. When we heard that Brazil had done it we sat in silence initially, then the language was choice from some of our players, including me. We were devastated. Then someone said "if only". I think that about sums up our 1974 World Cup finals effort.'

19

WHAT THEY SAID ABOUT HIM

DON REVIE MBE (Leeds United, England)
A marvellous skipper, leading by the example of his skill and
tenacity, temperament and fight. He's like Dave Mackay and
Frank McLintock both rolled into one. A born captain. Billy on
one leg is better than a lot on two. I get a warm feeling just
thinking about what he's done for this club – and what he's going
to do.

PELE (Santos, Brazil)
The majority of footballers (and people) are not always remembered, it takes somebody very special to be remembered as
someone great. Everyone in football from a generation knows
of Billy Bremner, he had an awe-inspiring reputation as a
determined achiever and winner. I knew about Billy Bremner
when I was playing, he was regarded as a great footballer. I don't
call many people great footballers, but Billy Bremner really was.
He was as difficult an opponent as I knew and when he
represented Scotland he always gave his best effort to win every
game.

JOHN CHARLES CBE (Leeds United, Juventus, Wales)
As a footballer he earned the utmost respect of his colleagues and
other professionals in the game, not only from those of his
beloved Leeds United, but from across the football universe.
He had an incredible appetite for the game and as a manager
he realised that the future success of the game was going to
be reliant on developing youngsters, long before others even

170

considered such matters. After he left the game I joined him on the after-dinner speakers circuit and we went all over the place to speak. We often travelled in his Jaguar which had the registration WJB. He loved that car. When we passed through towns and villages, if Billy saw a group of kids kicking a football around, he would stop the car and watch. All too often he got out of the car to offer words of wisdom and advice and sometimes he even joined in a game. It was great being with him, such a character and personality.

We were once on the outskirts of Kettering and Billy wanted to stop for a break. As we pulled into the town centre we were stuck in traffic and it was pouring down with rain. Billy noticed an old lady struggling with bags of shopping. She had dropped them a couple of times and made her way to a bus stop but she was soaking wet and looked upset. Billy jumped out of the car and asked her if she was alright then, after a few seconds, he flagged down a passing taxi, gave the driver the money for the fare and told him to take her home. The woman couldn't believe it, nor could the taxi driver who exclaimed, 'My God, you're Billy Bremner' and asked for an autograph.

That was Billy through and through, always helping other people and considering others' feelings. When he got back to the car we had a queue of traffic behind us, beeping horns and shouting at us to move. Billy was drenched through but turned towards the traffic and gave a bow and a wave and thanked them all for being so patient. He was such a lovely man and the image of this tough and rugged footballer is far removed from the person he truly was. An exceptional man, sorely missed.

JIM BAXTER (Raith Rovers, Rangers, Sunderland, Scotland)
I had a great affection for the wee man; he was an exceptional individual in every sense of the word. A great family man, a wonderful husband and father and grandfather, and a friend who I and so many others will sorely miss.

As a footballer he had the lot, ball control, vision, passing skills and what a finisher. In fact he could do most things with a ball at his feet. I shared a lot of fun times with him when we both played for our country, we both enjoyed a pint and a dram, sensible drinking only, mind you. I remember him giving some stick to Bobby Moore at Wembley, asking him if he was wearing a wig and whether he had a cushion stuffed down the back of his shorts as his backside looked so big in tight pants. The England man didn't like it one bit and swore at Billy and made fun of his height – he asked if he came from beneath the same mushroom as Nobby Stiles? Billy then stood on Moore's bootlaces causing one to come undone. He had to bend down to tie it up at which point Billy walked up to him and looking down on him whispered in his ear: 'This is no time to pray, Bobby. Its men vs men out there, and may the best man win.'

MARTIN BUCHAN (Aberdeen, Manchester United, Scotland)
Billy Bremner was a fine captain and leader of men. A great ambassador of the game and for Scotland. He loved nothing more than pulling on the Scotland jersey and representing his country. He was inspirational to us all and worshipped by supporters wherever he played.

GEORGE BEST (Manchester United, Fulham, Hibernian, Northern Ireland)
I hated playing against Billy Bremner, he was the toughest opponent I knew and I could never get the better of him. He read the game and my game in particular so well that I dreaded coming up against him. I tried everything to get one over on him but he was too sharp and strong. We often met up on the after-dinner speaking circuit and enjoyed reminiscing about old times. He was always a gentleman and did a lot for charities and underprivileged children. I do know he made anonymous donations to lots of good causes, and helped the Stirling football clubs with auction material and other donations. Sir Matt always reminded us that Billy Bremner was at his most devastating when staring adversity in the face and that he didn't understand the meaning of the word defeat. He was right. Billy Bremner was

one of the finest footballers of his generation and as a family man, a player or in management, he can never be replaced. He was an adversary on the pitch but a good man and friend to me off it.

BOBBY LENNOX MBE (Celtic, Scotland)
Billy and I go back along way, he was a good friend. There can be no doubting that he was one of the finest Scotsmen to ply his trade on the football pitches of England and Europe. As a player he worked hard and was determined and, regardless of the opposition, Billy would treat every game with similar respect and deservedly won many honours at club level with Leeds United.

At international standard he was a fine captain, a real general on the park, demanding 100 per cent commitment from those around him. I will never forget Scotland's 3-2 Wembley win over England in 1967. On that day he was a Colossus, running his legs off and continually pushing everyone to their very limits. It was a marvellous performance from the entire team, but Billy was outstanding and would always have it, that as long as we had beaten the World Champions, then the mantle should now belong to Scotland.

He was a gentleman off the field, a likeable man who will be missed by all those who knew him. I cannot think of one footballer I know who had anything but respect for him not only as a player, but as an individual. I am honoured to be able to pay tribute to one of the world's greatest footballers of all time.

SYD OWEN (Luton Town, Leeds United, England)
Billy Bremner was a dream to coach and train. He always listened intently to what he was told and acted out every instruction meticulously. I would sit and watch him take some serious beatings during a game, he was targeted from the second the ball was first kicked and he would have lumps kicked out of him. Afterwards, when many players went down and complained of injuries and cuts and bruises, Billy would ignore those he suffered, such was his determination not to miss any

game. I don't know of any footballer who had the stamina to run and run for the sake of his club. Billy gave every ounce of energy to Leeds United in every game. He genuinely cared and that's what made him stand out from other players of that era. A fantastic footballer and a nice man to know.

JIMMY JOHNSTONE (Celtic, Scotland)

To say that Billy and I were close friends is an understatement. We were both red heads, of the same build, and of the same temperament. We both played for the best two football teams of our era, Glasgow Celtic and Leeds United. We kept in regular contact during our careers and after; it came as a terrible blow to me when I heard the sad news of his death.

As a footballer he played with great pride and determination. Fiery he may have been, but he was the ultimate professional and was always the first to shake his opponent's hand after a game. He had a great desire to win, a passion which flooded through the great Leeds side and also into the Scotland international team – he was an inspiration to all those around him. An outstanding passer of the ball and a regular goal scorer, he was as complete a footballer as I can recall.

As a leader, he was one of the best. It was an honour to play alongside him at international level and he would give you a kick up the backside if he did not think you were performing to your best, but was also quick to praise when you were on top of your game. Football has lost a legend, life has lost someone very special, and I have lost a very good friend.

BRIAN CLOUGH OBE (Middlesbrough, Derby County, Leeds United, Nottingham Forest)

He made the Leeds team tick and without his consistency they may never have won the trophies they did. I was never an admirer of the rough tactics that team employed, but they were only acting to managerial instruction. Billy Bremner had more to his game than the rugged and over-the-top challenges that he is renowned for. He could play a bit as well and when he was in full flow there were few players who could stop him or prevent his exceptional passing game and finishing. Of course I would have liked to have professionally worked with him for much longer, but other factors prevented that from happening. I was certain that he would replace me as Leeds manager when I left them – he seemed the logical and ideal choice. I was surprised when they didn't give him the job, and later when he was given the position, I am told that the club was in a mess and he had his hands tied and was severely restricted with what he could essentially achieve. We may not have been personal friends, but he was a damn fine footballer and I have nothing but respect for his skill in that area; he was a player who any manager would want in their side.

BILLY MCNEILL MBE (Celtic, Manchester City, Aston Villa, Scotland)

Billy Bremner epitomised the Leeds United and Scotland sides of the 1960s and '70s, determined, hard but fair and professional. He was an all-round excellent footballer with vision and an abundance of skill in all departments. We kept in touch with each other right up until his death, which absolutely devastated me. I always felt that people like Billy Bremner would live forever; he was a true legend in every sense of the phrase.

If I could have picked a player who I would want to have played alongside me, then his name would be one of the first on my list. I know that the majority of managers and players would have wanted him in their team. As an opponent he could be devastating, his tackling was fearless and often bone shaking. His energy was incredible, as he would run his legs off for both Leeds and Scotland; I used to wonder where he found the sheer strength to compete at the highest standard for a full ninety minutes over a football season which could well last seventy odd games.

Billy had, since a boy, a healthy support for Glasgow Celtic. When Leeds were drawn against us in the semi-final of the European Cup it must have been something of a dilemma for him, but like he was in every game, he gave everything he had to beat us, he even scored at Hampden to level the tie. Afterwards he shook every Celtic player's hand and told them to go on and win the trophy. I regard him as one of the best passers of a football and tacklers of his era and he was without doubt one of the all-time great footballers to grace our game. I consider myself fortunate to have known him as both a player and a friend, and I know he will be remembered for a long time to come. What he achieved for his clubs and country is indeed, legendary.

BOBBY MURDOCH (Celtic, Middlesbrough, Scotland)

I could talk for hours about Billy Bremner and still could never provide sufficient positives to say about him. He was a man of honour, a true friend and a wonderful person. On the football pitch he was Leeds United's warrior; for Scotland he was our very own 'Braveheart'. I used to hate playing against him, whether at training or in a meaningful competitive match such as the European Cup semi-final. Billy treated every game the same, it was there to be won and everybody wants to be winners. He never shirked a challenge or lost a tackle, he caused players like myself, almost twice the physical size of him, to think twice before going up against him in a fifty-fifty challenge. He would laugh about it and try to wind me up, calling me a big softie.

I know he was immensely proud to play for Leeds against Celtic in that European Cup semi-final. In the tunnel before the game I had a word with him and reminded him that he was among his own kind and to remember his roots. He told me to piss off and reminded me that Leeds United were his pay-masters, Don Revie his boss and he wanted to win for the Leeds supporters. That was Billy for you, and of course he scored in that game, I'm sure some Celtic and Scotland supporters cheered when they saw it was the wee man who netted for Leeds. That was his moment and thankfully we won on the night, 2-1. He was the first to congratulate the boys in the dressing room afterwards and was magnanimous in defeat. He is a legend in Scotland and Leeds and quite rightly so.

176

WILLIE HENDERSON (Rangers, Sheffield Wednesday, Scotland)

Billy was a warm genuine man, and an outstanding footballer. He was a real character on and off the pitch and was an inspiration to us all. One game which particularly stands out among my memories is the World Cup qualifying game at Hampden Park on 9 November 1965. We were playing Italy and had to win to stand a chance of progressing further. There was 100,000 plus inside Hampden, every one of them a Scotland supporter. It was a strength-sapping game and we managed to sneak a goal to win the game 1-0. But what I most remember is the leadership of Billy during those last ten minutes of the game. I think every Scotland player that game was fit to drop from sheer exhaustion, we ran and chased everything that moved. It was the influence of Billy which pushed us to our very limits and kept us going, his type of play was instrumental in those last few minutes. Possession football, passing and running off the ball, creating space and pushing the Italians back into their own half, it was a superb display of leadership.

We would often room together at international matches; his practical jokes were a real source of amusement to all the squad. He was so full of energy, not only for football but for life. He enjoyed everything he did, but more so he wanted everyone else to enjoy themselves as well. It came as a terrible shock to me when I heard that he had passed away, I cannot think of anything negative to say about the man, he was good, honest and genuine, he loved his family and he loved his football and he will be sorely missed.

JOHN GREIG MBE (Rangers, Scotland)

Billy Bremner is a footballing legend. I knew him for a long time, right back to when we were Scottish international schoolboys together at the ages of fourteen or fifteen. Then later as under-23 internationals, when we shared a room when on such call-ups. Naturally, during this period we became very close and I am proud to say maintained our good friendship.

177

Billy was a fierce competitor who you always wanted in your team; in training sessions he was just as committed as during a full game, he pushed himself to the limit of his ability and always gave 100 per cent. His passing was tremendous and he could turn a game with a simple piece of skill which left his opponents bewildered. His ability to stop play, put his foot on the ball and spread it across the pitch is something very few footballers possess. In one movement he could dispossess someone, look up and pass a ball with precision to a team mate. I could never believe his stamina right through ninety minutes and often longer; he would continue to run and play football. I've lost count of the times he started moves in his own half and scored at the other end to finish it off. He loved the game very dearly. As a person he was different to the player on the pitch, greeting players with a smile and warm handshake, the on-the-field activity forgotten.

He had a warm character and was approachable on every front. I genuinely liked him as both a player and a person, and was deeply saddened by his sudden death. There are many people who will remember him for a long time to come as he helped so many during his short life.

DAVID BATTY (Leeds United, Blackburn Rovers, Newcastle United, England)

He encouraged me and taught me a great deal about football. He was a tremendous influence on my career. He was special as a person and as a footballer and manager.

GORDON MCQUEEN (St Mirren, Leeds United, Manchester United, Scotland)

One of the main reasons I joined Leeds United from St Mirren in 1971-72 was Billy Bremner. The large Scottish contingent at Elland Road was one of the healthiest in the English league, friends on and off the field, they were indeed united. As a young professional I knew I had a great deal to learn, and what better mentor could I ask for than Billy Bremner.

From day one he helped me with my game. He possessed a great wit and had a sharp sense of humour, which sometimes eased the passage through arduous training sessions, which were new to me. I recall how exhausted most players were after training; not Billy Bremner, he would sometimes remain out there training, practising crosses, shooting and passing accuracy.

The five-a-side training sessions we held during the week were to his particular liking. He thrived on the competition between his side and the rest, he would treat every tackle and move during these games as though it was of the utmost importance to him, and a few of us understood the ferocity of his sometimes bone-shaking tackle.

On the Saturday of a game he really came to life, especially when that whistle went. His love of football was as infectious as his personality. No matter who our opponents were, Billy would treat them all the same, whether it was a cup final or a friendly match, he gave his all. He was the undoubted master of the reverse pass and if any other player had tried this pass in such a manner I think they would have dislocated a joint, but such was his dexterity that he could commit such passes accurately and apparently without even thinking about it. He had everything, including an ability to single-handedly win games. I've lost count of the important matches he won for Leeds United through his own ability and determination. Together with Johnny Giles, he formed a formidable partnership in the Leeds midfield.

Football has lost one of its finest characters, but his memory will long remain with all who knew him.

HOWARD WILKINSON (Boston United, Leeds United, Sheffield Wednesday)
Billy Bremner epitomised the wonderful Leeds team of the 1960s and 1970s. He was a determined, loyal and honest footballer who always led by example. His passion for the game, and Leeds United and Scotland is now the stuff of legend. At Leeds he is still revered by supporters and throughout the football club. He will never be forgotten.

SIR BOBBY ROBSON (Fulham, West Bromwich Albion, Ipswich Town, PSV Eindhoven, Barcelona, Sporting Lisbon, Porto, Newcastle United, England)

The mention of his name conjures in my mind a fiery-haired, gritty and determined footballer, with an undeserved reputation for being hard. The Billy Bremner I knew was a kind and considerate human being, a person who would go out of his way to speak to you or to help you. I had many titanic struggles with him over the years but he was a footballer I would love to have signed, and he was inspirational and determined, qualities that are rarely seen in a player today. He used to joke about the Geordie accent saying he couldn't understand it, but when he reverted to his Scottish accent I would have to ask him to slow down so I could understand what he was saying. He would laugh and tell me that Geordies were as close to being Scottish as was possible.

I liked so much about Billy Bremner the man and Billy Bremner the footballer, he will hold a special place in football's heart.

PAUL HART (Blackpool, Leeds United, Nottingham Forest, Portsmouth)

What can be said about the complete footballer that has not already been said? Billy Bremner was the ultimate competitor, a truly magnificent player throughout his career, and a dignified human being long after. I played with him in Peter Lorimer's testimonial at Dundee, when his playing days had all but ended. I was astounded by his thirst and appetite for the ball which he pushed around in a majestic manner. It was a proud moment playing on the same pitch as him.

As a boy I would watch him playing on television and often dreamed of acquiring his skill and fight – I very much wanted to be like him. Sadly I never quite managed it, but how many players can attain such high standards? It came as a great shock to me when I heard of his death. Billy Bremner is one of the great footballing legends in the history of the game and I doubt if anyone will ever replace him.

180

TREVOR FRANCIS (Birmingham City, Nottingham Forest, Sampdoria, Sheffield Wednesday, Rangers, England)

Throughout my career I have played against many good teams, but undoubtedly the most outstanding has to be the Leeds team of the early '70s. Captain of that great team was Billy Bremner. He was inspirational as a captain, fiercely competitive, and always led by example. Billy had so many great attributes which helped to make him one of the greatest central midfielders of his generation.

DAVE BASSETT (Wimbledon, Sheffield United, Nottingham Forest, Leicester City, Leeds United)

I played against Billy Bremner just twice. I was a semi-professional with Wimbledon FC at that time, a virtually unknown club in the Southern League and, having overcome a number of hurdles in the preliminary rounds of the FA Cup, we found ourselves drawn to play at Elland Road against the mighty Leeds United, arguably the best team in England. In addition to Billy, the team was packed with international players, including the likes of Johnny Giles, Gordon McQueen, Allan Clarke and Joe Jordan.

What an occasion it was for us! We managed to force a 0-0 draw, thanks to a superlative performance by our goalkeeper, Dickie Guy, who, in addition to making a string of magnificent saves, topped it all by saving a Peter Lorimer penalty. Incidentally, I was the player who gave the penalty away! We lost the replay 1-0 at Selhurst Park, but we were well pleased with our two performances.

In both matches, Billy Bremner was his incomparable self — tough, uncompromising, competitive, fearless. As a footballer, he was a natural winner, as his playing record shows.

In more recent years, I got to know Billy on a more personal basis. We met on quite a few occasions at functions where we were after-dinner speakers, so we were able to enjoy a couple of drinks together and talk about football. He was a lovely man, a gentleman, with an inbuilt modesty that forbade him from talking about his heady achievements as a footballer. In addition to our professional interests, we had one significant thing in common – we were both adopted Yorkshiremen. Bill spent the major part of his professional life in Leeds, I have spent a major chunk of mine in Sheffield, where I still live.

Billy's untimely death is a great loss to football, but I am sure that the memory of the man and his achievements will live on for many years to come.

GRAHAM TAYLOR OBE (Lincoln City, Watford, Aston Villa, England)

Talent; leadership qualities; commitment; Billy Bremner had the lot. But what he had more than anything else was enthusiasm, and without that all other qualities mean nothing. Billy Bremner loved football passionately and it showed in everything he did on the football field. We will all miss him.

HOWARD KENDALL (Preston North End, Everton, Birmingham City, Stoke City, Blackburn Rovers, Sheffield United)

Billy Bremner was a member of that brand of footballers I would describe as hard but fair, certainly one of the most difficult opponents I have ever played against. His passion for the game both as a player, and later as a manager, continues to serve as an example for any player with ambitions to play the game at the highest level. Billy's immense pride when playing for Scotland was always evident whenever he wore his national colours.

This most pugnacious of players will always remind me of the great Leeds United side of the seventies, and whether he was winning trophies with Leeds or coping with the pressures of managing a lower league club Billy always managed to put on a smile.

SAMMY MCILROY (Manchester United, Stoke City, Bury, Macclesfield Town, Morecambe, Northern Ireland)

Billy, for me, epitomised the passion and desire required to be a winner in professional football. Add that to a very high skill factor and you are not far away from the perfect player. A man who gave his all for his team, he will be sadly missed, but never forgotten by anybody who had the privilege to see him play.

ALAN BALL MBE (Blackpool, Everton, Arsenal, Southampton, Manchester City, Portsmouth, Stoke City, Exeter City, England)
I, like everyone else, was shocked when I heard the news about the passing of Billy Bremner.

Being a person directly in contact with Billy, playing against each other for our respective teams, and after having played all over the world against the world's greatest players, I knew that every time I came face to face with Billy it would be the toughest game of my life. I also knew that at the end of the match we would have a marvellous short time, and occasionally a long time, sharing a drink and a laugh together.

It was an honour to have pitted my skills against Billy's throughout the years.

JOE ROYLE (Everton, Manchester City, Bristol City, Norwich City, Oldham Athletic, Ipswich Town, England)
I was a great admirer of Billy Bremner, the player, the man. He was a ferocious competitor and a gentleman with a sense of humour. Everyone in football misses him.

GEORGE BURLEY (Ipswich Town, Sunderland, Ayr United, Derby County, Heart of Midlothian,, Southampton, Scotland)
Billy Bremner will go down as one of the all-time great footballers to represent Scotland. He was a tremendous competitor with undoubtedly the greatest of ability and was a great servant for Scotland over many years.

JIMMY ARMFIELD CBE (Blackpool, Bolton Wanderers, Leeds United, England)
Billy and I got on very well, both during our time together at Elland Road and in the years after. Billy Bremner just lived for football. He loved the game for its own sake and for the

pleasure and privileges it handed him. Despite all the thought of his aggressive stance on the field, I always believed he played with a smile on his face. He was never happier than when he was playing football. Somehow I could never have imagined him as a manager, it would have been impossible for him to pass on the skills and commitment he had . . . and that must have brought frustrations to him. Kind, generous and always ready to put a smile on your face . . . Billy Bremner is already being missed.

JIM SMITH (Aldershot, Halifax Town, Lincoln City, Boston United, Birmingham City, Oxford United, Newcastle United, Portsmouth, Derby County)

I am delighted to say some kind words about Billy Bremner. To me, Billy Bremner epitomises everything that was good about football, with tremendous ability, enthusiasm, determination, and above all, a super person and companion.

I played in a game with Billy in the semi-final of the Northern Intermediate Cup, and he was playing on the right wing – I was playing for Sheffield United and they won 7-0. I always thought then that Billy must be a great player and he was!

DAVID ROCASTLE (Arsenal, Leeds United, Chelsea)

A lot of people say that my game is not too dissimilar to that of the great Billy Bremner. What an honour to be so recognised. When I went to Leeds I was told by so many that I was potentially the Billy Bremner of the modern era. I watched many games in which he played, he was exceptional. When I first joined Leeds, he was the first person to congratulate me and wish me every success. I loved my time at Leeds, it wasn't as if I was given the chance to prove myself, but everything about the place was good. I remember speaking to Billy once and he told me that he thought the manager had not recognised my ability, or used me in the right positions. That's exactly how I felt. When I was moved on I was devastated, and again, it was Billy Bremner who contacted me to tell me not to let the manager's inadequacies undermine my career, or tarnish the good name of Leeds United. What a man he was. Now, here I am at Hull City, following in his footsteps, but not quite so great a player as he was. He was an exceptional person who I will forever respect.

COLIN TODD (Sunderland, Derby County, Birmingham City, Bolton Wanderers, Bradford City, England)
When Billy passed away we lost a gentleman who I always found to be honest, genuine and very likeable. Billy was a gifted player as he proved in his many games for Leeds and Scotland. He was a feared and competitive opponent who gave no quarter and asked for no favours in return. I can recall many a stirring tussle with him during my time at Sunderland and Derby County, but in the bar after the game it was Billy's sense of humour that shone through. The many accolades he received both as a player and in management were well deserved and his passing was an undoubted loss to football.

BARRY FRY (Barnet, Birmingham City, Peterborough United)
Billy Bremner was an example to us all. He gave 150 per cent total commitment in every game he played in. His leadership of men was second to none.

JIMMY HILL OBE (Brentford, Fulham, Coventry City)
Billy Bremner was the kind of midfield player who in recent years appears to have become extinct. A tendency developed to bypass the skilful midfield artists when in possession and overburden them with defensive responsibilities when not. Billy displayed the perfect balance between aggression and creativity. He made life unpleasant for his opponents, whether they had the ball or he did. If you add to that his unrivalled will to win, whether playing for Leeds United or Scotland, you have a player of inestimable value. Whoever coined the phrase 'They don't make them like that these days,' must have had Billy in mind.

185

DAVE MACKAY (Heart of Midlothian, Tottenham Hotspur, Derby County, Doncaster Rovers, Birmingham City, Scotland)
There was no way you can manufacture what Billy had, skill and toughness. He was as bright as a shiny new button both on and off the field, an opponent to be fearful of for his tenacity and commitment. Away from the game, he was a nice person too, a person who would make time to stop and chat to all supporters and his friends. The world of football has lost a legend.

BILL SHANKLY OBE (Preston North End, Grimsby Town, Liverpool, Scotland)
An outstanding footballer, and when I say footballer I mean it in the true sense of the word, he had complete all-round skills. His mere presence on the football field caused many a team serious concern before a ball was ever kicked; such was the stature of the man. As a captain of Leeds and Scotland he was as determined a leader as I can recall, never giving up until the final whistle blew. He possessed an aura which commanded instant respect from other players, something which is indefinable, and which I witnessed very few times during my football career.

The Leeds team of the late sixties and seventies was very much a great side, a match for anyone. Billy Bremner epitomises everything to do with that side, a tough competitor on the field, not only physically, but mentally as well, and off the field a charming good-humoured man. Football needs more players like Billy Bremner.

IAN ST JOHN (Motherwell, Liverpool, Scotland)
Billy was a great person, someone whose company I really enjoyed and we shared a lot of laughs together. He put a smile on your face. In football he was a great player, one of the best. I hated playing against him as you knew he would force you to give the ball up on every occasion he could, he had so much energy I never knew how he kept running over ninety minutes, but he did. He could score goals as well, too often against sides I

represented, including Liverpool. For Scotland, well he has to be one of the best ever.

CRAIG BROWN CBE (Clyde, Preston North End, Motherwell, Scotland)

I remember Billy as an inspirational player and captain, one of the greatest ever to represent Scotland. On a personal note his very good friend and best man at his wedding, Alex Smith, who was assistant manager at Raith Rovers, is also a friend of mine and he speaks in glowing terms of Billy on every occasion. There are few people in football for whom I have more respect than Alex Smith, and I can assure you that his personal recommendation of Billy Bremner, as a man as well as a footballer, is good enough for me.

There have been many famous captains of Scotland but, arguably, Billy Bremner was one of the greatest, certainly highly respected and greatly admired as a footballer and as a leader of men.

ALBERT JOHANNESON (Leeds United, York City)

When I first came to Leeds, one of the people I met as soon as I got here was Billy Bremner and there was something about him which at once put me in awe of him. He was then physically the slightest of players but he possessed a strong personality and will, and in his mind he would not accept defeat at anything. He knew what he wanted and he expected the same commitment from everyone who played in his side, which was the same in training as it was in First Division matches or Cup games.

When he put on the shirt of Leeds United on a Saturday he wore it with pride and passion. He would never have anyone say a bad word about the club or any of its players; personal criticism was something he understood, and maintained that it should remain within the club.

When I played in the 1965 FA Cup final I know that I really badly underachieved on the day – it was a nerve-wracking experience and I confess I was terrified. Billy told me to forget the surroundings, forget what the newspapers were saying about me being the first black footballer to play at Wembley in an FA Cup final and not to dwell on how good our opponents that day were. 'Keep things simple, make the easy pass, and run until you cannot run any more.' It was good simple advice, he always made it look so easy, but it wasn't. Billy was a great player, one of the best I have ever seen.

Whenever someone within the club was suffering a loss of form or confidence, it was Billy who would first approach them and offer words of advice. Beneath that tough image there was a really nice man, he's a person I will always have lots of respect for.

CHARLIE GEORGE (Arsenal, Derby County, Southampton, England)

Billy and I go back a long way, there are few players who I could honestly say were top class but Billy Bremner is one of those who I place in this category. Whenever you played against him you knew you were in for a real battle, not only a physical battle, but a mental challenge. Sometimes I thought he was one step ahead of everyone else in his vision of the game. There were times when playing against him was like opposing him in a game of chess as he rallied his side and tried to outmanoeuvre your every move.

Physically he was as tough as they come; I can never recall him pulling out of a challenge, and likewise, I can never recall him going into a challenge half-heartedly. There were few footballers who could contemplate beating him in the tackle. As a footballer he was complete: vision, style, skill, ability, desire, and the absolute must for any world-class player – he was a match winner. I don't know how many times he would pull something a bit special out of the hat and take Leeds onto greater achievements.

No matter what attitude he displayed during the game, he was always the first one to console or congratulate the opposition after the final whistle. He was a genuine footballer. As a person he was full of life, a real character, if ever you were down he had the temperament and personality to lift you. I will always remember him because he made time to speak to anyone, and always had a smile on his face. Billy Bremner was a major part of the Leeds success story; it would be fair to say, Billy Bremner was Leeds United. He is greatly missed by thousands of people worldwide, and not only in the world of football.

BRIAN TALBOT (Ipswich Town, Arsenal, West Bromwich Albion, England)

I was sorry to hear of the sad news about Billy, but you can only remember him in the good times, and what a great player he was. I was only starting my career in the 1970s and I remember the battles we had when Ipswich played Leeds in the FA Cup epic, and Leeds were the best team in England, if not Europe. An all-action player who didn't know the meaning of defeat, he gave everything for his team in every game. A leader of men.

MICHEL PLATINI (St Etienne, Juventus, France, President of UEFA)

He was regarded as being tough and strong, everyone knows his name and who he is.

SIR ALEX FERGUSON (Dunfermline Athletic, Rangers, Falkirk, St Mirren, Aberdeen, Manchester United, Scotland)

Billy Bremner may have been small in stature but in terms of footballing ability, courage and enthusiasm he was a giant. In my opinion he was without doubt one of the greatest midfield players that Scotland has ever produced and unquestionably the finest captain Leeds United have ever had.

I got to know Billy Bremner through a mutual friend, Alex Smith, and I am proud to say that later we became friends also. He possessed such a single minded will-to-win character that I find it hard to think of anyone who came anywhere close to him in those terms.

What a marvellous servant he was to Leeds United. I understand that he played over 750 competitive games for the Elland

Road club and scored well in excess of 100 goals. Those statistics alone speak volumes, but at the same time tell only a small part of the story.

His determination to succeed sometimes overpowered him, particularly in his early days, but had you taken away the tigerish side of his personality then he just wouldn't have been the same individual. What he lacked in height and weight he made up for twice over with his 'never say die' attitude.

He also possessed a marvellous demeanour. I remember when he was sacked by Leeds United, he refused to show any resentment or utter a bad word against the club. There wasn't a trace of bitterness because Leeds was, and always would be, his club.

He will go down in Leeds United folklore as one of the all-time greats and no one could possibly change that. One thing that did delight me was to see several Manchester United fans present at his funeral. They had put aside that traditional rivalry between the two clubs to turn up and pay tribute to a very fine footballer and a great man. It was a marvellous gesture on their part and I felt immensely proud of their humanity.

Anyone who knew Billy Bremner will always miss him. I know I shall because he was a man who had a lasting effect on everyone he met.

JOE BAKER (Hibernian, Arsenal, Nottingham Forest, England)
I've played against some hard men in my time, players who would kick you off the pitch because that was the only way they know how to stop you. Although Billy Bremner was regarded as one of those sort of players, he was different. He could actually play football himself. He outwitted you with his skill and brain, and wound up anyone who displayed weakness on the pitch. Whenever I met him away from the pitch, he would always talk about how superior Scotland was over England, in everything. He once told me he thought I acted like I was Scottish – I never understand what he meant by that, until someone explained that we were standing at the bar and it was my round. Through

190

gritted teeth, I did buy him a drink. Lovely fellow, great company, and a devout Scot.

ALAN BIRCHENALL MBE (Sheffield United, Chelsea, Crystal Palace, Leicester City)

I played against him on many occasions for Sheffield United, Chelsea, Crystal Palace and Leicester in the old First Division. When I think, without doubt Leeds had the most awesome side of the late '60s and early '70s. If I can just tell this little story that sums up Billy.

I was playing against Leeds at Elland Road – let's say I tripped and as I rolled on the ground Billy accidentally used my head as a stepping stone. I carried on with the game but I had to be bandaged up as blood was pouring from four stud marks in my forehead. After the game I asked my old team mate at Sheffield, who was now playing for Leeds at the time, Mick Jones, if any of the Leeds players could drop me off at the station after the game as I was not travelling back with Chelsea to London. Billy offered to drop me off at the station and there I was sat beside him, my forehead wrapped in bandages with blood seeping through from the four stud marks. Not a word passed between us until we got to Leeds station. I thanked Billy for the lift, he turned to me and said in his own inimitable way, 'That looks nasty Birch, better get that seen to.' Great player, great character. Sadly missed.

I hope that little story about my memory brings a smile to your face as it does me when I tell it now.

DENIS LAW (Huddersfield Town, Manchester City, Torino, Manchester United, Scotland)

He was such a character, and I loved to be in his company both on and off the pitch. He was so bright and intelligent and when he talked he spoke a great deal of common sense, be it on football, management or life in general. As a footballer he was great, unique and Scottish. As a manager he never let anyone down and maybe should have been made boss long before he was. Billy was a great guy.

DON WESTON (Wrexham, Rotherham United, Leeds United)
Wee Billy Bremner has been the life and soul of Leeds United for over three decades now. I first met him when I joined the club from Rotherham in 1962, he had an awesome reputation even back then when his career was just starting. A gentleman off the field, he was ruthless and uncompromising on it; he had a winning mentality in everything he did. When it came to kick-off time, Billy would be focused and rallying round everyone, making sure they knew how important it was to win for the boss and for the fans. I remember him trying to square up to me once after a game, I missed a couple of sitters and he thought that I had let the pressure get to me; when I turned to look at him, he was almost a foot smaller than me, I couldn't help but laugh at the image of the pair of us, and gave him a big cuddle instead. Thankfully he saw the funny side of it too, and laughed with me. Billy will always remain Mr Leeds United.

KEITH NEWTON (Blackburn Rovers, Everton, Burnley, England)
As a footballer there are few who were blessed with so much talent as that of Billy Bremner. He could pass, shoot, head and score – he had everything. He was a passionate footballer keen to help his colleagues, and would run and run for his beloved Leeds United and Scotland until he had used every ounce of energy in his body. He did not know the meaning of the term 'lost cause' and would play out a full ninety minutes, refusing to accept defeat until the referee blew the whistle to end the game.

Versatility was synonymous to his game, he could play anywhere and give a sparkling performance. I don't really think he completely realised how many footballers and managers were in complete awe of him, and even after he stopped playing and managing, Billy Bremner remained a giant among his peers. I don't think there will ever be another footballer who could ever be like him.

GRAHAM CARR (Northampton Town)

I remember Billy Bremner the footballer with fondness, I always thought I was tough, but he epitomised spiritual toughness as well as strength, belief, and character. As a manager, he is class, quality, he just needs to walk into a dressing room and people shut up and listen. There isn't many people like him in the game, one of a kind, a genius of sorts.

GLENN AITKEN (Gillingham, Wimbledon)

What a character he was, on the pitch there were few who could or would try to stop him. A superb passer of the ball, a goalscorer, and a born leader, and a gentleman too, but not until the game was over. Billy always made you feel as though you were important, special almost. The game lost a true character and what makes British football so wonderful, when he passed away. He'll be forever missed and never replaced.

DICKIE GUY (Wimbledon)

You just have to say his name and people listen, Billy was such a character. It was a privilege to meet him and to challenge his beloved Leeds United in one of Wimbledon FC's greatest games of the era. We lost, but only just. Right after the game, the first player to shake our hands and congratulate us on some wonderful performances, was Billy Bremner. A truly memorable occasion, a truly memorable character.

ANON – BOOK OF FOOTBALL 1971

His bones might be constructed of steel and his muscles of reinforced concrete. His energy might be the by-product of an atomic power station. He just does not know how to stop. There are two men in football who have sometimes been likened to James Cagney. One is Billy Shankly, the other is Billy Bremner. But Cagney, even if he could play the game, could never have achieved what Billy has achieved without a machine gun in his hands.

ERIC THORNTON – Author *Leeds United and Don Revie*
It might be said that over a decade he has successfully completed the transition from a spitting wildcat to a matured international star . . . He's very much in love with Leeds United, and everything that goes with it. That includes the Boss, and one cannot say that about all players and managers.

ANON – Gates of Elland Road – 9 December 1998
Good night Billy. God Bless. Thanks x. From a Man U Fan.

PUDSEY WHITES – Gates of Elland Road – 9 December 1998
In memory of the greatest ever Scottish Yorkshireman. Love Always, from the Pudsey Whites.

ANON – Gates of Elland Road – 9 December 1998
King Billy. Simply the Best.

GRAHAM KELLY (Ex Chief Executive of the Football Association)
Billy was such an inspiring leader and competitor on the pitch for Leeds United and Scotland that it will be a long time before football people stop talking about players in the 'Billy Bremner mould'. The incredibly successful Leeds team of the 1960s and 1970s was clearly built around this brilliant midfielder.

In almost seventeen years as a player he totalled some 770 first-team appearances and won the lot: League Championship, FA Cup, Football League Cup, two European Finals and the 'Footballer of the Year' award in 1970.

Billy was one of the all-time greats who would command a fee of several million pounds in today's transfer market. He was a character and we will miss him.

JIM FARRY (Ex Chief Executive of the Scottish Football Association)
With fifty-four appearances in a Scotland jersey, Billy Bremner will be remembered as a powerful defender, a creative

194

playmaker and a leading captain of the national team. His experience was crucial in taking Scotland to its first World Cup Final tournament in a generation, in West Germany in 1974, and his leadership contributed greatly to Scotland's unbeaten record that summer. His portrait hangs in the SFA offices as the third member of Scottish Football's Hall of Fame, granted for those who reach fifty caps for Scotland. He therefore retains a special place in Scottish football and his memory will always be with us.

20

WHAT HE SAID ABOUT THEM

GARY SPRAKE

A frustrating bloody goalkeeper – if he had tried a bit harder and concentrated more fully on improving his game, instead of believing he was the best, then he would have made a decent keeper. As people we have our differences, I don't hide the fact that I have issues with some of things he has done in his life, but that's for Gary to consider and reflect upon. What's done is done. So far as a professional footballer goes, not one of the wisest or most respected; despite that, he could pull off some unbelievable saves. That's as positive as I can get about the man.

PAUL REANEY

A lovely man and so quick with a football at his feet. He had a level head and tended to keep his cool in most situations. He was a bit of a comedian though, and you could rely on him to break the ice on difficult discussions. He should have received far more recognition than he did. He had a great sense of humour as well and always saw the funny side of football and life. If you needed to lighten the atmosphere or lift the tension then Paul was the man who could do that, he was naturally very likeable.

TERRY COOPER

He was such a rounded player who could turn defence into attack with one tackle. Terry took the game seriously and I don't know many players who concentrated so intensely throughout an entire game. He was a great lad to have around, and a confidant, too, I respected him highly. To be honest, I would walk hundreds of miles to help and support Terry Cooper. I enjoyed playing alongside Terry and he instilled confidence with his mere presence.

JACK CHARLTON

What can I say about this giant of man that hasn't already been said? Jack was the ultimate professional. Known more for his heading and defending ability, his skill and control with a ball at his feet were also incredible, though I'm not always certain that he knew where he was going with the ball! Jack could head a ball as far many players could kick it, and his heading accuracy was awesome, I'm certain he would have been able to drop a headed ball onto a half crown piece from twenty yards. His antics used to have me in fits of laughter, he was so passionate about football, Leeds and England. The only thing was, when him and me used to have a go at each other, no other bugger could understand what we were saying: angry and passionate Geordies and Scots don't make for eloquent speeches.

NORMAN HUNTER

Not many footballers get by with having just one foot, I don't mean physically you understand, yet Norman Hunter did. Ask him to pass the ball with his right foot and it was always going to be a challenge for him. In training, if I wanted to put him off, I would always go for his left leg. Only joking of course; Norman was a class act, great in the dressing room, supportive on and off the pitch and he could play a bit as well. As an opponent, for England, Leeds (in training) or for Bristol City, he was a noisy bully who strutted round the pitch like he owned it; not many questioned that, not even me. Norman was one tough cookie, and a lovely man.

PETER LORIMER

A fellow Scotsman with a great sense of humour and a fantastic footballer, too. Peter was as determined to succeed as I was. He would do anything for the sake of Leeds United. I saw him score so many goals that he created for himself from nothing, others he scored through his ferocious shooting ability. I would do anything to get out of the way of his shots in training, it was said that some of the balls he fired off were moving upwards of seventy miles per hour. I think they were faster than that. A good and close friend.

ALLAN CLARKE
If there was a better goal getter in the British game than Allan Clarke then I never saw them play. Allan was like a ghost in the penalty area, he would drift in, almost unnoticed, behind defenders and finish so many of our moves with a goal. He had so many different aspects to his game. As a front man he could hold up the ball or split defences wide open with his passing. He scored plenty with his head too. I wouldn't have swapped him for anyone else, an honest hard-working footballer and man, a good and loyal pal. The best.

MICK JONES
If any one player in that Leeds team deserved to win more honours than they did then it was Mick Jones. He was much more athletic than I was and could jump almost a high as Big Jack (Charlton). Mick never said never, he chased every ball and was the perfect goal-scoring partner for Allan Clarke. His performances merited greater international recognition than he got, he was as good a forward in England at the time.

JOHN GILES
I was fortunate to be in the same team as this wonderful footballer and man. John Giles to my mind had it all, he had an authoritative presence on and off the pitch that could intimidate if you let it. Not that he ever deliberately imposed himself in such a way. He was a distinguished footballer who could do anything he wanted with the ball. Some of his ball tricks in training and during games were sublime. Between us we imposed ourselves on every game and every opponent but it

198

does make me laugh when people say we were a formidable force together. In my opinion John Giles was the driving force that pushed us on. He was an inspiration not only to me but to thousands of football fans. His football writing is second to none too, so be aware Mr Harrison, he is the role model you should aspire too.

EDDIE GRAY

I could talk about Eddie Gray and what he brought to Leeds United all day. I cannot recall hearing anyone say a bad word about him. His football skills were stunning; he seemed to dance round other players like they weren't there, all the while moving forward into the opponent's penalty area. That left-foot skill would be worth millions in football now, Eddie is one of the few players who caused my jaw to drop in awe at his skill. As a person they honestly don't come any nicer, albeit he could moan a fair bit, nearly as much as me some would say!

DAVID HARVEY

David Harvey was unlucky not to make more appearances for Leeds and for Scotland. He was, in my mind, the better of the two first-team goalkeepers we had at Elland Road during my time there. That's not through personal opinion but through professional opinion. He was solid, dependable and safe; he could be relied upon to do the right thing. He was agile and quite fancied himself as a forward; after that penalty miss in the Charity Shield final I think he gave up on the idea of swapping positions. I rate him so highly as to suggest that he could have been, and possibly is, one of Scotland's greatest ever goalkeepers.

MICK BATES

Mick could come in to the team and fill in any role that was asked of him, defender, midfield, forward and he always seemed to do well. At any other club he would have been a regular first teamer, but we had so much quality throughout that he tended to miss out on more appearances. Mick always had time for others, he would make sure that supporters always got the autograph and was an integral part of our team. Mick was a personable and likeable man, he could play football a fair bit too.

ALBERT JOHANNESON

Albert was in many ways the author of his own downfall. When he joined Leeds United the rest of the team stood open-mouthed, drooling over his ball skills and trickery. He was a bloody excellent player and had so much pace and strength, he was a great athlete. Over the years, we all worked closely with Albert, trying to keep him focused and motivated. Many a time during a game he would devastate other teams with his blistering pace and finishing, yet on other occasions he would hide and look timid and impotent. He was very much a confidence player and we certainly tried to instil plenty of confidence in him. As we got more successful, Albert seemed to drift away from us, he rarely showed the consistent performances we knew he could. Some of the racial abuse he would get from opposition players and fans was disgraceful. I would try to protect him from that, so would the rest of the lads. It's outrageous to know that you have fellow professional, highly respected and big club players, treating someone like they all too regularly did Albert, calling him 'Nigger' or 'Sambo'. I confess I have, over the years, delivered physical hurt and retribution to many of those who so damaged Albert. If I told you some of the names you would be mortified.

Eventually, we found out that he was drinking, not the odd snifter before a game or at half time, but whole bloody bottles of Scotch. We would often have a bottle with us in the dressing room, a quick dram before you went out onto the pitch before a game on a wintry afternoon never did any of us any harm. After one game, I think it was at Nottingham Forest, Albert had come off early. At full time we made our way back into the dressing room to find bottle empty, Albert had drank the f—— lot and was laid pissed on the floor. Thereafter, it was virtually all over for him at Leeds. The boss didn't like it. He had become a liability, a drain on us all. We all tried to get him off the sauce and to believe in himself, but it never seemed to work. Eventually he moved on to York City and never achieved anything else in the game. It's a crying shame as he was a lovely lad and a fine footballer on his day. The Leeds United ex-players association did an awful lot to help Albert after his career was over, but he always pissed the money we gave him up the wall. All very sad, I do feel for the fellow.

DON REVIE

Words cannot describe how great a man he was, he was massive, not only in physical height but in stature. People would cross the street to shake his hand and the Leeds supporters held him in the highest esteem. I think most of us would do as the boss asked – if he said run through that brick wall, then we would. He was a deeply caring person and did things that you never expected him to, certainly the football press have over the years described a totally different man and manager to the person we all knew. He wanted everything to be just right for his players, his ethic was that if he got the basics right then the players had nothing to contend with but playing for Leeds United. Right down to relaxing walks and diet, the boss concentrated on getting us to feel wanted and as one, and it worked. Some people have tried to diminish his professionalism and sold kiss-and-tell type stories for the sake of a few quid. I would never say anything negative about the boss, simply because there is nothing negative to say about him. He will always be loved and respected by those important to him. As for the rest, well they are insignificant and their thoughts don't really matter.

BRIAN CLOUGH

It's no secret that he and I are not the best of pals. In fact I will go so far as to say that I dislike him as much as I do Bob Stokoe. Isn't it peculiar how they both come from the North-East! Maybe it was a clash of personalities, maybe it was just the fact that he was a jumped-up arrogant sod of a man who wanted and generally got everything his own way, till he came to Leeds. Neither I, nor

Leeds United had anything to prove to Brian Clough, we were proven winners. At that time, he was not.

I despised the way he always publicly taunted us with being a dirty team. We had every right to feel reticent when he came in; everyone in the game knew that the club had made a balls-up of the whole thing. I think we all expected someone to be promoted from within the ranks, Johnny Giles or me maybe. I won't deny I wanted it. Brian was a prick, he tried to change everything overnight, our style, our personality, and to suffocate the memory of the boss (Don Revie). He went missing, before, during and after games; not us – we were there, a consistent. Player power didn't get him the sack, his arrogant attitude and total lack of attention to detail cost him his job. We were like a rudderless ship lost at sea. He knows full well how I felt about him when he was at Leeds. I couldn't hide it or keep quiet about it. He wrecked the team, created an attitude of mistrust and back-biting, and brought in his own stooges, all of whom didn't meet the high standards we had set. Some of them were decent players, just not good enough for Leeds, that's all.

Brian was out of his depth but would never admit it. I tried to help him, tried to give him advice, tried to listen. What more did he expect me to do? I was glad when he left the club. Whenever I bumped into him, we always acknowledged each other's existence – with a casual glance or a dirty look, always without ever speaking. I never liked him before he came to Leeds, and I sure as hell didn't like him thereafter – an overrated, highly strung autocrat.

PELE
A gentleman and idol to all Brazilian soccer fans and football lovers worldwide. We met Brazil in one of their warm-up games for the 1966 World Cup at Hampden. I was ordered to stick to him like glue, and even if he went off the field for attention then I had to be there to pick him up when he came back on. The first chance I got I had to let him know I was on the park. I hit him with a real bone-cruncher of a tackle. If I thought that would be

enough to unnerve him, I was to receive a real shock. We both went for a high ball jumping together and I thought I held all the aces and he would pull out. I was wrong, the next thing I knew I was on the ground with a cracker of a black eye! No matter how close I got, he somehow made space for himself. There is no player in the world who could mark him out of the game, then or now!

BOBBY CHARLTON

He moves so sweetly with the ball I could watch him play all day. His change of pace and direction are phenomenal and there are goalkeepers who can vouch for the terrific power and accuracy he has in either foot. When Bobby figures on the team sheet of our opponents the boss does not come any of the patter about 'not worrying about the others'. His instructions are sharp and right to the point: 'Cut out Bobby and we are halfway there.' And that is as big a tribute as Don Revie and Leeds United can pay to anyone.

ON THE CURRENT LEEDS UNITED (1995)

All the ex-players want Leeds United to do well. We are still very passionate. I'd love to see the club on the European victory trail again. The UEFA Cup is probably the hardest of all the European campaigns to win, partly because there are so many rounds.

FATHER (POP)

My father was the biggest influence on my football career, no one will ever come close to him, but Don Revie was a close second.

NOBBY STILES

Folk say I was a tough player but Nobby Stiles was far tougher than I ever was. He has the strength of a rhinoceros, especially when he went into the tackle, and clattered you from behind. Then he would get up; give you a cheeky smile, before helping you to your feet and shaking your hand, enquiring to see if you are okay. If you dared say you were okay, then he would come back at you for more, later in the game. He had masses of energy and skill and he knew how to spoil a game. His timing in the tackle and positional sense would suffocate many forward lines, and I know some centre forwards who were just scared of him. Despite everything, Nobby is a real character and a good football man, who I have a lot of time for.

JOCK STEIN

I honestly used to tremble when I was in his company; the man is a true legend of Scottish and European football. The Celtic boys worshipped him, and rightly so. Jock knew everything there was to know about Scottish football and he scoured the land looking for fresh up-and-coming talent. He was a seven-days-a-week manager, his life was Glasgow Celtic and Scotland. He and the boss had mutual respect for one another, though they could also be damning. I once saw Jock lay into a well-known Scotland forward at a Celtic reserve match. It was a nothing game, and the player clearly wasn't going to push himself to the extreme and risk getting hurt playing for the reserves. He pulled out of a tackle, allowing the opposition to get the ball. It wasn't a major sin. Yet afterwards, big Jock was fuming and told the player he was in the reserves for a month until he had earned the right to wear the Celtic first-team shirt.

WILLIE HENDERSON

I used to love being with wee Willie on my Scotland trips; he was a right joker and character, always good for a laugh. Put a football his way and he could do magic with it. There will only ever be one Willie Henderson; they broke the mould when he was created. You would never share a secret with him – it would be passed around the dressing room within minutes. Away from the game he liked a dram or two and we shared a fair number between us. The best thing about Willie was that he could always put a smile on your face.

BILLY MCNEILL

I learned so much from Billy McNeill during the early part of my Scotland career. What a captain he was, nothing ever passed him by and he really rallied the players and got us all motivated. Tough as rhino hide too, nothing hurt him, insults, kicks, punches, Billy laughed them all off and could give a stare that would terrify Frankenstein. Over the years I have been fortunate to play alongside many captains and leaders of men; Billy McNeill stands out as one of the best. You just had to respect him, he had a dressing-room presence that made you listen to him because he knew what he was talking about. Why he never really succeeded as a manager I cannot say, a mystery.

ALAN BALL

He should have joined Leeds when he had the chance – we would have worked great together. I really liked Alan as a footballer and as a person and, although it pains me to say it, he has done well for himself at other, lesser clubs than Leeds. He was so easy to wind up on the pitch, and his squeaky voice would always get heard by the referee. I once faced him in a league game at Elland Road when he was running rings round us. So I moved up behind him as a throw-in was about to be taken. I called him a puff and a light-weight who I could knock down without knowing it. He didn't like that and turned round to confront me, in that high-pitched tone he screamed, 'F—— hell, Bremner, I am going to do you in a minute.' Of course the referee heard and came over to warn him. That kept him quiet for the rest of the game.

BOB STOKOE

The man is just odd. I have to say, it never sat well with me how he ran to the newspapers to sell his story about the boss and after our altercation at the Park Royal hotel. I generally saw him as a twat and a money grabber thereafter. I wasn't alone in the game in having no respect for the man. He really rubbed it in when his Sunderland team beat us at Wembley in the 1973 FA Cup final. Of all the f—— games we didn't want to lose, it was that one. I have never heard any manager call opposition players and club staff such foul and abusive names as he did that day. Despite winning the Cup he was still very bitter, or could it be envious, certainly that is the only reason I can think why such an attitude prevailed.

FRANZ BECKENBAUER

What a man he was when he was playing. So thoughtful and yet so cynical he epitomised for me all that German football was about. Strong, disciplined and direct with clinical finishing. Franz orchestrated all that so that the players around him could deliver. He was as solid as a rock in the 1975 European Cup final and kept the referee on side with compliments on his fine decision making! As you know, it paid off and worked for them. I always thought he was a bit of a big girl's blouse though, looked the part but not altogether flawless.

SUPPORTERS OF LEEDS UNITED

I think they are the finest in the world, they stick with us through thick and thin and are fair enough to applaud good football, even if it comes from the other team. If we were able to win anything through passion then those supporters would have won us everything. They are the best.

BILLY BREMNER & LEEDS UNITED AFC

'I have hit the headlines often enough since making my debut for Leeds United, and not always in a manner which I would wish. For I am blessed (or should it be cursed) with a temperament that matches my red thatch. Despite my size I'm a robust player by nature. It's something born and bred in me, and I cannot change it. I doubt if I would, even if it were possible, because then I feel sure I would lose the spark which has helped me to make such a success of professional football.'

'I genuinely hate to see an opponent get the ball. It is my job to see that this doesn't happen, if possible. I go in hard, but fairly, but the temperament sometimes erupts in the heat of the moment.'

'I've taken a bit of stick in my time from opponents and their supporters, but there's one thing I would like to get clear right now. I do not go out looking for trouble. In fact the way some folk describe me you would think I was a regular fire-eater. The plain fact is that I set out to do a job as a footballer. It's as simple as that.'

'I make no apology for saying that I'm a Don Revie fan. To my mind, what this fellow has done for Leeds United since he took over as manager is little short of miraculous. I have known the boss ever since he took over at Elland Road, in his first managerial job, and I think along exactly the same lines as he does when it comes to soccer planning and tactics.'

'They say that I have become indoctrinated with the Leeds brand of soccer, and that's true. I have been with the club since I left school in Stirling and I have known United in the bad days as well as the good ones. After emerging from the Second Division and establishing ourselves in the top flight, we have gone on to make a positive contribution to entertaining football.'

'Team spirit is a big factor for any successful team and we have it here. Most of us were brought up together on the ground staff and that is an important factor in our success.'

'Football is not all about the skill factor. It is about whether you are determined enough and have a greater desire to win games than the opposition.'

'There has been so much more enjoyment for me in my football this season, and when we hardened professionals start to enjoy this game it's only a matter of time before the fans notice the difference. I never thought that the rather unfortunate image we had of back-chatting referees and refusing to accept decisions had an effect on my game. But it must have done. Once you show dissatisfaction and start to argue you're obviously not concentrating your whole attention on the game. You may as well be sitting in the dressing room.'

'Looking back I was fiery because if I saw someone kick my own players I got a bit upset about it. Some teams had vendettas against us. They disliked us intensely because we were the team to beat in that era, so they always tried harder against us.'

'It is rather fashionable these days to take a swipe at British football, but if there are things wrong with football, then it's these people, these onlookers with a death wish. There are, of course, things I would like to see altered, but a change in attitudes is the quality I would most like to see. I look round the game now and see that, technically and in fitness, it has never been more advanced.'

'I loved Leeds and Leeds United, but boy, believe me, Scotland has everything any man could ever want. It's the world's greatest country.'

'Side before self every time.'

'If there was things I could change in my career? I would love that loose ball to go into the net (and not just wide) against Brazil in the World Cup finals; we deserved to win that game, I should have scored.'

'I should never have taken the stick and abuse from Brian Clough and Bob Stokoe, I should have laughed in their faces before kicking them both in the bollocks and reminding them that there really was only one "Boss".'

'I would love to have lifted the European Cup trophy, as winners, for every Leeds United supporter in the land, and for my Pop.'

'I would shake the hand of every Leeds United supporter and tell them to stick with the club and to always laugh in the face of adversity, you deserve the best, stay strong.'

'Always remember, football is a wonderfully emotive game, and it's important, but your family is more important and all encompassing. Love and respect your family, love and respect your team thereafter.'

Billy Bremner was an idol to thousands of football supporters around the globe. Tenacity, enthusiasm, and absolute quality are attributes we rarely see in one footballer, yet Billy possessed the lot. He was an exceptional role model. I doubt if the great Leeds success story of the '60s and '70s would be have been so dramatic or occurred at all had it not been for him. He single-handedly masterminded many victories which ultimately took Leeds onto greater glories. Elland Road and football will never be the same without him.

Paul Harrison

PLAYING CAREER TABLES

SCOTLAND INTERNATIONAL PLAYING RECORD

ECQ: – European Championship Qualifier. WCQ: – World Cup Qualifier WCF: – World Cup Finals

Date	Competition	Venue	Opponent	Score	Attendance	Other
8.5.1965	Friendly	Hampden Park	Spain	0-0	60,146	Debut
13.10.1965	WCQ	Hampden Park	Poland	1-2	107,580	
9.11.1965	WCQ	Hampden Park	Italy	1-0	100,393	
7.12.1965	WCQ	Naples	Italy	0-3	79,000	
2.4.1966	ECQ	Hampden Park	England	3-4	134,000	
18.6.1966	Friendly	Hampden Park	Portugal	0-1	24,000	
25.6.1966	Friendly	Hampden Park	Brazil	1-1	74,933	
22.10.1966	Home International	Cardiff	Wales	1-1	32,500	
16.11.1966	Home International	Hampden Park	Northern Ireland	2-1	45,281	
15.4.1967	Friendly	Wembley	England	3-2	99,063	
22.11.1967	Friendly	Hampden Park	Wales	3-2	57,472	
24.2.1968	Friendly	Hampden Park	England	1-1	134,000	
16.10.1968	Friendly	Copenhagen	Denmark	0-1	12,000	Captain
6.11.1968	WCQ	Hampden Park	Austria	2-1	80,856	Captain, 1 goal
11.12.1968	WCQ	Nicosia	Cyprus	5-0	10,000	Captain
16.4.1969	WCQ	Hampden Park	West Germany	1-1	115,000	Captain
3.5.1969	Home International	Wrexham	Wales	5-3	18,765	Captain, 1 goal
6.5.1969	Home International	Hampden Park	Northern Ireland	1-1	7,483	Captain
10.5.1969	Home International	Wembley	England	1-4	89,902	Captain
17.5.1969	WCQ	Hampden Park	Cyprus	8-0	39,095	Captain

Date	Competition	Venue	Opponent	Score	Attendance	Notes
21.9.1969	Friendly	Dublin	Republic of Ireland	1-1	30,000	Captain
22.10.1969	WCQ	Hamburg	West Germany	2-3	72,000	Captain
5.11.1969	WCQ	Vienna	Austria	0-2	11,000	Captain
15.5.1971	Home International	Cardiff	Wales	0-0	19,068	Booked
22.5.1971	Home International	Wembley	England	1-3	91,469	Captain
13.10.1971	ECQ	Hampden Park	Portugal	2-1	58,612	Captain
10.11.1971	ECQ	Pittodrie	Belgium	1-0	36,500	Captain
1.12.1971	Friendly	Amsterdam	Netherlands	1-2	18,000	Captain
20.5.1972	Home International	Hampden Park	Northern Ireland	2-0	39,710	Captain
24.5.1972	Home International	Hampden Park	Wales	1-0	21,332	Captain
27.5.1972	Home International	Hampden Park	England	0-1	119,325	Captain
29.6.1972	Brazilian Independence Cup	Belo Horizonte	Yugoslavia	2-2	4,000	Captain
2.7.1972	Brazilian Independence Cup	Porto Alegre	Czechoslovakia	0-0	15,000	Captain
5.7.1972	Brazilian Independence Cup	Rio de Janeiro	Brazil	0-1	130,000	Captain
18.10.1972	WCQ	Copenhagen	Denmark	4-1	31,000	Captain
15.11.1972	WCQ	Hampden Park	Denmark	2-0	47,109	Captain
14.2.1973	Friendly	Hampden Park	England	0-5	48,470	Captain
16.5.1973	Home International	Hampden Park	Northern Ireland	1-2	39,018	Substitute
19.5.1973	Home International	Wembley	England	0-1	95,950	Captain
22.6.1973	Friendly	Berne	Switzerland	0-1	10,000	Captain
30.6.1973	Friendly	Hampden Park	Brazil	0-1	70,000	Captain
26.9.1973	WCQ	Hampden Park	Czechoslovakia	2-1	100,000	Captain
14.11.1973	Friendly	Hampden Park	West Germany	1-1	58,235	Captain
11.5.1973	Home International	Hampden Park	Northern Ireland	0-1	53,775	Captain
14.5.1974	Home International	Hampden Park	Wales	2-0	41,969	Captain
18.5.1974	Home International	Hampden Park	England	2-0	94,487	Captain
1.6.1974	Friendly	Bruges	Belgium	2-1	7,769	Captain

SCOTLAND INTERNATIONAL PLAYING RECORD—*contd*

Date	Competition	Venue	Opponent	Score	Attendance	Other
6.6.1974	Friendly	Oslo	Norway	2-1	18,432	Captain
14.6.1974	WCF	Dortmund	Zaire	2-0	30,000	Captain
18.6.1974	WCF	Frankfurt	Brazil	0-0	62,000	Captain
22.6.1974	WCF	Frankfurt	Yugoslavia	1-1	56,000	Captain
20.11.1974	ECQ	Hampden Park	Spain	1-2	92,100	Captain, 1 goal
5.2.1975	ECQ	Valencia	Spain	1-1	60,000	Captain
3.9.1975	Friendly	Copenhagen	Denmark	1-0	40,300	Captain

Career total – Fifty-four appearances, Three goals

One appearance, Scotland v Scottsh League XI, 1963

One appearance, Rest of the World v Wales, 1968

FOOTBALL LEAGUE CUP (LEEDS UNITED)

Date	Round	Venue	Opponent	Score	Attendance	Other
23.11.1960	3	Saltergate	Chesterfield	4-0	2,021	1 goal
5.12.1961	4	The Dell	Southampton	4-5	13,448	
13.9.1961	1	Elland Road	Brentford	4-1	4,517	
4.10.1961	2	Elland Road	Huddersfield Town	3-2	10,023	1 goal (pen)
12.12.1961	3	Millmoor	Rotherham Utd	1-1	10,899	
15.12.1961	3 replay	Elland Road	Rotherham Utd	1-2	6,385	
22.10.1963	3	Elland Road	Swansea City	0-2	10,748	
23.9.1964	2	Elland Road	Huddersfield Town	2-3	9,837	
13.9.1966	2	Elland Road	Newcastle Utd	1-0	18,131	
4.10.1966	3	Deepdale	Preston NE	1-1	15,049	
12.10.1966	3 replay	Elland Road	Preston NE	3-0	17,221	
7.11.1966	4	Upton Park	West Ham Utd	0-7	27,474	
13.9.1967	2	Elland Road	Luton Town	3-1	11,473	
15.11.1967	4	Roker Park	Sunderland	2-0	29,536	
13.12.1967	5	Elland Road	Stoke City	2-0	24,558	1 goal
17.1.1967	Semi F 1st leg	Baseball Ground	Derby County	1-0	31,904	
7.2.1968	Semi F 2nd leg	Elland Road	Derby County	3-2	29,367	
2.3.1968	Final	Wembley	Arsenal	1-0	97,887	
4.9.1968	2	The Valley	Charlton Athletic	1-0	18,860	
25.9.1968	3	Elland Road	Bristol City	1-2	16,359	
24.9.1969	3	Elland Road	Chelsea	1-1	21,933	
6.10.1969	3 replay	Stamford Bridge	Chelsea	0-2	38,485	

FOOTBALL LEAGUE CUP (Leeds United)—*contd*

Date	Round	Venue	Opponent	Score	Attendance	Other
8.9.1970	2	Bramall Lane	Sheffield Utd	0-1	29,573	
8.9.1971	2	Baseball Ground	Derby County	0-0	34,023	
27.9.1971	2 replay	Elland Road	Derby County	2-0	29,132	
6.10.1971	3	Upton Park	West Ham Utd	0-0	35,890	
20.10.1971	3 replay	Elland Road	West Ham Utd	0-1	26,504	
6.9.1972	2	Elland Road	Burnley	4-0	20,857	
4.10.1972	3	Villa Park	Aston Villa	1-1	46,185	
11.10.1971	3 replay	Elland Road	Aston Villa	2-0	28,894	
31.10.1971	4	Anfield	Liverpool	2-2	44,609	
22.11.1971	4 replay	Elland Road	Liverpool	0-1	34,856	
8.10.1973	2	Portman Road	Ipswich Town	0-2	26,385	
9.10.1974	3	Gigg Lane	Bury	2-1	16,354	
13.11.1974	4	Sealand Road	Chester	0-3	19,000	
9.9.1975	2	Elland Road	Ipswich Town	3-2	15,318	
8.10.1975	3	Elland Road	Notts County	0-1	19,122	
1.9.1976	2	Victoria Ground	Stoke City	1-2	22,559	

Leeds career total: Thirty-eight appearances – Three goals

FOOTBALL ASSOCIATION CUP (LEEDS UNITED)

Date	Round	Venue	Opponent	Score	Attendance	Other
7.1.1961	3	Hillsborough	Sheffield Wednesday	0-2	34,281	
6.1.1962	3	Elland Road	Derby County	2-2	27,089	
10.1.1962	3 replay	Baseball Ground	Derby County	1-3	28,168	1 goal
4.1.1964	3	Ninian Park	Cardiff City	1-0	13,932	
25.1.1964	4	Elland Road	Everton	1-1	48,286	
28.1.1964	4 replay	Goodison Park	Everton	1-3	66,167	
9.1.1965	3	Elland Road	Southport	3-0	31,297	
30.1.1965	4	Elland Road	Everton	1-1	50,051	
2.2.1965	4 replay	Goodison Park	Everton	2-1	65,940	
20.1.1965	5	Elland Road	Shrewsbury Town	2-0	47,740	
10.3.1965	6	Elland Road	Crystal Palace	3-0	45,384	
27.3.1965	Semi Final	Hillsborough	Manchester Utd	0-0	65,000	1 goal
31.3.1965	Semi Final replay	City Ground	Manchester Utd	1-0	46,300	1 goal
1.5.1965	Final	Wembley	Liverpool	1-2	100,000	
22.1.1966	3	Elland Road	Bury	6-0	30,384	
12.2.1966	4	Stamford Bridge	Chelsea	0-1	57,384	
28.1.1967	3	Elland Road	Crystal Palace	3-0	37,768	
11.3.1967	5	Roker Park	Sunderland	1-1	55,763	
15.3.1967	5 replay	Elland Road	Sunderland	1-1	57,892	
20.3.1967	5, 2nd replay	Boothferry Park	Sunderland	2-1	40,546	
8.4.1967	6	Elland Road	Manchester City	1-0	48,887	
29.4.1967	Semi Final	Villa Park	Chelsea	0-1	62,378	

FOOTBALL ASSOCIATION CUP (Leeds United)—*contd*

Date	Round	Venue	Opponent	Score	Attendance	Other
27.1.1968	3	Elland Road	Derby County	2-0	39,753	
17.1.1968	4	Elland Road	Nottingham Forest	2-1	51,739	
9.3.1968	5	Elland Road	Bristol City	2-0	45,227	
30.3.1968	6	Elland Road	Sheffield Utd	1-0	48,322	
27.4.1968	Semi Final	Old Trafford	Everton	0-1	63,000	
4.1.1969	3	Hillsborough	Sheffield Wednesday	1-1	52,111	
8.1.1969	3 replay	Elland Road	Sheffield Wednesday	1-3	48,234	
3.1.1970	3	Elland Road	Swansea City	2-1	30,246	
24.1.1970	4	Gander Green Lane	Sutton Utd	6-0	14,000	
7.2.1970	5	Elland Road	Mansfield Town	2-0	48,093	
21.2.1970	6	County Ground	Swindon Town	2-0	27,500	
14.3.1970	Semi Final	Hillsborough	Manchester Utd	0-0	55,000	
23.3.1970	Semi Final replay	Burnden Park	Manchester Utd	1-0	56,000	1 goal
11.4.1970	Final	Wembley	Chelsea	2-2	100,000	
29.4.1970	Final replay	Old Trafford	Chelsea	1-2	62,078	
11.1.1971	3	Millmoor	Rotherham Utd	0-0	24,000	
18.1.1971	3 replay	Elland Road	Rotherham Utd	3-2	36,890	
15.1.1972	3	Elland Road	Bristol Rovers	4-1	33,565	
5.1.1972	4	Anfield	Liverpool	0-0	56,300	
9.2.1972	4 replay	Elland Road	Liverpool	2-0	45,821	
26.2.1972	5	Ninian Park	Cardiff City	2-0	50,000	
18.3.1972	6	Elland Road	Tottenham Hotspur	2-1	43,937	
15.4.1972	Semi Final	Hillsborough	Birmingham City	3-0	55,000	
6.5.1972	Final	Wembley	Arsenal	1-0	100,000	
13.1.1973	3	Carrow Road	Norwich City	1-1	32,310	

Date	Round	Venue	Opponent	Score	Attendance	Goals
17.1.1973	3 replay	Elland Road	Norwich City	1-1	36,087	
29.1.1973	3, 2nd replay	Villa Park	Norwich City	5-0	33,225	
24.2.1973	5	Elland Road	West Bromwich Albion	2-0	39,229	
17.3.1973	6	Baseball Ground	Derby County	1-0	38,350	
7.4.1973	Semi Final	Maine Road	Wolverhampton Wanderers	1-0	52,505	1 goal
5.5.1973	Final	Wembley	Sunderland	0-1	100,000	
5.1.1974	3	Molineux	Wolverhampton Wanderers	1-1	38,132	
9.1.1974	3 replay	Elland Road	Wolverhampton Wanderers	1-0	42,747	
26.1.1974	4	London Road	Peterborough Utd	4-1	28,000	
16.2.1974	5	Ashton Gate	Bristol City	1-1	37,000	1 goal
19.2.1974	5 replay	Elland Road	Bristol City	0-1	47,128	
4.1.1975	3	Elland Road	Cardiff City	4-1	31,572	
24.1.1975	4	Elland Road	Wimbledon	0-0	46,230	
10.2.1975	4 replay	Selhurst Park	Wimbledon	1-0	45,071	
18.2.1975	5	Baseball Ground	Derby County	1-0	35,298	
8.3.1975	6	Portman Road	Ipswich Town	0-0	38,010	
11.3.1975	6 replay	Elland Road	Ipswich Town	1-1	50,074	
25.3.1975	6, 2nd replay	Filbert Street	Ipswich Town	0-0	35,195	
27.3.1975	6, 3rd replay	Filbert Street	Ipswich Town	2-3	19,510	
3.1.1976	3	Meadow Lane	Notts County	1-0	31,129	
24.1.1976	4	Elland Road	Crystal Palace	0-1	43,116	

Leeds career total: – Sixty-nine appearances – Six goals

FA CHARITY SHIELD (LEEDS UNITED)

Date	Round	Venue	Opposition	Score	Attendance	Other
2.8.1969	Final	Elland Road	Manchester City	2-1	39,835	
10.8.1974	Final	Wembley	Liverpool	1-1	67,000	Sent off

Leeds career total: Two appearances

EUROPEAN CLUB RECORD (LEEDS UNITED)

EUROPEAN CUP

Date	Round	Venue	Opponent	Score	Attendance	Other
17.9.1969	1, 1st leg	Elland Road	SK Oslo	10-0	25,979	2 goals
1.10.1969	1, 2nd leg	Ullevaal Stadion	SK Oslo	6-0	7,595	
12.11.1969	2, 1st leg	Elland Road	Ferencvaros	3-0	37,291	
26.11.1969	2, 2nd leg	Stadion Albert Florian	Ferencvaros	3-0	5,400	
4.3.1970	3, 1st leg	Stade Maurice Dufrasne	Standard Liege	1-0	38,000	
11.3.1970	3 2nd leg	Elland Road	Standard Liege	1-0	48,775	
1.4.1970	Semi Final, 1st leg	Elland Road	Celtic	0-1	45,505	
15.4.1970	Semi Final, 2nd leg	Hampden Park	Celtic	1-2	136,505	1 goal
6.11.1974	2, 2nd leg	Elland Road	Ujpesti Dozsa	3-0	28,091	1 goal
5.3.1975	3, 1st leg	Elland Road	Anderlecht	3-0	43,195	Subbed
19.3.1975	3, 2nd leg	Parc Astrid	Anderlecht	1-0	37,000	1 goal
9.4.1975	Semi Final, 1st leg	Elland Road	Barcelona	2-1	50,393	1 goal
15.4.1975	Semi Final, 2nd leg	Camp Nou	Barcelona	1-1	110,000	
28.5.1975	Final	Parc des Princes, Paris	Bayern Munich	0-2	48,374	

Leeds career total – Fourteen European Cup appearances – Six goals

EUROPEAN CUP WINNERS CUP (LEEDS UNITED)

Date	Round	Venue	Opposition	Score	Attendance	Other
13.9.1972	1, 1st leg	Ankara 19 Mayis Stadium	Ankaragucu	1-1	20,000	
27.9.1972	1, 2nd leg	Elland Road	Ankaragucu	1-0	22,411	
25.10.1972	2, 1st leg	Ernst Abbe Sportfeld	Carl Zeiss Jena	0-0	18,000	
8.11.1972	2, 2nd leg	Elland Road	Carl Zeiss Jena	2-0	26,885	
7.3.1973	3, 1st leg	Elland Road	Rapid Bucharest	5-0	25,702	
11.4.1973	Semi Final, 1st leg	Elland Road	Hadjuk Split	1-0	32,051	
25.4.1973	Semi Final, 2nd leg	Stari Plac	Hadjuk Split	0-0	30,000	

Leeds career total – Seven European Cup Winners Cup Appearances – No goals

INTER CITIES FAIRS CUP/UEFA CUP (LEEDS UNITED)

Date	Round	Venue	Opponent	Score	Attendance	Other
29.9.1965	1, 1st leg	Elland Road	Torino	2-1	33,852	1 goal
6.10.1965	1, 2nd leg	Stadio Comunale	Torino	0-0	26,000	
24.11.1965	2, 1st leg	Zentral Stadion	S.C.Leipzig	2-1	8,000	
1.12.1965	2, 2nd leg	Elland Road	S.C.Leipzig	0-0	32,111	
2.2.1966	3, 1st leg	Elland Road	Valencia	1-1	34,414	
16.2.1966	3, 2nd leg	Estadio Mestalla	Valencia	1-0	45,000	
2.3.1966	4, 1st leg	Elland Road	Ujpesti Dozsa	4-1	40,462	1 goal
9.3.1966	4, 2nd leg	Szusza Ferenc Stadium	Ujpesti Dozsa	1-1	30,000	
20.4.1966	Semi Final, 1st leg	La Romareda	Real Zaragoza	0-1	35,000	
27.4.1966	Semi Final, 2nd leg	Elland Road	Real Zaragoza	2-1	45,008	
11.5.1966	Semi Final, replay	Elland Road	Real Zaragoza	1-3	43,046	
18.10.1966	2, 1st leg	Spieringhorn	D.W.S. Amsterdam	3-1	7,000	1 goal
26.10.1966	2, 2nd leg	Elland Road	D.W.S. Amsterdam	5-1	27,096	
18.1.1967	3, 1st leg	Elland Road	Valencia	1-1	40,644	
8.2.1967	3, 2nd leg	Estadio Mestalla	Valencia	2-0	48,000	
22.3.1967	4, 1st leg	Stadio Renata Dall'Ara	Bologna	0-1	20,000	
19.4.1967	4, 2nd leg	Elland Road	Bologna	1-0	42,148	
19.5.1967	Semi Final, 1st leg	Elland Road	Kilmarnock	4-2	43,000	
24.5.1967	Semi Final, 2nd leg	Rugby Park	Kilmarnock	0-0	28,000	
30.8.1967	Final, 1st leg	Stadion Maksimir	Dynamo Zagreb	0-2	40,000	
6.9.1967	Final, 2nd leg	Elland Road	Dynamo Zagreb	0-0	35,604	
3.10.1967	1, 1st leg	Stade Josy Barthel	Spora Luxembourg	9-0	2,500	1 goal

INTER CITIES FAIRS CUP/UEFA CUP (Leeds United)—contd

Date	Round	Venue	Opponent	Score	Attendance	Other
29.11.1967	2, 1st leg	Stadion Partizana	Partizan Belgrade	2-1	10,000	
6.12.1967	2, 2nd leg	Elland Road	Partizan Belgrade	1-1	34,258	
20.12.1967	3, 1st leg	Elland Road	Hibernian	1-0	31,522	
10.1.1968	3, 2nd leg	Easter Road	Hibernian	1-1	30,000	
26.3.1968	4, 1st leg	Ibrox Park	Rangers	0-0	80,000	
9.4.1968	4, 2nd leg	Elland Road	Rangers	2-0	50,498	
1.5.1968	Semi Final, 1st leg	Dens Park	Dundee	1-1	30,000	
5.5.1968	Semi Final, 2nd leg	Elland Road	Dundee	1-0	23,830	
7.8.1968	Final, 1st leg	Elland Road	Ferencvaros	1-0	25,268	
11.9.1968	Final, 2nd leg	Stadion Albert Florian	Ferencvaros	0-0	76,000	
18.9.1968	1, 1st leg	Stade Maurice Dufrasne	Standard Liege	0-0	35,000	
23.10.1968	1, 2nd leg	Elland Road	Standard Liege	3-2	24,178	1 goal
13.11.1968	2, 1st leg	Elland Road	Napoli	2-0	26,967	
27.11.1968	2, 2nd leg	Stadio San Paolo	Napoli	0-2	15,000	
18.12.1968	3, 1st leg	Elland Road	Hanover 96	5-1	25,162	
4.2.1969	3, 2nd leg	Niedersachsen Stadion	Hanover 96	2-1	15,000	
5.3.1969	4, 1st leg	Elland Road	Ujpesti Dozsa	0-1	30,906	
19.3.1969	4, 2nd leg	Szusza Ferenc Stadium	Ujpesti Dozsa	0-2	40,000	
15.9.1969	1, 1st leg	Sarpsborg	Sarpsborg	1-0	10,000	
29.9.1969	1, 2nd leg	Elland Road	Sarpsborg	5-0	19,283	2 goals
21.10.1969	2, 1st leg	Elland Road	Dynamo Dresden	1-0	21,292	
4.11.1969	2, 2nd leg	Rudolf Harbig Stadion	Dynamo Dresden	1-2	35,000	
2.12.1969	3, 1st leg	Elland Road	Sparta Prague	6-0	25,843	1 goal
9.12.1969	3, 2nd leg	Generali Arena	Sparta Prague	3-2	30,000	
14.4.1970	Semi Final, 1st leg	Anfield	Liverpool	1-0	52,877	1 goal

Date	Round	Venue	Opponent	Score	Attendance
28.4.1970	Semi Final, 2nd leg	Elland Road	Liverpool	0-0	40,462
28.5.1970	Final, 1st leg	Stadio Comunale Vittorio Pozzo	Juventus	2-2	45,000
3.6.1970	Final, 2nd leg	Elland Road	Juventus	1-1	42,483
15.9.1970	1, 1st leg	Herman Vanderpoorten Stadium	SK Lierse	2-0	17,000
22.9.1971	Play-off for Inter Cities Fairs Cup Trophy	Camp Nou	Barcelona	1-2	35,000
3.10.1973	1, 2nd leg	Elland Road	Stroemgodset	6-1	18,711
24.10.1973	2, 1st leg	Elland Road	Hibernian	0-0	27,145
7.11.1973	2, 2nd leg	Easter Road	Hibernian	0-0	36,150
28.11.1973	3, 1st leg	Elland Road	Vitoria Setabul	1-0	14,196

Leeds career total – Fifty-five Inter Cities Fairs Cup/UEFA Cup appearances – Ten goals
Leeds career total – One appearance Inter Cities Fairs Cup play-off
Total appearances in European competition for Leeds United:
   European Cup – Fourteen appearances, Six goals
   European Cup Winners Cup – Seven appearances, No goals
   Inter Cities Fairs Cup/UEFA Cup – Fifty-five appearances, Ten goals
   Inter Cities Fairs Cup play-off – One appearance, No goals
   Career total – Seventy-seven appearances, Sixteen goals

FOOTBALL LEAGUE CUP (HULL CITY)

Date	Round	Opponent	Venue	Score	Attendance	Other
31.8.1977	2	Southport	Haig Avenue	2-2	3,864	
14.9.1977	2, replay	Southport	Bootherry Park	1-0	4,846	1 goal
25.10.1977	3	Oldham Athletic	Bootherry Park	2-0	6,923	
29.11.177	4	Arsenal	Highbury	5-1	25,922	

Hull City Career total – Four appearances – One goal

FA CUP (HULL CITY)

Date	Round	Opponent	Venue	Score	Attendance	Other
8.1.1977	3	Port Vale	Bootherry Park	1-1	9,694	
10.1.1977	3 replay	Port Vale	Vale Park	3-1	10,688	
7.1.1978	3	Leicester City	Filbert Street	1-0	12,374	

Hull City Career total – Three appearances – No goals

FOOTBALL LEAGUE PLAYING RECORD
(ALL CLUBS)

Season	Club	League	Apps	Goals
1959-60	Leeds United	First Division	11	2
1960-61		Second Division	31	9
1961-62			39	11
1962-63			24	10
1963-64			39	2
1964-65		First Division	40	6
1965-66			41	8
1966-67			36	2
1967-68			36	2
1968-69			42	6
1969-70			35	4
1970-71			26	3
1971-72			41	5
1972-73			38	4
1973-74			42	10
1974-75			27	1
1975-76			34	5
1976-77			4	0
1976-77	Hull City	Second Division	30	2
1977-78			31	4
Career Total			**648**	**96**

MANAGERIAL RECORD

Club	From	To	Games	Won	Lost	Drawn
Doncaster Rovers	25/11/1978	01/10/1985	319	115	121	83
Leeds United	11/10/1985	28/09/1988	143	59	52	32
Doncaster Rovers	03/07/1989	02/11/1991	115	33	54	28

SHIRT NUMBER WORN LEAGUE FIXTURES
(LEEDS UNITED)

Season	Number 4	Number 7	Number 8	Number 9	Number 10	Number 12
1959-60		11 games				
1960-61		6 games	12 games		13 games	
1961-62		19 games	19 games	1 game		
1962-63	2 games	5 games	16 games		1 game	
1963-64	39 games					
1964-65	40 games					
1965-66	39 games		1 game		1 game	
1966-67	36 games					1 game
1967-68	36 games					
1968-69	42 games					
1969-70	35 games					
1970-71	24 games	1 game				
1971-72	41 games					
1972-73	38 games					
1973-74	42 games					
1974-75	27 games					
1975-76	34 games					
1976-77	4 games					
	479 games	42 games	48 games	1 game	15 games	1 game

SHIRT NUMBER WORN OTHER GAMES
(LEEDS UNITED)

Competition	Number 4	Number 6	Number 7	Number 8	Number 9	Number 10
FA Cup	66 games		2 games			1 game
Football League Cup	32 games	1 game	1 game	4 games		
Europe	75 games				1 game	
Charity Shield	2 games					
	175 games	1 game	3 games	4 games	1 game	1 game

Games where Billy Bremner was substituted (Leeds United)

8 January 1969 – FA Cup 3, replay v Sheffield Wednesday (Elland Rd); Belfitt
1 April 1970 – European Cup semi-final v Celtic (Elland Rd); Bates
27 September 1971 – Football League Cup 2, rep v Derby County (Elland Rd); Mann
17 March 1973 – FA Cup 6 v Derby County (Baseball Ground); Bates
13 November 1974 – Football League Cup 4 v Chester (Sealand Rd); Bates
5 March 1975 – European Cup 3, 1st leg v Anderlecht (Elland Rd); Yorath
24 January 1976 – FA Cup 4 v Crystal Palace (Elland Rd); Hunter

Game where Billy Bremner was substitute (Leeds United)

15 May 1967 – Division 1 v Sheffield Wednesday (Elland Rd); Replaced Gray

OTHER AWARDS

Manager of the month Doncaster Rover October 1979
Doncaster Rover September 1980
Doncaster Rovers September 1981

Golden Boot XI Was selected by his peers in the First Division team of the season
for five consecutive seasons between 1970-1975. He was the first
and only player of this era to receive five consecutive selections.

Selected to represent Scotland in the Glasgow Charity Cup at Hampden Park
versus Glasgow Select XI (1-1) Attendance 18,000

Billy had a racehorse named after him. Billy Bremner was owned
by Mrs Anne-Marie Banks and trained by Frank Carr at his
Malton stables. The two-year-old was ridden by Lester Piggott in
the Acomb stakes at York in 1971, and won by 8 lengths. It was
sold and exported to Venezuela. Of its eight races in England,
Billy Bremner won four times.